"An entirely honest and entirely affirming treatment of the challenges facing LDS believers. Mason brings a historian's training and sophistication together with a disciple's compassion and sensitivity to bear on an urgent topic. The result is a provocative and inspiring framework for faith."

—FIONA AND TERRYL GIVENS
Authors of *The Crucible of Doubt:*
Reflections on the Quest for Faith

"Patrick Mason has carefully listened to the diverse community of Latter-day Saints. He has heard the love and the faith as well as the bewilderment and the pain. This book is his moving response. His deeply intelligent call to mutual understanding and his compelling invitation to faith and fellowship have had a transformative effect on me."

—DAVID HOLLAND
Associate Professor of
North American Religious History
Harvard Divinity School

"Before reading this book, I anticipated a masterful discussion about how to intellectually and spiritually navigate the messier moments in church history. To my delight, Patrick Mason not only met my expectations; he exceeded them. This insightful, personable, and thought-provoking book places the complexities of faith and doubt within the context of discipleship. It reminds us of the importance of establishing and maintaining a Christlike community, despite—and because of—the many struggles we face. *Planted* is a must-read."

—RACHEL COPE
Assistant Professor of
Church History and Doctrine
Brigham Young University

"Patrick Mason is a brilliant historian who has thought hard about the tough questions of faith and doubt. Now he has written about those questions with humor, refreshing candor, and genuine empathy. Readers all along the 'belief spectrum,' so to speak, will be surprised to find how movingly this book speaks to them. That's a tribute to the inclusive spirit that pervades *Planted* and will inspire everyone who picks up the book."

—J.B. Haws
Author of *The Mormon Image in the American Mind: Fifty Years of Public Perception*

"Every Latter-day Saint knows someone who grapples with faith, is dismayed at facts or rumors concerning the church's history and policies, or feels bereft of a comfortable place in Mormon culture. Such people may chafe at the stigma of doubt, persuaded that no one understands their concerns. Patrick Mason shows he does understand. His book offers a safe space where legitimate questions are honored and where provisional answers will engage many an open mind and heart. Mental integrity and spiritual sanity, in a Mormon context, may look something like this."

—Philip Barlow
Leonard J. Arrington Professor of Mormon History and Culture at Utah State University
Coeditor of the *Oxford Handbook of Mormonism*

"In an age where the Internet has made all things present, confronting questions about church history and theology is the new norm. How we respond to those who doubt is, according to Mason, our generation's test of true discipleship. He provides compassionate, wise, and reassuring advice for both those confronting doubt and those who minister to them. To find peace in the church one must find Christ there, for only there can we find fertile soil to plant our faith."

—Boyd Petersen
Program coordinator for Mormon Studies at Utah Valley University
Editor of *Dialogue: A Journal of Mormon Thought*

"In this honest, compassionate, and personal exploration of Latter-day Saint history, beliefs, and practices, Patrick Mason reaches out to those who might feel 'switched off' from the bright light of faith that once animated their spiritual life, and those who sometimes feel 'squeezed out' from their faith community because they might not fit the mold. Mason walks with his readers through nettlesome aspects of Mormon history without dismissing or downplaying difficulties. His approach is at once candid and pastoral—a welcome method that sheds warm light into dark corners. *Planted* articulates a vision of a capacious church that offers ample space for the marginalized and disenchanted to not merely stay, but to find joy in doing so. Ultimately, Mason believes in Zion—its ideals, and its redemptive vision anchored in Christ. He offers compelling reasons for others to find belief and belonging, too. Mormons of all stripes should read this book and savor its messages."

—W. Paul Reeve
Author of *Religion of a Different Color: Race
and the Mormon Struggle for Whiteness*

"A remarkable and unmatched resource for preserving faith and restoring empathy in a secular world. For Latter-day Saints who experience pressing doubts, isolation, or even disaffection, *Planted* is a healing balm that liberates people to engage with difficult, legitimate questions about LDS history and theology. And for those who live with more certainty, this book teaches how to empathize with others in their faith transitions. Patrick Mason's narrative is humble and nurturing, never dismissive or condescending. He reminds us that the very difficult process of creating communities where doubt, faith, and differences coexist is an important means of developing Christlike character."

—Andrea G. Radke-Moss
Author of *Bright Epoch: Women and
Coeducation in the American West*

"A triumph! Patrick Mason has crafted a singular book that will speak to many Latter-day Saints, from the most confident church members to any who struggle with questions. With compassion toward those who feel to leave the fold, Mason exemplifies great competence in the church's rich history, showing why faithful study is a requirement, not an elective, for contemporary members. *Planted* provides compelling reasons—intellectual, as well as those couched deep in the heart—to foster one's faith in the latter-day gospel."

—Blair G. Van Dyke
LDS Seminaries and Institutes of Religion
Author of *Holy Lands: A History of the
Latter-day Saints in the Near East*

"In *Planted*, Patrick Mason successfully navigates the often challenging shoals between faith and reason that many Latter-day Saints encounter in this generation. He deftly combines historical accuracy, intellectual honesty, and genuine personal faith. While he provides useful strategies for dealing with major issues regarding the history of the church and its place in modern society, his greatest contribution is helping us distinguish between the host of secondary issues and focusing on what is truly, salvifically important: being firmly planted in the Risen Lord, Jesus Christ."

—Eric D. Huntsman
Professor of Ancient Scripture
Coordinator of Ancient Near Eastern Studies
Brigham Young University

"This deeply informed and meditative treatment of 'belief in an age of doubt' can truly help those experiencing a loss of faith. Patrick Mason envisions the LDS tradition as a return to 'sacred cosmos' in a 'secular age.' He situates current loss of belief within a larger historical shift from inheritance to agency—from being 'held by religion' to learning how to 'hold on to religion.' In this context, doubt is not a problem but a healthy process in a life where 'faith and doubt are constant traveling companions.' Mason's insights resonated in my mind, soul, and heart like a spiritual communion of light, intelligence, and truth, married with wisdom, comfort, and bonding. He is both scholar and brother."

—Maxine Hanks
Theologian and independent scholar
of women's studies in religion

PLANTED

PLANTED

Belief and Belonging in an Age of Doubt

Patrick Q. Mason

Image credits:

Page 181: *A Conversation with the Master*, © 2008 Nathan Florence. Used by permission. Visit nflorencefineart.com.

Page 183: *Wedding Feast*, © 1996 John August Swanson. Used by permission. Los Angeles artist John August Swanson is noted for his finely detailed, brilliantly colored paintings and original prints. His works are found in the Smithsonian Institution's National Museum of American History, London's Tate Gallery, the Vatican Museum's Collection of Modern Religious Art, and the Bibliothèque Nationale, Paris. Visit www.JohnAugustSwanson.com.

Book design: Andrew Heiss

Library of Congress Cataloging-in-Publication Data

(CIP on file)

ISBN 978-1-62972-181-1

Printed in the United States of America

RR Donnelley, Harrisonburg, VA

10   9   8   7   6   5   4   3   2   1

To my mother

We live in an age of doubt, but we need not be overcome.
When we are planted in the Savior, we can be nourished as much
by our questions as by the answers.

Contents

Introduction

I'M A MEMBER OF THE CHURCH OF JESUS CHRIST of Latter-day Saints, and I wrote this book for you, my fellow church member, whether you feel your faith is rock solid or whether you sometimes wonder if this church is the place for you. Some of the things I'll address are applicable for all people of faith trying to chart a course in the modern world, so other people are welcome to listen in. But Mormonism looks and feels a lot like a big family.[1] At its heart, this is a family matter, and right now people are leaving our family. Some of them are angry or hurt and don't desire to come back. It's not entirely clear how many exactly, but abstract numbers don't really matter because we suffer the loss if even one seat is empty at the table—or to use Jesus's metaphor, if even one sheep leaves the fold (see Luke 15:1–7). To be sure, our family boundaries have always been porous with people coming and going, sometimes in a trickle and other times in waves. It helps to remember that every generation faces its respective challenges to faith. This book is meant to address some of the unique challenges that our family of faith is facing in this generation.

This is an exciting time to be a member of the church. We are having conversations about things we've not previously talked about in the open, which is one sign of a church membership that is more committed and less casual about the role of faith and the church in their lives. To help facilitate and inform these discussions, in recent years the church has addressed a number of traditionally challenging historical and doctrinal matters by releasing a series of essays on the Gospel Topics portion of the official website (go to www.lds.org/topics). As authorized conversation starters, I welcome the Gospel Topics essays as a real blessing to a maturing church coming forth "out of obscurity" (D&C 1:30)—and will come back to them throughout this book.

These recent efforts notwithstanding, right now a number of church members are either questioning their place in the church or leaving it altogether because they feel, in the words of Latter-day Saint historian Richard Bushman, either "switched off" or "squeezed out." In either case we are talking about longtime members of the church, not those who are baptized by the missionaries and then stop coming within a matter of weeks. (That could be the subject of a different book!) Perhaps the following descriptions will seem familiar because they depict you or someone you care about. The switched-off group includes those who, after a life of service in the church, encounter troubling information online or somewhere else, usually regarding our history or doctrine. This new knowledge does not square with what they had previously learned over the years at church—sometimes by way of direct contradiction but usually by revealing parts of the story that we don't usually tell in our three-hour Sunday meetings. When a person realizes that at least part of what they are learning for the first time is factually true, not simply the malicious invention of anti-Mormon propagandists, then they sometimes start to wonder what else they haven't been told. They often go off in search of other "hidden knowledge," sometimes forgetting the basic principles and experiences that they had originally built their testimony upon. They begin to see duplicity rather than sincerity in the church's presentation of its doctrine and history. Skepticism and doubt begin to overcome trust and faith. Even when reminded of the many good things about the church, including its positive impact in their own life and the ways that they touched others' lives through their service and testimony, their answer becomes "Yes, but . . ." Shaken by intellectual challenges to their understanding and faith, their relationship to the church becomes tenuous. Some withdraw, and others leave, feeling that they cannot participate with integrity in church meetings where certain details are either neglected or denied. In short, they become switched off, both in terms of their commitment to the church and sometimes in their entire testimony.

The second group feels squeezed out, like they just don't fit in at church. Usually this comes about more because of present issues than past ones, though historical concerns may be a contributing factor. Like most families, we Latter-day Saints have our own particular culture. This culture varies somewhat depending on country, region, and even ward, but there are certain shared elements that provide stability and unity across the worldwide institution. Most aspects of the institutional church are either indisputably essential, such as belief in the Savior's atonement or the proper performance of priesthood ordinances. Other aspects are understandably cultural and comparatively minor in the grand scope of things, such as men wearing white shirts and women wearing dresses to church. The concerns of the squeezed out tend to fall somewhere in the middle of that continuum. Oftentimes our squeezed sisters and brothers fully embrace the basic principles and ordinances of the gospel. But sometimes they feel alienated by things like the dominant political conservatism among the members (at least in the United States), or the sense that church membership is an all-or-nothing proposition (and even what it takes to do be "all-in"), or heartfelt questions about whether girls and women have all the opportunities for spiritual growth and recognition in the church that boys and men do, or how the church ministers to our LGBT (lesbian, gay, bisexual, and transgender) brothers and sisters.[2] Some people who can bear testimony of all the basic principles of the restored gospel but who disagree with certain aspects of the dominant social, cultural, economic, political, or ideological views held by most other members sometimes feel that their presence is unwelcome, or that the things that they feel strongly about are not only dismissed but in some ways held in suspicion by fellow members. Feeling isolated, alienated, and sometimes pressured, they sense that there is simply no place for them in the church in spite of their core commitments. And they leave us.

Because categorizing people this way risks oversimplification, I hasten to add that these two broad categories—switched off and squeezed out—do not capture the wide range of reasons why people find themselves on the margins of the church or leave it altogether. But since no book can do everything, this book is oriented specifically toward those two patterns of disaffection and disaffiliation from fellowship. My conversations with people from places across the United States and Europe suggest that we are not talking about just a localized smattering of malcontents. Maybe you find yourself in the position of many parents, grandparents, siblings, friends, Relief Society presidents, and bishops around the church worried about the people they love who are struggling to remain or have chosen to leave. Maybe you are the one struggling to stay or wondering if you should leave. In either case, this book is written for you.

How did I become involved with addressing these issues? Like many of my fellow LDS scholars, in recent years I have spoken at numerous firesides, lectures, and other presentations addressing these issues of faith and doubt in the contemporary church. I always leave time for discussion with the audience at the end of my talks. On almost every occasion, one or more individuals have expressed that my remarks helped them or would help someone they know. This book thus grows out of many conversations with many real people and a sincere desire to help lift some of the burdens that so many feel.

My insights here are built upon a foundation of responsible, faithful scholarship for which I can personally claim little or no credit. For many decades a small but committed group of devoted Latter-day Saints have applied their professional scholarly training to the study of Mormon history, theology, and culture. These scholars have demonstrated persuasively that a thorough and honest examination of Mormonism can enhance rather than detract from a life of deep faith and committed discipleship. In particular, the entire membership of the church owes a debt of gratitude for the outstanding work being currently done within the Church History Department. Two of the department's many projects deserve special mention. The Joseph Smith Papers Project seeks to gather, annotate, and publish accurate transcripts of all existing historical documents produced by or closely related to Joseph Smith.[3] It is a massive undertaking being performed by highly trained specialists and has been recognized by national organizations and non-LDS scholars as truly exemplary in its commitment to historical accuracy and documentary editing. The underlying message of the project is that Latter-day Saints are not afraid to provide a completely open, honest, and transparent accounting of our founding prophet's life and history. We have nothing to hide.[4]

In addition, I am especially grateful for and reliant upon the Gospel Topics essays that have recently been produced by the Church History Department and published on the church website.[5] Each of these essays has been researched and written by experts on the topic as a collaborative effort between LDS Church employees and independent scholars, most of whom are professors at colleges and universities around the

United States. Every essay has been reviewed by the highest councils of the church and approved by the First Presidency and Quorum of the Twelve. In short, these materials can be trusted by the membership of the church, both for accuracy and message. As of this writing, the church has released over ten essays, many of which received extensive media coverage. The topics covered include "Are Mormons Christian?," "First Vision Accounts," "Race and the Priesthood," "Plural Marriage and Families in Early Utah," "Book of Mormon Translation," "Book of Mormon and DNA Studies," "Becoming Like God," "Peace and Violence among 19th-Century Latter-day Saints," "Translation and Historicity of the Book of Abraham," "Plural Marriage in Kirtland and Nauvoo," and "The Manifesto and the End of Plural Marriage."[6] Perhaps most importantly, the material contained in these essays is now being incorporated into the church curriculum and leadership training resources, thus ensuring wider distribution of this information to youth and adults throughout the church.[7]

The Gospel Topics essays are not perfect nor are they the final word. Entire books have already been written on virtually every one of these subjects, so it is impossible to say everything in a few thousand words. I believe some of the essays' interpretations can be responsibly disagreed with. Nevertheless, I welcome them as a further indication not only of the church's increased transparency but also of our religion's increased maturity. We are confident enough in the truthfulness of the gospel and the divine mission of the church that we can have hard conversations and need not shy away from difficult issues. Indeed, the very fact that this book is being copublished by Deseret Book and the Neal A. Maxwell Institute for Religious Scholarship in its Living Faith series is another indication of a positive change of atmosphere within the fold, where questions can be aired and faith strengthened through candid discussion of important issues.

As soon as I decided to write this book, I reached out to Claudia Bushman, Richard Bushman, and Spencer Fluhman—three highly respected scholars and seasoned church members who have also been laboring in the trenches and talking with people about keeping the faith. My thinking and framing of the issues here has been profoundly shaped by my interactions with and work alongside these friends and colleagues. Upon request, each of them has sent me material from their own related firesides, lectures, and presentations, which they have generously allowed me to draw freely upon. Although I occasionally refer to Claudia, Richard, or Spencer directly, for the most part I seamlessly wove their words in with my own with their permission. I remain solely responsible for the content of the book, but I am deeply indebted to these three friends for many of the insights herein.

I have not designed this book as a series of prepackaged answers to gospel-related questions or problems. I will refer to many of the challenging historical and doctrinal issues treated in the church's Gospel Topics essays, but I don't take the time here to fully assess the evidence or even offer ironclad solutions. For readers who are unfamiliar with any issue that I mention, I recommend that you turn first to the relevant Gospel Topics essay prepared by the church and continue your research from there. Although in the coming chapters I occasionally weigh in on these issues, my purpose here is somewhat broader than to relay the facts and then tell you what you should think about the Book of Abraham or the Mountain Meadows Massacre, for instance. I am less concerned right now with delivering definitive answers than with having a conversation. To use fancier terms, I have written this less as a work of formal apologetics and more as a pastoral dialogue. I value honest and sincere conversation more than scoring points in debates that can probably never be decisively won. It is true that criticisms of church history and doctrine will continue to be made, and it sometimes helps to have some basic factual responses at hand.[8] I believe that the most effective conversations, however, are to be had face-to-face. I therefore want *Planted* to retain something of that character—two people sitting down and talking openly and even with a certain amount of vulnerability, probably over the course of several meetings, ideally while sharing good food (sold separately). More than anything, this book is intended as an act of friendship.

Discussing the gospel—especially with our friends—is never simply a matter of having the right information in our heads. In my conversations with people going through personal struggles related to issues in church history, doctrine, or culture, I have found that it's not necessarily about giving the right answers—although having a good and ready answer to people's questions is always better than having no answer, which itself is better than having a bad answer. Members of the church should follow the apostle Peter's advice to "be ready always to give an answer to every man that asketh you a reason of the hope that is in you with meekness and fear" (1 Peter 3:15).⁹ In most cases, however, the facts are not really in dispute. Oftentimes the person we are ministering to already knows what the party line is or how he or she would expect a church leader to respond. That doesn't mean we shy away from those faithful, basic answers, but we must be prepared to address that individual's specific follow-up questions and concerns, which come as much from the heart as the head.

Before giving answers, then, I have found that it is most important at every point to listen—to really, truly listen. The Bible offers a useful example here. When Job's friends heard that Job was suffering affliction, they "made an appointment together to come to mourn with him and to comfort him." It seems they thought a quick home teaching visit could resolve whatever problems Job was having. When they realized the depth of his suffering, any pat answers they may have prepared beforehand evaporated. The relationship between them came before the proffered solution. They wept and they grieved with him. For seven days and nights they simply "sat down with him . . . and none spake a word unto him: for they saw that his grief was very great" (Job 2:13–15). Though this powerful example of compassion is overshadowed somewhat by their impatient responses in later chapters, we learn from Job's friends a profound lesson about the limits of the spoken word.¹⁰

For most doubts, there are no magic words or ready-made formulas that will immediately make them go away. Doubt is thus less a problem in need of a solution than a common part of the mortal experience that should, like all things, be treated with charity and ultimately consecrated to God. Oftentimes, simply having a conversation with someone who needs to talk through personal questions is enough. Real conversation is more an art than a science. It is unpredictable, and we can't always tell the end from the beginning or easily measure efficiency or impact; statistics aren't helpful here. But most people don't really want to be solved. They want to be heard, valued, and as much as possible understood.

For many people, some aspects of being a member of the church are difficult. This is true not just because of the lists of commandments or persistent conflicts with the external culture but also because of internal stresses as well. The quest for faith, with its accompanying doubt and uncertainty, is a crucible that tests our mettle, as Terryl and Fiona Givens have so eloquently articulated.[11] The quest happens in real time with real people. Latter-day Saint faith never exists in the abstract. It can never be divorced from its history on the one hand and community on the other. Those aspects that are part of the core strength of our religion also provide challenges for those who are switched off or squeezed out by their inherent challenges and paradoxes.

This book is thus structured to address issues pertaining to both belief and belonging in the church. The first few chapters focus on the challenge of maintaining faith in the face of disconcerting information and in the context of a secular age when religious knowledge in general is increasingly questioned. I offer basic principles that can help in addressing historical and doctrinal challenges to Mormon belief. A slight shift in perspective can not only help us accommodate difficult information but can also allow us to emerge on the other side with a deeper and more mature faith centered on the redeeming work of Jesus Christ.

The later chapters reflect more specifically on the importance of the church as an institution and community. Some of our greatest challenges—but also most important lessons—appear while we work in the laboratory of love that we call the church. Maintaining belief is essential, but Christ also calls upon us to live out our discipleship within the context of a flesh-and-blood community that makes demands of us and gives us assignments and opportunities to take a lively interest in other people. Perhaps the most important thing we can do in the face of our current challenges is to make the church a more welcoming place for those who struggle, creating the conditions in which they can feel comfortable while they work through questions and doubts in the midst of the body of Christ rather than feeling excluded from it. A more embracing Mormonism may thus be the most important factor in helping people more fully embrace Mormonism.

This book *Planted* is therefore written with two distinct but overlapping audiences in mind: those who actively doubt, whether they are on the precipice or have already made the decision to leave the church, and those who do not doubt, who consider themselves solid, active, believing members of the church. If you are a member of this latter group, serious doubt may be a stranger in your own heart, but I am certain that it nevertheless manifests itself somewhere in your family or ward, thus making the issue of "faith crisis" just as important for you as if you were going through it yourself. Because this book is addressed to a dual audience, a given passage or line of reasoning may resonate with some readers more than with others. My belief, however, is that we all need to have the conversation together. We can't set up camp on two sides of an arbitrary divide with believers on one side and doubters on the other and then talk at (and usually past) one another. That approach only exacerbates the problem with a tragic sense of division in the body of Christ. Too often we have used religion as a means of building a "wall of partition between us," of introducing "enmity" within the family of God. But the ministry of Jesus Christ is one of reconciliation. As we're reminded in the New Testament letter to the Ephesians, Christ "is our peace"—he has broken down the walls and abolished the enmities that exist among us. He has "preached peace" both to those who are near to the church and those who are "afar off." Through him we "have access by one Spirit unto the Father." He reveals the reality of who we really are, both to God and to one another—not "strangers and foreigners, but fellowcitizens with the saints, and of the household of God" (Ephesians 2:14–19). The solution to any enmity that may exist among us is to become more firmly planted in Christ.

In an era in which we recognize that no author is objective or writes from nowhere, it has become fashionable to disclose something of one's own perspective. In short: I am a believer and a belonger. When it comes to Mormonism, I'm "all in," to incongruously use the poker term, and have been my entire life. I like being in. I go to church every Sunday, and (mostly) enjoy it. I know it is good for me. I know that I find redemption and sanctification in the gospel of Jesus Christ proclaimed by The Church of Jesus Christ of Latter-day Saints through its prophets and members.

It's difficult for me to fully articulate the origin, nature, and depth of my belief. The experiences, thought processes, and life journey that have shaped and solidified my faith are intensely individual and in some ways inscrutable. It is impossible for me to download my belief from my heart into anyone else's—even my own children's. Any testimony I can give is only an approximation. In this regard at least I feel

I'm in good company. Moroni, Joseph Smith, and a host of other more illustrious spiritual communicants than I am have been similarly frustrated with "the little narrow prison" of "a crooked broken scattered and imperfect language."[12]

I approach the issues of doubt and uncertainty from a position of belief and, yes, certainty. That does not mean I have a clear-cut answer for everything, and I am judicious in my use of the phrase "I know." Certain aspects in the church's past and present trouble me, and I am still seeking understanding about many important issues, including some I will mention in this book. Nevertheless, I am fully comfortable in and with my Mormonism. While I can imagine deepening my faith and most of all my commitment, I can't imagine being more convinced that God has ordained The Church of Jesus Christ of Latter-day Saints to accomplish its divine mission, laid out in the preface of the Doctrine and Covenants: to help all people speak in the name of Jesus Christ, to increase faith in the earth, to establish the everlasting covenant, and to proclaim the fulness of the gospel to the ends of the world (D&C 1:20–23). I fall short in fulfilling my Christian duties as much as any other member of the church. But while I interact easily with friends, neighbors, and coworkers of all faiths and of no faith, at the core of my being I'm a Mormon.

This book will discuss some hard things. It will probably raise some new questions for some readers. Frankly, I worry about sowing doubt rather than belief. I don't wish to undermine faith in any way. Faith is a gift and a precious commodity in any age, but an increasingly rare one in our modern world in which, as the famous theorists Marx and Engels so aptly described, "All that is solid melts into air, all that is holy is profaned."[13] And so if you feel this book is hurting more than it is helping, put it down. Please forgive me. And then find another way to find belief and belonging, another way to plant yourself in Christ. But if you find any comfort or wisdom in these pages, I hope you can share it with others while you remain planted in your corner of the vineyard.

1

Faith and Trust in a Secular Age

HANS MATTSSON WAS A THIRD-GENERATION MORMON, a senior priest-hood leader who spent decades serving and defending the church. He and his wife raised their five children in the gospel, and the family was a pillar of the church in Europe. Because of his leadership position, other members would often come to Mattsson with questions. Some of their concerns were based on troubling information they found on the Internet that seemed to contradict what they had heard about church history and doctrine. Mattsson originally dismissed the online material as anti-Mormon lies. He reached out to other church leaders for their assistance in responding to the members' doubts but did not receive any answers that satisfied him. So he began his own investigation. He realized that some of the claims he had previously dismissed as baseless propaganda were supported by credible historical evidence he had been unfamiliar with. The doubt that he had worked to dispel in others now began to overcome him. "I felt like I had an earthquake under my feet," he said. "Everything I'd been taught, everything I'd been proud to preach about and witness about just crumbled under my feet. It was such a terrible psychological and nearly physical disturbance." Repeated efforts by other church leaders and historians have not assuaged his sense of betrayal. Although he still feels attached to the church that he spent so many years serving, Mattsson is no longer active.[1]

Half a world away, in Utah, another member was similarly struggling with his faith after learning about certain events in church history that he had never heard about despite a lifetime of church activity.

At a priesthood leader's suggestion, he called a scholar who was also serving as a bishop and complained, "How could I be a high priest and serve all these years and never know this?" The two talked for a long time that day. At the end of the experience, the questioner remains in the church. His questions were not resolved. The bishop didn't have any magic words that made his concerns go away. But the bristling sense of betrayal the man harbored at the beginning of the conversation was gone. He felt valued. He felt like he was heard. He felt like he had a place to go, a place to stay.[2]

Anatomy of a faith crisis

Experiences like this have been repeated numerous times throughout the contemporary church. Although the experiences are as unique as the individuals who have them, there are enough recurring patterns that people have come to describe and understand the phenomena in terms of "faith crisis." That umbrella term is certainly too broad to fit every case, but it is an unavoidable fact that the language—and for many the experience—of faith crisis has become a recent fixture in the Mormon spiritual landscape.[3]

While all humans have their doubts and questions and troubles, not all members of the church go through a faith crisis of existential proportions; most, in fact, do not. Crisis is not a necessary or universal step on the path to spiritual understanding. For inexplicable reasons, some people seem simply hardwired to believe, and the same things that rock other people's belief only seems to strengthen theirs. Perhaps this is what is meant by the gift of faith—even what Moroni calls "exceedingly great faith" (Moroni 10:11). But this brand of unquestioning faith is unusual. For most people, faith is work, and oftentimes it is hard work. It is a journey, with its peaks and valleys. It requires constant nurturing, but even when planted in good ground it is vulnerable, far from impervious. By its very nature faith is not based on tangible, empirical proof. Fundamentally, faith is a matter of hope and of trust, not much different than love.

When two people fall in love and start telling each other "I love you," they surely want to believe it, and it thrills them to believe it, but in the beginning they have little more to go on than hope and trust. In successful relationships, that hope and trust is validated with time and experience. When the tender bond of trust is violated, however, relationships deteriorate and sometimes dissolve. Even a lifetime of marriage can be undermined by certain actions or revelations—sometimes dug up from long ago in the past, before the relationship even began. Especially in the case of those past transgressions, it may not be so much the act itself as the withholding of information that precipitates the loss of trust. People feel lied to, betrayed. "What else are you not telling me?" "Has everything been a lie?" "How can I entrust you with my heart, my soul, and my affections?"

The dynamics of faith crisis are remarkably similar, especially because Mormonism is a religion that exerts such a strong claim on people's hearts, souls, and affections. Of course, Latter-day Saints have experienced dissension and disaffiliation from our earliest days; the church was practically ripped apart by faith crisis in Kirtland, then as now basically over the question of what it means to have a living prophet.[4] The most recent wave has come with the advent of the age of the Internet. Sometimes it's hard for us to remember what it was like before we all went online. Most news was local news, and diversity of opinion was diminished by the fact that most people's conversations were had with their immediate neighbors. For most of its history, therefore, Mormonism was fairly parochial. Isolated primarily in the American Intermountain West, church members got most of their information about the church from materials published and distributed by the church and its leaders. Divergent views were easily dismissed as anti-Mormon.

All that has changed in the past two decades. The online information explosion has exposed the now-global community of Latter-day Saints to a wider range of available facts about their religion and its past. For some, this has been exhilarating, since it has provided enhanced access, with incredible speed, to an avalanche of information about Mormon history and scripture. For many, though, this improved access has proven to be destabilizing, disorienting, or even corrosive to their faith. On a host of websites ranging from the scholarly to the explicitly hostile, people are encountering information that they didn't learn in Sunday School or seminary where lessons frequently focus on inspirational stories and positive examples rather than various difficulties, and they often don't know how to reconcile such things with what they have been taught all their lives. Caught off guard, they are unsure what to make of information that conflicts with what they already believed. Every person's set of troubling questions is different, but many of the same difficult historical and doctrinal topics come up over and over again. These include polygamy, the race-based priesthood-temple restriction before 1978, women and the priesthood, the church's relationship to modern science (including biological evolution and DNA studies), the translation or historicity of the Book of Abraham and the Book of Mormon, and the existence of multiple accounts of Joseph Smith's first vision.

If these trigger issues are fairly consistent across the cases, so is the general process that leads to a person's crisis of faith. More often than not it begins with a simple Google search. Ironically, it is frequently active, committed church members like Hans Mattsson who go online to find the answers that will help satisfy their friends' or family members' doubts and misgivings who are then surprised and troubled by what they discover. At first they deny what they have read. But when they start doing more research they learn that some of the claims they have newly learned are indeed based in fact, not just scurrilous lies made up by anti-Mormons. Now they're confused and not quite sure where to go or whom to talk to in order to make sense of their troubling discovery. They might approach their bishop, another priesthood leader, or perhaps an institute teacher. Sometimes their uncertainties are validated if not confirmed, as with the high priest in the opening vignette. In too many other cases, however, they are met with searching questions about their worthiness, with the not-so-subtle suggestion that their doubts are really a cover for or symptom of immoral behavior. Honest questions and sincere doubts are thus equated with a lack of faithfulness. Some members have been told by well-meaning individuals that even their very questions are sinful. If the bishop or the institute teacher does not know the answer to their questions—which is often the case in a church with lay leadership and a seminaries and institutes faculty that frequently have received little to no formal academic training in church history and theology—the questioner is counseled simply to study their scriptures more, pray harder, serve more diligently, and put their doubts out of their mind.

But it's not that simple. Remember, most of these searchers are already active Latter-day Saints who have spent countless hours reading their scriptures, praying, and serving. They are returned missionaries, Gospel Doctrine teachers, Relief Society presidents, bishopric members. They have predicated their lives on the belief that the church is true and that it has the answers to eternity's grandest questions. So when their church leaders and teachers don't have good answers to their historical and doctrinal questions, it feels to them like evasive action, a dismissal or nonacknowledgment of the very things causing them concern. They wonder if they've even been heard or if they were simply judged. Shamed by the implication that their questions are inappropriate and not to be discussed in public, they go back to the Internet, where a few keystrokes can bring up inexhaustible libraries of information in only fractions of a second. They quickly find online forums where other people are struggling with similar issues. They have now discovered a "community" of like-minded questioners who also have found no satisfactory answers in their conversations with their LDS family members, friends, teachers, and leaders. Finally, they feel, they have found people who understand where they are coming from and who seem to care about the whole truth and nothing but the truth, no matter where it leads them.

Facts and emotions are never so far apart, of course. Throughout this process, new feelings have arisen in the questioner's heart—sometimes emerging gradually and almost imperceptibly, sometimes hitting immediately and like a ton of bricks. In a word, they feel betrayed by the church that they have served so faithfully for so many years. The most common question is, why was I never told any of this? They feel that the church has lied to them. Even worse, they feel that they have lied to others on behalf of the church, whether it was to the investigators on their mission, to the people in the Sunday School or elders quorum classes they teach, or even to their own children. Feeling that they can't get straight answers—or worse, that there aren't good answers to be had—they decide they can no longer trust the church or its leaders, past or present. The cords of confidence that connected them to the church have become frayed, or even severed.

Many of these people end up staying in the church, usually for family reasons, but they withdraw into themselves. Every time they hear a testimony, talk, or lesson that doesn't square with what they are reading online, it reinforces their sense of the church's duplicity and the naïveté of ordinary members. Other questioners can no longer bear to attend, and they drift into inactivity. Some become angry and rage against the church, both online and in person, their trust broken and faith shattered.

For some people, their crisis of faith leads them to doubt the grounds of their testimony. Given that they spent years testifying, "I know the church is true," and given that they now no longer believe that declaration, they call into question everything they ever knew. The old ways of knowing have become suspect. They ask, Can I trust past spiritual experiences? When the edifice of faith seems to be trembling, what authorities or sources or voices or experiences can I rely upon to settle such pressing questions? How do I know that God lives? How do I know that Jesus was resurrected and atoned for my sins? For that matter, how do I know what is sin and what is righteousness? How do I know that the moral standards taught by the church are the best way to live my life? How can I know anything at all?[5]

For many people who undergo a faith crisis of profound proportions, their whole world comes crashing down because that world had been built on the truthfulness of the church and the structure that the church provided in their lives. Their predicament entails more than just a few unanswered questions about church history. It is a crisis of who they are and how they make sense of this life. It is one of the most confounding things that can happen to a person, especially to someone who has been a committed member of the church for many years. It's no wonder, then, that a faith crisis often becomes deeply disruptive not only to a person's spiritual life but also to the character and quality of his or her relationships with other people, especially with that person's spouse, parents, friends, and fellow (or former) church members.

Understandably, these family members and friends, particularly those who remain active members of the church, are concerned about the person and what his or her doubts mean for their enduring relationships. Parents are worried about having an empty spot at the family dinner table—whether at Thanksgiving or worse, in the celestial kingdom. Spouses are terrified about what this means for their marriage, especially when it began with covenants made in the temple that their partner no longer attends or even recognizes as sacred. If the covenantal foundation of their marriage is shaken, what of the relationship can be salvaged? Since so much of their life together was based on church activity—callings, service, church attendance, temple nights, dinners with friends in the ward—what will fill that hole? And what about the children? Will one parent's loss of faith undermine the other's sincere desire to continue raising their children in the church? Will other parents not want their children to play with theirs for fear of their own children being negatively influenced? At the most basic level, friends and family members wonder what to do and say. They feel at a loss, having been rebuffed when they suggested to the person in crisis that they might consider reading their scriptures more, praying harder, and serving more diligently. What else is there?

What not to do

The rest of this book will offer some frameworks and suggestions both to those struggling with doubt and to the circle of sincerely concerned people around them, including parents, spouses, bishops, and friends. But it is important to establish immediately what generally does *not* help.

Essentially, we must recognize at the outset that in the majority of these cases, not only is the pain and struggle real, but so are the issues. Because spiritual knowledge is prized as such a virtue in Mormon culture, doubt seems deviant, and the people who struggle with doubt are suspected of actually covering up some deeper sin or preferring to indulge some kind of lifestyle not approved by the church. The assumption is that the person won't admit that she is having an affair or that he really just wants to go boating on Sundays, so he or she made up a convenient story about being existentially grieved over Brigham Young's Adam-God teachings. Indeed, sometimes expressions of doubt are a cover for part of a larger complex of beliefs and behaviors that the person knows runs counter to church teachings. If a person's spiritual discipline is lax, she may be less inclined to receive the quiet assurances that often accompany a life of saintly striving. But in most cases it is not our place to render a verdict on the state of another person's soul, and we will be far more effective (and better Christians) when we give people the benefit of the doubt. To simply assume that someone with doubts is guilty of some grave moral transgression or to cause that person to feel in any way unfaithful or unworthy merely because of his questions displays a lack of charity. If someone gathers enough courage to raise a question with a parent, spouse, bishop, seminary teacher, or friend and then is met with judgment or scorn, he or she will likely be left feeling isolated and alienated, with nowhere to turn other than back to the Internet. In a recent general conference address, Rosemary M. Wixom, general president of the Primary, shared the words of a woman who had struggled with doubt before returning to full activity in the church: "I did not separate myself from the church because of bad behavior, spiritual apathy, looking for an excuse not to live the commandments, or searching for an easy out. I felt I needed the answer to the question, 'What do I really believe?'"[6]

Perhaps not quite as immediately damaging, but usually just as unconstructive, is for people to take evasive action when confronted with a friend's or family member's doubts. A response of "read your scriptures and pray," while certainly good advice in principle, is often unhelpful in such cases for two reasons. For one thing, chances are the person has already tried reading her scriptures and praying about her questions. For another, a formulaic answer demonstrates a lack of concern for the person and his actual problems. While reading scriptures and praying are always necessary, they are rarely sufficient for the range of profound human dilemmas, whether it be financial disaster, a failing marriage, death or chronic illness, or a crisis of faith. To love others, to be in a true relationship with them, is to mourn with them when and how and where they are mourning, to comfort them when and how and where they need comfort, to know in depth and detail what their burdens are so you can help lighten them (see Mosiah 18:8–9). Avoiding tough situations, dismissing concerns as insignificant, or giving prepackaged answers without thought or care all come off as naive or worse, as insensitive and uncaring. When the people we love are in pain, our first response is not to blame them or dismiss them or trivialize their hurt. We go to them. We embrace them. If words fail us, we simply sit with them, as did Job's friends. Mostly, we love them regardless of their beliefs or place in the church.[7]

Honest doubt is not just a phase, like teenage acne or disco. Nor is doubt itself necessarily a tragedy. It can become a tragedy when someone's faith crisis is precipitated or deepened because they cannot find an open, candid, and supportive place to work through his or her sincere questions. Stigmatizing doubt to the point that people feel guilty for even having questions is not conducive to spiritual growth. Neither is it helpful to ignore questions as if they are invalid, unimportant, and wrongheaded. After having spent time in the scholarly trenches with many if not all of the issues that typically trouble people, and as one who has had countless conversations with those who feel their faith is teetering on the edge, I can strongly assert that the challenges are real and that most of the people who face them are earnest. How we deal with doubt in the church today is one of the most pressing tests of our collective discipleship.

A secular age

Mormons are not alone in striving to preserve faith in a time of doubt. This is simply part of what it means to live in an era defined by one prominent scholar as "a secular age."[8] For those of us living in the modern world, especially in the West, we are awash in a sea of secularism. Though Mormons and many other religious believers often interpret the word *secular* with negative connotations, it is important to remember that we are all the beneficiaries of many aspects of secular modernity, including the scientific method, religious freedom, and constitutional democracy. Even if we personally spend most of our time consciously rowing in the raft of religion, we recognize that there's a difference between religion being the raft (as it is in modern times) and religion being the ocean (as it was in premodern times).

In the next chapter we will take a closer look at differences between the past and our present secular age. For now, consider the common misconception that religion has no place in a secular age—that religion and secularism are inexorably locked in conflict in what amounts to a zero-sum game. This was the assumption of a number of scholars in the early to mid-twentieth century who propounded what was called the secularization theory. They argued, and found evidence to support their claims, that religion would disappear as society modernized and people became more enlightened. Science would explain all the mysteries of the universe that prescientific humans could only

make sense of by inventing religion. Religion, in this view, was a ves-
tigial remnant of antiquity—the societal equivalent of the human
appendix. The high point of this way of thinking came in the 1960s.
Even *Time* magazine, which had traditionally been friendly to religion, printed a cover that asked the penetrating question—displayed
in blood-red letters against a jet-black background—"Is God Dead?"

But the past half-century has proven, as the old Christmas carol
says, that "God is not dead, nor doth he sleep."[9] Religion experienced a
remarkable resurgence around the world beginning in the 1970s, with
the public rise of evangelical Protestantism in America, the Islamic
Revolution in Iran, and Catholic-inspired democratic movements in
Poland, Latin America, and the Philippines, just to name a few. Secularization theorists began to backpedal. A French scholar incisively
captured these new developments in the title of his book *La Revanche
de Dieu*, or *The Revenge of God*.[10]

Yet somewhat paradoxically, at the same time that religious movements have been reclaiming their privileges in the public sphere, many
places, including western Europe and America, have witnessed steady
declines in religious belief, affiliation, and confidence. A number of
recent studies have pointed to the rise of the "nones" as one of the most
significant religious developments in modern America. When asked
about their religious affiliation in a survey, these are the people who
respond "none." The nones—not to be confused with nuns—are not
necessarily agnostics or atheists. In fact, they often describe themselves
as "spiritual but not religious." Many report that they still believe in
God and retain some kind of personal spiritual practice but at the same
time choose not to affiliate with any organized religion. In the early
1970s, only about 5–7 percent of the American population reported
no religious preference; by around 2005 that number was closer to
17 percent. Some survey estimates put their numbers near 21 percent
today. When viewed generationally, the rise of the nones is even more
striking. The percentage of nones has approximately doubled with each
generation in modern America, from about 5–7 percent among those
who came of age before 1960, to about 10–20 percent among the baby
boomers, then rising again to 20–30 percent among those who reached
adulthood in the 1990s and 2000s. Nearly a quarter of college freshmen
in 2009 reported not attending a single church service in the previous

year, compared to about 8 percent in 1965.[11] A 2015 study revealed that more than one out of three Americans born between 1981 to 1996 (the "Millennials") are religiously unaffiliated, with the majority of those simply stating that when it comes to religion, they are "nothing in particular."[12]

It is not just the number of people in the pews that has declined. Trust in religious institutions has also dropped precipitously over the past forty years. In 1973, "the church or organized religion" claimed the top spot in an annual Gallup poll measuring Americans' confidence in institutions. In a period of generally declining public trust—these were, after all, the years following Watergate and the Vietnam War—religion consistently garnered more respect than any other institution in America, including the military and the Supreme Court, until the mid-1980s. Then a series of scandals involving prominent televangelists shook the public's confidence in religion. The bottom dropped out in the early 2000s, when the sex abuse crisis in the Catholic Church and religiously inspired terrorism (the September 11 attacks being the most notable case) caused trust in religion to plummet. By 2012, only 44 percent of Americans reported having high confidence in religious institutions, the lowest tally since the poll began.[13]

So we have the resurgence of religion on the one hand and declining rates of religious participation on the other. How do we explain this paradox? Scholars have spilled lots of ink on this question, but for our purposes a couple of observations are sufficient. First, religion is thriving in many places around the world, including in the United States. Predictions that modernity would squeeze religiosity out of the human soul were not only premature but fundamentally wrong. Billions of people around the globe prove every day that it is possible to be genuinely modern and authentically religious at the same time. Second, the reasons people leave churches and lose faith in religion are as varied as the individuals themselves. There are probably always both "push" and "pull" factors that can be identified. What often seems to be the case is that people leave because they feel that their religion isn't what they want or expect it to be. Therefore it is overly simplistic to claim that people leave churches because they are lured away by the siren song of secularism. Recall that most of the nones still believe in God and aren't giving up on spirituality altogether. The ranks of atheists in America have grown somewhat in recent years, but their voices are louder than their still-modest numbers would suggest. Most people want a connection to God, and they go elsewhere (or nowhere) when they feel that religion has failed to deliver on its promise to foster that connection. In short, they feel failed by religion. So when it comes to declining rates of faith, affiliation, and trust in religion—or what we might refer to in shorthand as a faith crisis—the secularism of the modern world is more context than cause. The vast ranks of eminently modern believers prove that living in a secular age does not in itself compel one to give up on belief.

Seeking the truth, together

Contemporary Mormonism has not experienced a widespread public scandal that has led people to flee in droves for the exits. Yet privately, many church members have become troubled by their recent discoveries about church history and doctrine, and some have either left the church or are seriously considering doing so. Most of the issues that distress people, some of which I cited above, are not newly unearthed. Rather, the availability of information online has brought these subjects to more people's attention than ever before. The very fact that something can be found on the Internet typically means that it is not actually news—someone else had to know it and then put it there. Often what appears online to be an exciting and novel conversation is actually a rehash of a debate scholars have been having for decades. That is the case, for instance, regarding the translation of the Book of Abraham. Bloggers, posters, and commenters have recently dedicated a significant amount of bandwidth to laying out all kinds of arguments for and against the authenticity of Joseph Smith's translation of the papyri. This is all rather exciting until one realizes that the basic contours of the debate were established forty to fifty years ago and that not much has changed since. This is not to claim that the issues are settled or that nothing new can be said—far from it. It is simply to say that when someone stumbles across some controversy about church history and doctrine being furiously debated online, the issue might be a revelation to that person, but it's more than likely that plenty of others have been down that road before—and many of them have remained faithful Latter-day Saints.

Online discussions of Mormonism often feature many of the same falsehoods, half-truths, and statements taken out of context that have fueled anti-Mormon literature since Joseph Smith's day. But not everything critical of the church or its history and doctrine is a lie. Neither is it always posted with malicious intent. There are troubling episodes in our past. As President Dieter F. Uchtdorf has noted, "There have been times when members or leaders in the Church have simply made mistakes. There may have been things said or done that were not in harmony with our values, principles, or doctrine."[14] There are inconsistencies and missing information and injustices that we have yet to fully grapple with, let alone reconcile. In this generation, ours is not primarily a problem of lies or the misrepresentation of our history—though no doubt they are still rampant in some corners. Rather, it falls to us to come to grips with the complex *realities* of our past, of "things as they really are" and were (Jacob 4:13).

The ensuing chapters will take a closer look at some of these realities, but there isn't space to tackle them all in depth. What I think matters most is to familiarize ourselves with useful methods of questioning and pondering and analyzing that can be employed in our own wards and branches and homes. Scholars and other faithful members of the church have been examining these issues "by study and also by faith" for literally decades (D&C 88:118). If you or someone you know has doubts or questions about historical or doctrinal issues in the church, there are answers to be found. Unfortunately, too many of our past answers, for instance on the priesthood-temple restriction, have been inadequate and even wrong, despite often being well-intentioned.[15] But there are in fact good answers, intellectually rigorous and honest answers, faithful answers. Because our knowledge is always incomplete and imperfect, the answers we have will not satisfy everyone nor will they solve every problem. We are learning and will continue to learn. But there are ways we can talk faithfully, constructively, and honestly about difficult things, even when our knowledge is imperfect. We can live with loose ends. We can have hard conversations. Indeed, for many reasons—not the least of which are the many challenges attendant to living in a secular age—we *must* have them.

2

Testimonies

> The Church of Jesus Christ of Latter-day Saints is a place for people with all kinds of testimonies. There are some members of the Church whose testimony is sure and burns brightly within them. Others are still striving to know for themselves. The Church is a home for all to come together, regardless of the depth or the height of our testimony. I know of no sign on the doors of our meetinghouses that says, "Your testimony must be this tall to enter."[1]
>
> —President Dieter F. Uchtdorf

THE WORLD IS A SYMPHONY OF DIVERSITY. The variety of plant and animal life alone is staggering. Add the infinite range of human personality, talent, and experience, and we begin to appreciate the boundlessly creative mind of God, who is both the Organizer of all that diversity and the Chief Delighter in it.

One of the grand truths of Mormonism is that humans, at our very essence, are coeternal with God. The spark at the core of our being—what we call "intelligence"—is uncreated, indestructible, and self-existent, just as is the intelligence at the core of God's soul. Apparently our first consequential act was to enter into a relationship with God, whom we recognized was "more intelligent than [us] all" (Abraham 3:19). Joseph Smith pulled back the veil and offered a glimpse of this defining moment in the premortal cosmos: "God Himself found Himself in the midst of spirits and glory. Because He was greater He saw proper to institute laws whereby the rest, who were less in intelligence, could have a privilege to advance like Himself and be exalted with Him, so that they might have one glory upon another in all that knowledge, power, and glory. So He took in hand to save the world of spirits."[2] The beginning of our eternal progression thus preceded "the beginning" described in Genesis 1:1. Before God created the heavens and the earth, he offered growth, exaltation, and glory to an innumerable host of preexistent intelligences. The nature of personality at that stage of our existence is a mystery, but it is clear that we possessed sufficient agency to make a meaningful choice to eternally associate ourselves with God. He thereafter became the Father of our spirits. For all intents and purposes, the possibility of life began not with the violent explosion of the Big Bang but rather earlier, with the benevolent invitation of a loving exalted being to those intelligences that would become his children. Predicated on a reality of infinite diversity, the moral universe begins with grace. In John's words, "We love him, because he first loved us" (1 John 4:19).

The independence and agency that our individual spirits exercised in our premortal existence become magnified through our particular earthly experiences. Through a combination of premortal and genetic inheritances, all of us enter mortality with unique gifts, predilections, and dispositions. These are then filtered through an infinite range of environments, choices, and encounters, some intense but most mundane, which makes us who we are. Since God so clearly rejoices in the variety of his creation and in the souls he seeks to exalt, it seems paradoxical that slicing through the panoply of human diversity is the divine mandate to focus our entire hearts, minds, and souls on the One. Indeed, one of the primary ways that Christianity scandalizes the twenty-first-century mind is in its insistence that all people, whatever the location or condition of their birth, must believe in and follow the singular Way, Truth, and Life that is Jesus Christ (see John 14:6). The scriptures repeatedly affirm that Jesus's atonement is the only "means whereby salvation cometh" and that "there is none other salvation . . . neither are there any conditions whereby man can be saved." Before the call to repentance, ordinances, and obedience comes the invitation— even the imperative—to "believe in God" (Mosiah 4:8–9).

This chapter contemplates the nature of testimony in a world of spiritual and experiential variety. My reflections on testimony here lead to two propositions: first, that human diversity dictates a somewhat more open view of what testimonies are and how they come (or in some cases don't); and second, that the commitment to live a religious life with integrity is related but not reducible to the act of having discernible "spiritual experiences." Given a cosmos defined by infinite variation, we have perhaps been too limited in conceptualizing how people experience God and live religiously—which in LDS parlance we usually collapse into the single term *testimony*. Testimony is always and ultimately a highly personalized reflection of a singular relationship between a unique eternal intelligence and God. In a church that seeks to encompass and seal together the entire human family, we will better fulfill our mission by embracing the notion, in President Uchtdorf's words, that the church is truly "a place for people with all kinds of testimonies."

From sacred cosmos to secular age

Before considering testimony in the contemporary church, let's pause for a moment and take a step back to consider how we got here. Up until rather recent times, religious belief itself was not a problem for humans. People in different societies believed different things, but they virtually all believed. The ancient world contained a staggeringly diverse parade of gods: the Egyptians had Ra (and others), the Greeks had Zeus (and others), the Mesopotamians had Marduk (and others), the Indians had Ganesha (and others), the Hebrews had Jehovah (and others). As times changed, so did people's gods. About a millennium and a half ago, the Arabian peninsula was radically transformed from feverish polytheism to staunch monotheism as people accepted the message of Islam delivered by the prophet Muhammad. In the age of colonization, religious change swept the Americas as European explorers, missionaries, and colonists introduced—and too often imposed—Christianity. Religions have always been on the move, and religious beliefs and traditions have never been entirely stable. But the striking fact is that in the midst of this religious maelstrom, in every premodern society that we have a record of, practically everyone believed in a world beyond this one. And more often than not, they believed pretty much the same things that their close neighbors did.

In the premodern world, the notion of a lone individual switching religions, let alone leaving religion altogether, was exceptionally rare and in most times and places inconceivable. This was true for many reasons, not the least of which because religion in the way we understand and practice it today didn't exist. For our ancestors, religion was not a separate category of human activity; many cultures didn't even have a word for it. Rather, everything—the naming of infants, the crop cycle, disease and healing, the succession of kings, literally every moment and every activity from birth until death—was infused with spiritual meaning. Of course, there were always those who slept through the sermon or skimped on their sacrifices. But the majority of humans throughout most of history operated in what we might call a sacred cosmos. They had no sense that some things were "sacred" and other things "secular." An early revelation to Joseph Smith captured this notion when the Lord affirmed that "all things unto me are spiritual, and not at any time have I given unto you a law which was temporal" (D&C 29:34). In a sacred cosmos, people recognized that they were surrounded by a world of spirits that they could neither see nor control but nevertheless knew was quite real. A person could no more elude the sacred than they could escape the air around them.

Obviously, that's not the world we live in today. Rather than living in a sacred cosmos, we live in what the philosopher Charles Taylor has dubbed "a secular age." As Taylor describes, in the space of a few short centuries we went "from a society in which it was virtually impossible not to believe in God, to one in which faith, even for the staunchest believer, is [only] one human possibility among others." Faith has gone from being "unchallenged" and "unproblematic" to being a conscious choice, one that is "frequently not the easiest to embrace."[3]

Many differences between our ancestors and us are evident, but one of the most significant is that when it comes to religion, we know we have other options available to us—including the option of opting out. Every one of us has a brother, a cousin, a friend, a workmate, a daughter, a parent—or perhaps ourselves—who has chosen the option of unbelief and disaffiliation that not very long ago would have been literally unavailable. Today, it's not just a matter of choosing from a menu of different beliefs; it's a matter of whether we will enter the cafeteria of belief at all. Every day you and I decide, even if implicitly, not only *what* we believe but *whether* and *why* we will believe. My dissertation advisor and mentor put it this way: in traditional societies we were held by religion, whereas in our modern, secular world, we have to hold on to religion.[4]

As much as any other modern religion, Mormonism holds on to us. From the moment of our birth (or spiritual rebirth for adult converts), we are enveloped in not just a church that we attend but also a total religious culture that will carry us from cradle to grave if we allow it. Rosalynde Welch captures the rootedness of Mormon belonging when she locates her religiosity less in mystical spiritual experiences than in "the loving community I've found in my wards and my family, opportunities to serve and be served, the consecrated ideal of building Zion, the comforting warmth of religious ritual, [and] rooted connection to family and church histories."[5] However we came to the religion, as moral agents we each hold on to Mormonism through personal testimony, reasoned belief, and individual commitment. At the same time, Mormonism holds on to us through ordinances, obligation, culture, history, (often) family, and good society. Of course, sometimes religion has held on to people through coercive means; we should always reject anything that looks like ecclesiastical abuse or "unrighteous dominion" (see D&C 121:36–40). But short of that, we should not be ashamed that our religion seeks to hold on to us, as if that gives us some kind of second-class type of faith. Being held onto is what it means to be in relationship, in society—and humans are ultimately hardwired for relationships and society.

Different modes of belief

As we go about living our lives in the church and in the world, we discover fairly early on that belief isn't a one-size-fits-all proposition. People believe in different *things*, but they also believe in different *ways*. The Book of Mormon illustrates some of these diverse ways of believing, particularly as we consider the differences between some of the book's major faith heroes. Here I'll reflect briefly on the experiences of Nephi and the father-son duo of Alma the Elder and Younger.

Just about anyone who has ever picked up the Book of Mormon has read the first verse in which Nephi tells us that he was "born of goodly parents" (1 Nephi 1:1). Though the youngest of Lehi's four sons at the beginning of the story, Nephi is the most faithful. Prior to acting on the Lord's commandments, Nephi believed what the Lord said through his father, the prophet. Nephi later admits struggling with sin, as we all do. Yet he seemingly never struggled with doubt. Interestingly, there is no record of what we might call a momentous religious conversion for Nephi. From his very first breath he was cradled in the pervasive religiosity of his family and his culture, and he obviously delighted in it. Nephi seemingly came out of the womb a believer. He desired to see his father's visions for himself because he completely trusted they were real, not out of a skeptical "I'll believe it when I see it" attitude. It's no wonder, then, that his prophetic writings focus on obeying God's commandments, making and keeping covenants, and enduring to the end, no matter the cost. For Nephi, the struggle was never whether to believe but rather how one should behave based on religious truths that were plain as day. In other words, faith is not nearly as important a concept for Nephi as is faithfulness. Like Isaiah (whom he quotes liberally), Nephi focuses not so much on conversion as he does on covenant.

Compare that to what we learn from the Almas. Both Alma the Elder and Younger come to God as adults, after they preached a false gospel or preached against the gospel in their younger years. For each of them, belief came not simply by virtue of being born and nurtured in the covenant. Rather, in both cases, conversion came about as a profound change of heart: in the father's case, a softening of the heart; in the son's case, more like God ripping out his heart and replacing it with an entirely new one. The metaphor for Alma the Elder's conversion is being "awakened . . . out of a deep sleep" (Alma 5:7), while the image for Alma the Younger's conversion is being "racked with eternal torment" until the mercy of Jesus filled his soul with exquisite joy (Alma 36:12).

Like Nephi, the experiences of both Almas conditioned their theology, or their beliefs about God. If Nephi's writings focused on covenants, Alma the Younger's preaching fixated on conversion: "And now behold, I ask of you, my brethren of the church, have ye spiritually been born of God? Have ye received his image in your countenances? Have ye experienced this mighty change in your hearts?" (Alma 5:14). Recall that Alma was preaching to the members of the church. Being a member of the right club wasn't going to be good enough.[6] Indeed, it is in Alma's writings that we first see converted Lamanites. The message is that it doesn't matter who your parents are, what neighborhood you grew up in, or what your passport says. What really matters is "if ye have experienced a change of heart, and if ye have felt to sing the song of redeeming love," and if "your garments have been cleansed and made white through the blood of Christ, who will come to redeem his people from their sins" (Alma 5:26–27). If Nephi with his covenant theology is the Isaiah of the Book of Mormon, then Alma with his conversionist theology is the Book of Mormon's Paul.

Taken together, these portraits of faith from the Book of Mormon suggest that each one of God's children has a different pattern of testimony. There is no cookie-cutter version of belief, even for those within the church. Some people are like Nephi, held by the faith from their birth. Other people are like the Almas, for whom religion didn't take hold until a dramatic adult conversion experience. Just as King Benjamin didn't have time to number all the diverse ways and means of sin (Mosiah 4:29), the Book of Mormon doesn't number all the different types of belief. The patterns proliferate, with each faith journey as unique as the person experiencing it. It is therefore important to give place for others' blossoms just as we give place to the seed of faith planted in our own hearts (Alma 32:28).

The reality of doubt

In this modern world, we no longer live in a sacred cosmos where belief is a given. Some are persuaded by the philosophy espoused by Korihor, who taught that God is "a being who never has been seen or known, who never was nor ever will be," that religion is "the effect of a frenzied mind," and that "when a man was dead, that was the end" (Alma 30:16–17, 28). Others are spiritually lost, whether "blinded" or "kept from the truth because they know not where to find it" (D&C 123:12). Some people confess they don't know where they stand on matters of belief. They are like the "numberless concourses of people" in Lehi's dream who wander as if in mist, without a firm sense of location or direction (1 Nephi 8:21–23). This does not necessarily constitute for them a rejection of spiritual things. It is merely where they find themselves in the spiritual maelstrom of modern life, and it generally says far more about the circumstances of their birth or their life experiences than it does about the quality of their soul.

Not everyone is a Nephi or an Alma, but that doesn't mean that they are a Korihor or a lost soul either. For some people, the best and perhaps only way that they can describe their relationship to spiritual things is through the language of sincere doubt. We often fear doubt and keep it at arm's length. In many cases this is appropriate—for instance, a marriage can be unnecessarily poisoned by persistent doubts about a spouse's fidelity, even when there is no evidence to warrant such suspicions. Unmet doubt can be corrosive to both human and spiritual relationships; for this reason the Lord counseled the early church to "doubt not, fear not" (D&C 6:36). While we do not want to encourage unnecessary doubt—doubt for doubt's sake—we also want to avoid the opposite reaction: denying or even demonizing its existence, not just among "unbelievers" but even among Latter-day Saints. The fact that one person does not experience serious doubts need not invalidate the fact that someone else does. In the event that doubts generate fear or even sorrow, we can exercise our discipleship by "mourn[ing] with those that mourn" (Mosiah 18:9).[7] So the question is not whether doubt exists in a secular age, but whether we can deal with it constructively. Doubt need not be a badge of honor nor a mark of shame. We have to ask ourselves if we really believe that God can make "all things"—including our doubts—"work together for good" (Romans 8:28). Substantial spiritual doubt will not and need not be experienced by everyone; it is not a necessary stop on the personal path to God. But its presence among us actually does important things for us, both as individuals and as a church community. Doubt dislocates us from our comfortable places. It asks hard questions of us and forces us to deal with hard issues. It refuses to let us get spiritually sluggish with the lazy assumption that "All is well in Zion" (2 Nephi 28:21).

As a church and a people we have not always dealt in the most productive ways with the doubts and questions in our midst. Because we have been blessed with an outpouring of truth from the spirit of revelation, we often speak in terms of what we know. We typically frame our public testimonies that way. It is a beautiful thing for us as individuals and as a people to be so confident in the knowledge that God has blessed us with. Yet sometimes in our "I know" culture, we haven't always been as generous or understanding toward those who can't honestly use those words. We sometimes treat doubt as a character flaw rather than simply a part of many people's struggle to live with belief in a secular age. Even in the nineteenth century Joseph Smith recognized his miraculous experiences would be difficult for some people to accept. "I don't blame any one for not believing my history," he told a congregation in Nauvoo shortly before his death. "If I had not experienced what I have, I would not have believed it myself."[8] Like the Prophet, we can eschew blame and instead seek understanding. Recently I had a conversation with a man who, with tears in his eyes, told me about how he had been rejected by his own family when he expressed questions about his faith. Their shunning of him, sadly, did not work to increase his desire to believe; quite the opposite happened.

For many, the struggle with doubt is the very definition of their journey of belief. One writer said of our modern predicament, "Even as faith endures in our secular age, believing doesn't come easy. Faith is fraught. . . . We don't believe instead of doubting; we believe *while* doubting. We're all Thomas now."[9] I offer my own brief meditation on Thomas's example in the book's interlude,[10] but here the basic point is that for all of us in the modern world, including the most faithful, belief exists in a context of pervasive doubt. In a secular age, faith and doubt are constant traveling companions. Even if belief is preeminent in your own heart and mind, the fact remains that uncertainty, puzzlement, and doubt constitute the primary spiritual condition for many others.

My own experience is that while some people choose belief from a range of possible options, and other people choose skepticism from the same menu, there are many people for whom faith or doubt appear more as an unearned inheritance than a personal choice. To be sure, as moral agents we decide what to do with the various givens in our life—but we don't get to choose our givens. Although controversial, some scientists have even identified a genetic component to faith, which if true means that doubt is also at least partly found in the cards we are dealt at birth.[11] Some people who crave spiritual experience are left wanting; other people can't seem to shake God and religion even when they try. We have to consider, then, what it means that faith and doubt are, within the broad spectrum of the human family, seemingly the products of both agency and inheritance—or in theological terms, works *and* grace. In this dual paradigm of conscious choice on the one hand and unchosen givenness on the other, doubt emerges as a mortal reality—perhaps even a divinely appointed one that God can turn to our benefit—just as much as does faith.

Come be my light

The scriptures often use the metaphor of light to describe spiritual intuitions: "That which is of God is light; and he that receiveth light, and continueth in God, receiveth more light; and that light growth brighter and brighter until the perfect day" (D&C 50:24). We are reminded of the different modes of receiving light by two of God's modern servants, Elder David A. Bednar and Mother Teresa. Elder Bednar teaches that for some people, revelation is received instantly, like flipping on a light switch in a dark room. The experience is "immediate and intense," and the darkness that once filled the room now completely disappears. In other cases, however, light comes more subtly, akin to the sun gradually rising on the horizon. The difference in light from one moment to the next is almost imperceptible, yet it is real: "Gradually and steadily the intensity of the light increased, and the darkness of night was replaced by the radiance of morning. Eventually, the sun did dawn over the skyline. But the visual evidence of the sun's impending arrival was apparent hours before the sun actually appeared over the horizon." This process is one of "subtle and gradual discernment of light."[12] While the light-bulb metaphor approximates the dramatic conversion experiences of both Almas, the sunrise metaphor offers a helpful variation on Nephi's belief-from-birth. That kind of belief seems obvious and inevitable in retrospect, but in reality it has to be acquired "from grace to grace," as was the case with Jesus (D&C 93:13).

Contrast that with the experience of Mother Teresa, the modern paragon of selfless devotion to God and neighbor. Shortly after her death, some of her private writings were published. The collection of journal entries, with the prayerful title *Come Be My Light*, was shocking to most readers—not because of any misbehaviors or scandals (indeed, it seems that some few people really are living saints) but because of something perhaps even more surprising. It turns out that this celebrated archetype of faith was internally tortured with pain and doubt because she felt God's absence, not presence, in her life. As one reader noted, here we see "a woman who sought God with tears and cried out for years for some small taste of the divine, for some tiny assurance in her soul of God's love and presence in her life, but, like so many of the rest of us, received nothing but silence in response."[13] My heart breaks for Mother Teresa as I read a wrenching passage like this:

> Lord, my God, who am I that You should forsake me? The child of your love—and now become as the most hated one—the one You have thrown away as unwanted-unloved. I call, I cling, I want—and there is no One to answer—no One on Whom I can cling—no, No One.—Alone. The darkness is so dark. . . . Where is my faith?—even deep down, right in, there is nothing but emptiness and darkness. . . . I am told God loves me—and yet the reality of darkness and coldness and emptiness is so great that nothing touches my soul.[14]

Of all people in the world, didn't Mother Teresa, that quintessence of service to "the least of these," deserve at least the occasional nod from the God to whom she had so thoroughly consecrated herself? On a personal level, I hope she got a really, *really* long hug from God once she passed to the other side of the veil. More theologically, I appreciate what philosopher Michael Rea suggests about the positive goods that can come out of "divine hiddenness, divine silence." He suggests several possibilities, including the preservation of human freedom and the integrity of moral choice—in many ways, the function of the veil in Mormon theology; the cultivation of personal virtues such as patience, hungering and thirsting for God, and gratitude for the spiritual communications we do receive; and learning the lesson that "God cannot be manipulated by us—that God is not at our beck and call." These options are all good takeaways from divine hiddenness, Rea suggests, but he ultimately concludes that perhaps the most meaningful response to divine silence is to recognize that perhaps God values *communion* with us as much as he does direct *communication*—that being *with* us does not always entail talking *to* us.[15] That may not fully satisfy the person for whom God's extended silence is exceedingly painful and indeed feels a lot like absence. But when we recall the many nonverbal and nonphysical ways that we mere mortals show love and compassion for other people, it's worth considering how God might do the same.

Scripture affirms our ability to withdraw ourselves from God's spirit, but this doesn't seem to explain Mother Teresa's agonizing emptiness, even granting that she was surely guilty of some small sins along the way (see Mosiah 2:36). If divine communication requires absolute human sinlessness, the heavens would be forever closed to a fallen world. Believing that is not true, like Rea we must consider other ways in which God's silence—whether temporary or prolonged—is meaningful, even if we cannot always explain it. While the feeling of estrangement isn't as pronounced as Mother Teresa's in every instance, there are many members of the church who doubt, or at least question, whether they really feel the Holy Ghost or that God answers their prayers in any identifiable way. Many of them have feelings and experiences that other people attribute to the Spirit, but they are not so sure. When they find a lost set of car keys, is it because of luck, a subconscious memory of where they left them, or because God answered their silent prayer (perhaps by inducing their recall of that subconscious memory)? When they get tingles on the back of their neck and spine in sacrament meeting, it seems obvious that it's the Spirit, until they remember they had the exact same sensation at the Bruce Springsteen concert the night before. Embedded within the very experiences that we might identify as religious, then, is the omnipresence of doubt—not incapacitating, faith-destroying doubt, but something more gentle and prone to even greater illumination. As one friend said to me, "Since my conversion to the church I've identified a feeling and reaction that I call the Holy Ghost, but there's always the problem of how do I really know, and know that I know? As a result, I've been both faithful and faithfully skeptical every single time that I call this reaction 'feeling the Spirit.'" For my friend, the searching question, how do I really know? is the essence of his faith life, not its antithesis. The question becomes as important as the answer—and in the absence of a definitive answer, even more so. These feelings of uncertainty can be lasting and painful, or periodic and subtle.

I go to church with people who see God in the little things—when their car breaks down and someone on the freeway stops to help them or in the check that inexplicably arrives in the mail when times are tight. Other active Mormons don't live that way and instead find God in scripture, the temple, the sacrament, church social events, or personal meditation. Others still, whom we might call religious but not spiritual, are drawn to and anchored by the community, tradition, and structure of Mormonism but infrequently have transcendent "spiritual experiences" to bear testimony of.[16] The fact is that we already have a diversity of spiritual experience (and nonexperience) within the church; we just don't very often identify it or use language to express and validate it. With such a strong culture of explicit and identifiable divine communication, leading to confident proclamations of "I know," those who do not experience God and religion in that way can feel shut out. We do not have to devalue anyone's very real and profound spiritual encounters or do away with expressions of authentic spiritual knowledge, but in our collective ministry perhaps we would do well to also acknowledge and find language for the diversity of religious experience already present among us.

Included in that more encompassing posture would be an embrace of the Teresas among us who rarely if ever hear the voice of God. We should recall that in feeling separated from God, Mother Teresa was in good company. Jesus on the cross and Joseph Smith in Liberty Jail both expressed anguish at feeling forsaken by God, though their periods of divine abandonment were mercifully shorter, if no less exquisite, than Teresa's long drought (see Matthew 27:46 and D&C 121:1–4). Many other spiritual stalwarts have experienced the "dark night of the soul," sometimes for decades.[17] Yet their doubt, inner turmoil, and absence of divine communication did not deter or disqualify them from dedicated service to God and his children. Mother Teresa would have been a terrific Relief Society president, even if she couldn't testify of any burnings in her bosom.

It is evident that God speaks to both the just and the unjust, and that by the same token he is silent toward both the wicked and the righteous. We rightfully rejoice when the voice of God comes to us, recognizing that every parcel of divine revelation is an utterly precious grace. At the same time we appreciate that his hiddenness does not constitute abandonment or even necessarily a rebuke. Toward those who feel God does not speak to them and who walk in the valley of the shadow of doubt, the wells of sympathy stir deep within our hearts. When we hear the heart-wrenching cries of Jesus on Calvary, Joseph in Liberty Jail, or Teresa in Calcutta, we wish we could embrace them and weep with them. We instinctively know that nothing we could say would be adequate and that the worst thing to do would be to tell them to buck up and stop complaining and try harder. We would never question the quality of their soul or their worth in God's eyes or in the kingdom. For those who suffer from doubt and divine hiddenness, our principal response to them must be compassion and deep sympathy.

The nature of Jesus's forsakenness on the cross, or Mother Teresa's decades-long famine of hearing a word from the Lord, may in many respects be distinct from the kind of doubt experienced by someone rocked by learning troubling details about Joseph Smith's polygamy. Yet I am not convinced that the depth of sorrow, pain, and feeling of abandonment is qualitatively different or requires a completely separate pastoral response within the church. From Teresa we learn at least two lessons. First, a life of faithful perseverance is possible for the doubter—albeit a different kind of religious life than the "average" believer. Teresa's discipleship was a life choice based on her commitment to Jesus and was not reliant on constant reaffirmations. Second, the body of Christ is immeasurably stronger, and indeed even more redemptive, because of the willing service of a woman who for very long stretches never received answers to her prayers. The tragedy is that Teresa suffered alone and in silence. Perhaps she feared that her questions, like dandelion seeds, could carry in the wind to the hearts of other believers and thus spread her anguish to others. Or perhaps she feared that had she openly admitted her feelings of divine absence, she would have been seen and treated as a second-class citizen by some people within her church, not worthy to do the work entrusted to her. The world, and especially the people to whom she imparted God's grace and care, would then have lost so much.

It was necessary for Jesus to feel abandoned on the cross so that he could truly "know according to the flesh" (Alma 7:12) what it means to feel doubt and separation from God. He had to be forsaken, however temporarily, so that he could succor and redeem the Teresas of the world. In our wards and families, can we, in our pale imitation of Christ, develop deep empathy for those struggling with doubt, disbelief, feelings of betrayal, or suffering from God's silence? Can the church be a place for people who cannot now, always, or ever say "I know"?

To some is given one, and to some is given another

Perhaps the first step toward developing empathy for others is learning to resist using our own personal experiences as the ultimate measuring stick to judge other people. It is only natural for us to begin by seeing the world through our own eyes—the only pair we have been given. Yet discipleship also calls upon us to go beyond our own experience to recognize the legitimacy and value of others' lives, however different they are from our own.

The development of my own beliefs has more in common with Nephi's experience than Alma's. From birth, Mormonism has been my place and my people. I have never had a dramatic conversion experience. Though I have had a handful of powerful experiences in which God's Spirit unmistakably spoke to my spirit, I very rarely get a "burning in the bosom." Belief is more organic and less spectacular for me. I apprehend God and his work in the world not through sudden divine affirmations that come like lightning from heaven, but rather, in Alma's words, by recognizing those things that "enlarge my soul . . . enlighten my understanding . . . [and are] delicious to me" (Alma 32:28).

Along the way I have learned that other people come to believe in other ways—sometimes because of the very visions, voices, and burnings that are relatively infrequent in my life. For some, testimony comes only after passing through a period of doubt, sometimes for years. Others feel that they never receive enough certainty about spiritual matters to honestly say they "know" anything. Some people's relationship to the divine is primarily mystical, for others it is experiential, and for others still it is intellectual. Spirituality is intensely individual, even for members of the same family or the same church.

Nephi taught, "The Lord God giveth light unto the understanding; for he speaketh unto [his children] according to their language, unto their understanding" (2 Nephi 31:3). It's not just that God speaks English, Spanish, Arabic, Tagalog, and Swahili—though of course he does. God knows how to speak the individual language of the soul of every one of his children. God transmits on different frequencies and uses different modes of delivery to give us the light and understanding we need. He might even "speak" to us in silence. We need to understand how he is trying to deliver light and understanding to us, while appreciating and respecting that it may well be different for the person next to us, who is just as unique and precious to him as we are.

My own belief is the result of a combination of many acts of grace and many acts of will. It is the product of study, experience, and encounters with God—both directly and through his children. At the most basic level, however, the reason I believe is because God gave me the spiritual gift of faith. I humbly count this as a precious gift from God. I do not take my gift of faith for granted. I don't deserve it. I didn't earn it. I can't explain why, but I was born, like Nephi, naturally inclined to religion, more so even than two of my siblings who were raised in the same home by the same parents and who attend church but struggle with it more than I do. Religion has come fairly naturally for me, church has generally been a comfortable place for me, and God has always been real for me. I have spent a lot of time with troubling historical and even anti-Mormon material, but I have never experienced a faith crisis. I have not always been immersed in God's spirit, but I have never felt totally forsaken. That doesn't make my story of faith any better or worse than anyone else's—it just happens to be mine.

Regrettably, however, I haven't always applied my gift of faith to the best ends. Ironically, at times it has even impeded my efforts to be a disciple of Christ, particularly when I assumed that my set of gifts and experiences was the standard by which to judge everyone else. As a missionary, my youthful understanding of what true testimony had to look like was stretched by one companion in particular. He slept in, grumbled through companionship study, and dragged his feet when I dragged him out the door. He didn't even like teaching, which is the one part of a mission that almost everyone enjoys. I thought he was faithless, unbelieving, and hardhearted. At one point in my "righteous" exasperation I declared that he should just go home. In a moment of honest vulnerability, this small-town Idaho farm boy admitted to me that he was miserable. He believed in the gospel and the church, but he hated putting on a shirt and tie, knocking on doors, and talking to people. He wished that instead of being called to proselytize in Seattle the church had asked him to go dig wells or build houses somewhere in Africa.

That didn't compute for me. Having a testimony meant one thing for this nineteen-year-old Mormon boy: you put on a white shirt and black name tag and talked to people who didn't want to talk to you.[18] It made even less sense to me when my companion called a Navy recruiter and tried to become a SEAL. (Our mission president talked him out of it.) At the time, and for a long time after, I considered him one of the worst missionaries I ever knew. Now I want to apologize to him for my lack of charity—or to be blunt, for being a self-righteous jerk. Sure, maybe he could have had a little better attitude and made lemonade out of lemons. But because I had a limited understanding of the nature and fruits of testimony, I fought against rather than working with a guy who genuinely wanted to dedicate his life to service—if not always in the church, then at least for Uncle Sam. I didn't even care about what gifts he had, let alone find a way to channel them so that together we could more effectively serve others. I've lost track of him—for all I know he could be digging wells in Africa right now or serving orphans in Calcutta. I just hope my narrow view of true religion didn't in some way push him out of the church.

Mormonism affirms the dignity and worth of every living soul. In an early revelation to Joseph Smith, the Lord revealed that all humans are the bearers of spiritual gifts from him. These gifts are just as varied as are God's children: "To some is given one, and to some is given another, that all may be profited thereby." We are instructed not to hoard our spiritual gifts, as if they are some kind of personal entitlement, because they come to us "from God, for the benefit of the children of God" (D&C 46:11–12, 26). God's bestowal of spiritual gifts on all his children underscores the divine purpose in human diversity. In the Qur'an God pronounces, "O humankind, We [God] have created you male and female, and made you into communities and tribes, so that you may know one another" (Qur'an 49:13). In other words, God created us in all our sexual, racial, and cultural differences, precisely so that we could learn from the unique gifts of others and then glorify God for the gift of his diverse creation. Part of what it means to have charity is to learn to cherish the unique gifts found in all our sisters and brothers—even those outside our own household of faith, and even and perhaps especially those within our faith community who see things differently than we do.[19]

That faith also might increase

For those of us who feel we have found the path leading to the tree of life, whether because we were set on that path from birth or after extensive exploration, our job, in Joseph Smith's words, is to "waste and wear out our lives" in bringing people out of darkness and into the light (D&C 123:13). In his preface to the Doctrine and Covenants, section 1, the Lord outlines four charges to his modern-day disciples that suggest how we can bring people to the light. Our purpose in the restored church, according to this revelation, is to speak the name of Christ the Lord throughout the world, to proclaim his gospel to the ends of the earth, and to establish his everlasting covenant. In The Church of Jesus Christ of Latter-day Saints we dedicate an enormous amount of time and energy to proclaiming the gospel of Jesus Christ to all the world and to extending the blessings of gospel covenants to all who will receive them. But there is a fourth purpose to our labor— "that faith also might increase in the earth" (see D&C 1:19–23). When he gave this revelation in November 1831, God knew that of all the calamities that would befall humanity in the past two centuries, a loss of faith would be among the most profound. We are called to increase faith, however and whenever we can.

A couple years ago I was invited to appear as a panelist for a talk show broadcast on a global Muslim satellite network. I was the only non-Muslim participant, and they introduced me as a Mormon (which probably made no sense to their viewers in Pakistan). The topic of the episode was about how we could avoid modern-day idols and focus on worshipping the one true God. I felt impressed that my task that day, in line with the Lord's commission in Doctrine and Covenants 1, was to increase faith in the earth. I wasn't there to proclaim the name of Jesus Christ or to invite Muslims around the world to be baptized; doing so would have been wildly inappropriate and offensive. My calling in that moment was to encourage the Muslims in the sound of my voice to be better Muslims, to set aside the idols of money and sex and cars and celebrities and the Lakers (seriously, we talked a lot about Kobe Bryant), and to grow instead in the faith and love and worship of God. Although many of our specific beliefs are different, for that hour my fellow panelists and I united in seeking to increase faith in an increasingly faithless world.

We live in an age when doubt is part of our collective spiritual condition more than in times past. But honest questioning and lack of surety are not the same as the active unbelief so often warned against in scripture. As a necessary part of living on this side of the veil, doubt itself is neither good nor bad necessarily. While it sends some careening, for many others it sparks deeper spiritual yearnings and more mature reflection on the complexities of mortality. Doubt can therefore operate as faith's partner as much as its enemy, depending on our response to it. The quest to eradicate all doubt becomes counterproductive to God's call for us to live by faith in a mortal existence where uncertainty is so often the norm. Once we recognize with Nephi that it is not wrong to not know all things (1 Nephi 11:17) and we acknowledge that testimonies come in different shapes and sizes, we are prepared to embrace both those within our faith and those beyond with love rather than judgment. Comprehending that faith is a process, a journey, a spectrum—choose your own metaphor—we realize that neither faith nor doubt are all-or-nothing propositions. People can (and most people do) hold both faith and doubt in their minds and hearts simultaneously.

The call to belief is not a decree to deny our doubts. It is rather to "give place for a portion" of God's light—whatever portion we have received, in whatever form—to be planted and then grow within us. Desire is enough; "a particle of faith" is sufficient. God's plea is simple and direct: do not cast out the seed of faith, whatever yours looks like, by your unbelief (Alma 32:27–28). President Dieter F. Uchtdorf expressed this idea in his October 2013 general conference address:

> It's natural to have questions—the acorn of honest inquiry has often sprouted and matured into a great oak of understanding. There are few members of the church who, at one time or another, have not wrestled with serious or sensitive questions. One of the purposes of the church is to nurture and cultivate the seed of faith—even in the sometimes sandy soil of doubt and uncertainty. Faith is to hope for things which are not seen but which are true. Therefore, my dear brothers and sisters—my dear friends—please, first doubt your doubts before you doubt your faith. We must never allow doubt to

hold us prisoner and keep us from the divine love, peace, and gifts that come through faith in the Lord Jesus Christ.[20]

It is possible to have questions and doubts enliven your faith life rather than squelch it. On the other side of the coin, for those whose testimony is sure, recognizing and even appreciating that doubt is a reality of this mortal probation will better allow you to embrace your brothers and sisters with charity, to minister to them with empathy, "that faith also might increase in the earth" (D&C 1:21).

3

Foolishness and Scandal

THOUGH MANY OF HIS POLITICAL OPPONENTS DISAGREED, labeling him an "infidel" and an "atheist," Thomas Jefferson considered himself a Christian.[1] Yet Jefferson was also one of the Enlightenment's most precocious students, and he could not stomach the supernaturalism of scripture. So in early 1804, having just doubled the size of the United States through the Louisiana Purchase, Jefferson found time in his presidential schedule to trim the New Testament—specifically, the four Gospels. His goal was to free the precious truths taught by Jesus from all the superstitious accretions and corruptions piled on by later scribes and authors (including the apostle Paul). In an actual cut-and-paste job, Jefferson took a razor to the King James Bible, with nothing but his own reason to guide him in what he called the "obvious and easy" task of retrieving Jesus's genuine teachings. Only about one in ten verses survived his (literal) cuts; he later commented that the authentic words of Jesus were "as easily distinguishable as diamonds in a dunghill." In the resulting "Jefferson Bible" there was no virgin birth, no wise men following a star, no angels, no miracles, and of course no resurrection. As one scholar has observed, what remained of Jesus after Jefferson was done with him was a philosopher who "did little more than wander around Galilee delivering pithy moral aphorisms."[2]

Jefferson died in 1826, a year before the angel Moroni allowed Joseph Smith to retrieve the gold plates from Cumorah. There is little doubt, however, that had he lived to see them, Jefferson would have placed Mormonism's founding visions and revelations squarely in his "dunghill," the supernatural world of those nine-out-of-ten verses that didn't make the cut. There were plenty of others, of course, who were willing to take up Jefferson's mantle, declaring Mormonism to be the "most shocking humbug" of the age and Joseph Smith to be little more than a "miserable impostor."[3] From its beginning Mormonism has always lived under a cloud of suspicion that its founding miracles were too fantastic and its doctrinal claims unworthy of serious theological consideration.

While we could certainly do without the contempt inherent in most dismissals of Mormonism, from religious and irreligious antagonists alike, perhaps there is wisdom in accepting the substance of their critiques rather than being offended by them. Mormonism is too large to fit within the confining worldview of Jefferson's secular bible. It simply doesn't fit within his tithe of scripture. It demands a grander, more capacious view of God and his workings in the world, where there is a reality beyond the readily observable material world. At the same time, Mormonism cannot be expected to fit within the theological molds of other, older religions. One of the fundamental claims of the restoration was that extant religious forms and doctrines were insufficient—creeds were called an "abomination" in Jesus's impolitic words (Joseph Smith—History 1:19). A new dispensation of revelation, not mere reform, was needed in order to capture the enormity of what God had to tell and do in the world.[4]

In chapter 1 I discussed the sense of betrayal that many people feel upon encountering aspects of church history and doctrine they had not previously learned at church. This chapter considers a related but distinct aspect of many (though not all) faith crises: the disenchantment with elements of Mormon history and doctrine that do not readily conform to either purely rational or widely accepted religious categories of understanding. In this view Mormonism seems all too vulnerable to critiques leveled by DNA studies and Egyptology on the one hand, and theologies of scriptural inerrancy and prophetic infallibility on the other.

Yet to reduce Mormonism to what can be explained rationally or on the grounds set by any other religion is to render it something other (and arguably less) than what it is and claims to be. Mormonism is sui generis—that is to say, it offers its own unique set of questions and answers for the world that overlaps with but is not identical to any other set of questions and answers, whether those posed by modern science or creedal Christianity. What this also means, however, is that while Mormonism is internally coherent, intellectually rewarding, spiritually satisfying, and theologically profound, when viewed solely through any other lens it will appear flawed, foolish, and even scandalous.

Wisdom and foolishness

Mention in casual conversation that a carpenter named Jesus was the Son of God and that he rose from the grave on the third day: while not everyone will agree with you, scarcely anyone will call you crazy. This was not true for the earliest Christians, who had to endure not only injury but also insult for their beliefs that flew in the face of so much of what their contemporaries thought they knew about how the world actually worked. The apostle Paul's ministry to regions dominated by Greek culture and thought was emblematic of early Christians' struggle for cultural legitimacy. Many things about Christian belief offended the Greeks, not least the devotion to a single god and the claim that God took on flesh and suffered pain, humiliation, and ultimately death. It was not so much that Christianity was a grave threat, though it was a bit of a nuisance to the business interests of the Ephesian silversmiths and other idol makers. Rather, in the Hellenistic mind Christianity was simply laughable. It was an affront to the most advanced intellectual culture of the ancient world. Gods are not born in stables, do not live in obscurity among peasants in a colonial backwater, do not preach about turning the other cheek, and then give themselves up to be scourged and crucified as enemies to the state. Furthermore, although the world was filled with wonders, people did not ordinarily turn water into wine, heal blindness with spit and leprosy with a touch, walk on water, or raise people from the dead. Such things were foolish superstitions held by unlearned provincials. The religion of Jesus preached by Paul was, to borrow a phrase from another skeptic, little more than "the effect of a frenzied mind" (Alma 30:16).

Had it been others of the early apostles who encountered such condescending ridicule, there might have been fireworks—one suspects, for instance, that the impetuous fisherman Peter may not have had much patience for the self-satisfied glories of the Athenian academy.

But the cosmopolitan Paul perfectly understood the stakes. And he called the Greeks' bluff. You call my religion "strange" (Acts 17:18) because I preach Jesus and the resurrection? You think my faith is absurd? Well, you're right. It is—by your standard of wisdom. I'm here for one purpose, Paul told the Greeks: to proclaim the gospel of Christ crucified. I cannot do so simply with the "wisdom of words," because on the basis of Greek philosophical reasoning alone, the "preaching of the cross" is nothing less than "foolishness." In a culture where wisdom was ascertained principally through rational argument, all Paul had at his disposal was "the foolishness of preaching" (1 Corinthians 1:17–21).

Of all the New Testament writers, Paul can hardly be accused of being antirational. But his rational arguments were almost entirely made within the confines of faith. In his masterful letter to the Saints at Corinth, Paul reminded them that the faith of a believer in Jesus relied not simply on "the wisdom of men" but also on "the power of God." Human wisdom is an excellent, divinely granted gift. But it has its limits. For those who see and feel and recognize a world beyond this material world, there are some things that can only be "spiritually discerned." There might not be strictly scientific evidence for many spiritual things, but there are other kinds of evidence—things that can be known without being empirically measured or verified.[5] From Paul's perspective, it was the Greeks' rejection of this spiritual way of knowing, with its unique access to the vastness of God's wisdom, that constituted the mark of true foolishness (1 Corinthians 2:4–14).

With Paul's blessing, then, perhaps we can stand ready to accept the charge (minus the condescension) that Mormonism indeed features much that can only be described as foolish when viewed entirely in the context of the Enlightenment-infused culture of Western modernity. Mormonism is an affront to a dominant modern mode of thought, in the same way that the cross of Christ was foolishness in first-century Greece. Angels do not appear to boys and deliver gold plates inscribed by ancient prophets. Obscure carpenters do not multiply loaves and fishes, calm raging seas, atone for the sins of all humanity, and resurrect after three days in the tomb. Those sorts of things simply don't happen in the normal world.

The cross of Jesus is foolishness, as are Joseph's seer stones. But as soon as you open up to the spiritually abundant world of the Gospels, full of all the marvel and strangeness of God working providentially in and through history, then—as Paul predicted—what you had previously thought was wisdom now appears as foolishness, and what you considered to be absurdity is now reality. Frankly, once you've gazed with wonder into the empty tomb of Christ, allowing for a prophet to gaze into a stone at the bottom of a hat is mere child's play.[6]

Facts and interpretation

Given the foolishness of belief, those who lose their faith in the church sometimes become skeptical of those who remain and wonder, "Are they seeing something that I don't see?" That question can then quickly morph into the more judgmental query, "Why don't they see what I see?" Given all the troubling facts in church history, or the lack of archaeological evidence for the Book of Mormon, or continuing questions about gender equality in the church, they wonder how their friends and family can possibly stay in such an institution. Disbelievers may feel that believers have too many vested interests to follow courageously where reason clearly leads. They don't want to disappoint family, friends, and fellow ward members. Rather than painfully cut all ties, they persuade themselves they have a reason to go on believing. That also helps explain all the Mormon intellectuals who are lifelong members of the church—they are well informed and surely have doubts in their hearts, but they simply can't bring themselves to renounce the faith of their mothers and fathers and friends.

There may be some truth in this hypothesis in certain instances, but there is another explanation for why some believe and others do not, even when they are looking at the same evidence. Whether because of my natural disposition or my professional training as a historian, or both, I typically do not think in black-and-white terms. Things don't seem as certain and obvious to me as they often do to others. Some people are absolutely certain the church is absolutely true when they are on the inside, and then just as absolutely certain it is absolutely false when they shift to the outside. Such people say that historical facts make it impossible to believe that Joseph Smith was a prophet. How could he be if he thought he was translating the words of Abraham when he was probably simply looking at a conventional Egyptian funerary document?[7] How could he be a prophet of God when he took a fourteen-year-old girl as a plural wife?[8] To some people such facts seem to make it logically impossible to believe Joseph Smith was inspired by God. They feel forced by the facts to leave.

To me, however, the evidence does not so obviously lead to that outcome. It is possible to think of a prophet who genuinely hears God's voice and yet is still mistaken on some things. (This is a theme taken up in greater depth in chapter 6.) What one does with seemingly damning facts is a matter of judgment. Facts do not compel us to a certain conclusion. They have to be interpreted and may take on a different aspect when viewed from another angle. This is no mere apologetic sleight of hand. Interpretation is at the heart of human cognition. Making sense of the raw data produced by our senses requires it.

Think, for instance, of the optical illusion that reveals a stylish, beautiful woman from one perspective, but a gnarled old hag from another. The facts—the lines on the page—have not changed at all. The only thing that changes is our perspective. Recognizing both options, we can choose to see either image. One view is not more factually correct than the other. At that moment interpretation becomes in no small part an act of will.

None of us are blank slates. When we encounter some troubling aspect within the church, whether in its past or present, our response

to it will be shaped by a million different choices we have made, things we have learned, experiences we have had, and people we have known throughout our life. It is only natural that our judgment will be dependent on a host of natural biases, some that we can readily identify and others that are embedded in our subconscious. None of us are purely objective; indeed, objectivity is not even desirable, as it would make us something less than human, with all of our wonderful passions, memories, joys, and hurts. One incontrovertible result of our God-given diversity is that we will perceive and then interpret the available facts differently. But in a moral universe predicated upon agentive choice, we are never compelled to disbelieve any more than we are forced to believe.

The scandal of religion

When it comes to how we interpret matters of faith, the stakes are of course far higher than they are when we look at an optical illusion. Because religion is a matter of ultimate concern, everything is on the line: our personal commitments, worldview, and relationships here on earth and what lies beyond this life as well. One might grant that religion requires a certain suspension of disbelief—after all, what else is faith? But to many, Mormonism still seems to strain credulity, not just because of its stubborn supernaturalism or theological innovations but also because of all the apparent contradictions and conundrums in the church's history, doctrine, and positions on current issues. How can we reasonably expect someone to believe that God is specially working through The Church of Jesus Christ of Latter-day Saints when they can readily identify the church's manifest flaws? We all acknowledge there is at least some of the attractive lady and some of the decrepit hag in each of us and in all our human institutions. But shouldn't the church, if it is really God's and really true, be somehow immune or at least elevated?

Paradoxically, the scriptural answer to that question is a resounding "no." Consider the following verse, from Paul's Epistle to the Romans: "As it is written, Behold, I lay in Zion a stumblingstone and rock of offense: and whosoever believeth on him shall not be ashamed" (Romans 9:33). Paul here is paraphrasing Isaiah and applying his prophecy messianically to the ministry of Christ. This concept of the stumbling block, snare, or cause of offense is denoted in this verse and others by the Greek word *skandalon* or the Latin word *scandalum*, which together are the roots of our modern English word *scandal*.[9] Paul and Isaiah are essentially saying, "I place in Zion a scandal, and whoever believes in Christ will not be put to shame."

For many in our secular age, religion itself is a scandal. The late Christopher Hitchens, one of the outspoken proponents of the New Atheism movement, wrote in his book *God Is Not Great* that "religion poisons everything" and, even less subtly, "religion kills."[10] In a post-9/11 world, we are more attuned than ever to the scandal of religious extremism. Exclusion, intolerance, violence, and other bad behavior have historically been the scandal of every religion. Too often we Christians have used Christ as a bludgeon rather than an olive branch. We have partaken too readily in the spirit of the Roman emperor Constantine, who had a vision of a cross in the sky inscribed with the words, "Conquer by this," after which he went out and slaughtered his enemies. That the religion of the Prince of Peace has so often been spread or enforced by threat, intimidation, or coercion is one of Christianity's great scandals, and a stumbling block for non-Christians around the world.[11]

As Isaiah and Paul wrote, in Zion we always find stumbling blocks, snares, and offenses—in other words, scandal. Scripture is many things, but one of its purposes is to be a faithful record of God working with, through, and against the scandals of Zion and the people who perpetrate them. Consider how this looks in just one of our standard works. Of all the sacred texts accepted by Latter-day Saints as scripture, the Old Testament, or Hebrew Bible, is the one in which the characters are most evidently human—which is what makes it great literature too. There are few angels here among the mortals. Even the book's exemplars are deeply and often tragically—we might say scandalously—flawed. Adam and Eve fall, Noah gets drunk, Abraham lies, Sarah is jealous, Jacob deceives, Joseph deceives, Moses murders, Joshua and Saul commit genocide, David commits adultery, Jonah runs from God, Elisha summons bears to kill forty-two children for calling him bald—and these are the good guys! The stunning thing is that *this* was the narrative that was consciously preserved and held sacred by the Jews and then adopted by Christians as a meaningful and faith-promoting record of humanity's relationship to God. Indeed, if there was ever written a tell-all history replete with religious scandal, the Old Testament is it.

Scripture contains plenty of admonitions directed toward those who fall outside the covenant, but for the most part the prophets have their hands full calling their own people—the people of Zion, even Zion itself—to repent, to quit their scandals, to be redeemed and reconciled to God and to one another. A consistent message of scripture seems to be that in the Zion we live in—as opposed to the Zion we aspire to and only rarely achieve—we will always find snares, stumbling blocks, and offenses. In a fallen world, scandal constantly dogs the covenant. The recurrent inability of God's people to learn their lessons can be a bit depressing, to be sure, but overall the message is one of hope: Zion's scandals can disappoint and disturb us without baffling or confounding us. After reading the Old Testament, we should not be particularly surprised that our modern-day Zion has snares, stumbling blocks, and offenses. I am, and should be, troubled anytime I see scandals in Zion, just as many of the events recorded in the Old Testament are deeply troubling to me. But scripture reminds me not to be surprised by Zion's failings and to believe that God can redeem his people in spite of their many missteps.

The "scandal" of Jesus

While Paul's appropriation of Isaiah's prophecy is helpful in thinking constructively about the scandals in Zion, his direct meaning was even more specific: he identified Zion's "stumblingstone and rock of offense" as the very One in whom we should believe and "not be ashamed." In other words, Jesus Christ is the great *skandalon*, or scandal, laid in Zion.

This is a hard message for us Christians to hear because we understand Jesus to be the solution to our problems, not a problem himself. We can comprehend why his messiahship was a hard thing for people at the time to accept; after all, Nathanael was not the only one to ask, "Can there any good thing come out of Nazareth?" (John 1:46). But we have the benefit of so many witnesses, ancient and modern, that it is relatively easy for us to believe in Jesus. To the contrary, it's fairly hard to find anyone nowadays who doesn't at least respect him and his teachings, even if they don't consider him divine. Christians who worship

Jesus as the Son of God and Savior of the world are joined by Muslims who consider him a great prophet, Jews who revere him as a master rabbi, Hindus who regard him as a preeminent yogi, and secularists who appreciate him as an ethical philosopher.[12] Indeed, admiring Jesus may be the modern world's least scandalous form of religious belief.

But the malleable and customizable Jesus of modernity is only a faint shadow of the Jesus revealed in scripture. The Jesus of the New Testament—the unabridged version, not Thomas Jefferson's rendering—does indeed provide comfort to the afflicted, but he is also a terrible affliction to the comfortable. If he does not scandalize you and your modern sensibilities, it means you're not paying attention.

He is born of a virgin, conceived by the Holy Ghost. He survives a forty-day fast, at the end of which he talks to the devil. He turns water into wine. He heals the vilest of diseases with a simple touch. He casts out devils and puts them into pigs, who run in a frenzy into the sea. He curses a fig tree for no apparent reason. He walks on water. He calms storms with a word. He feeds five thousand men, plus women and children, with five loaves and two fishes—with twelve baskets left over. He reads people's thoughts. He has conversations with long-dead prophets. He raises the dead. He rises from the dead.

And then there are the stumbling blocks of Jesus's teachings. He tells you to turn the other cheek when someone hits you, to give more to the person who sues you than what they demand, to give to whoever asks it of you. He urges you to "love your enemies, bless them that curse you, do good to them that hate you, and pray for them which despitefully use you, and persecute you" (Matthew 5:44). He commands you to be perfect. He says not to lay up earthly treasures and not to give any thought about where your clothing or your food will come from. He proclaims he was God before he was born. He declares that it's easier for a camel to go through a needle's eye than for a rich man to get into heaven. He tells a rich man to give away all his possessions. He teaches that he will save those who eat his flesh and drink his blood. He insists that he is the only way to heaven.

None of the above actions or teachings corresponds to the way the real world works. Seriously, read them again, like you were hearing it for the first time. If a guy named Bob came up to you and claimed any of this about himself, you would think he was crazy and walk away, but then call the authorities if he persisted. Any one of these statements should be a stumbling block to a reasonable person. Taken together, they are foolish and scandalous. They also constitute the core of the historic faith of billions of Christians worldwide.

To believe in the Jesus of scripture should be a demanding thing. It should assault our modern sensibilities. We should be shocked every time we open the Gospels. We should be ripped out of the normal rhythms and patterns of our everyday lives and plunged headlong into a world that requires us to rethink our sense of what is real. We should be profoundly disoriented before we find any kind of reorientation. We should be confronted with the fact that the kingdom of heaven proclaimed by Jesus looks little to nothing like the world as we commonly know it. We should find what we read virtually impossible to understand if we rely only on our reason and our modern judgments about what is real, right, and rational. We should be scandalized by Jesus.

But Christ does not scandalize us simply for the sake of scandal, or even to make a point. He scandalizes us so as to prepare us to be disciples. Paul urged the Roman Saints to "not be ashamed of the gospel of Christ" (Romans 1:16); one wonders if he had Peter's triple denial and his later triple affirmation by the sea at least in the corner of his mind. But it is not enough to be unashamed. We must embrace the *skandalon* of the Son of God and crucified Christ and participate in it with all our heart, might, mind, and strength. In doing so we realize that the *skandalon* was placed only to trip up our clumsy attachments to this world and is really meant to serve as a stepping stone to a higher life in the kingdom of God. That is what it means to be a disciple of Jesus. That is what it means to straightway leave our nets and follow him (Matthew 4:20). That is what it means to become a fool for Christ (1 Corinthians 4:10).

The scandal of Mormonism

None of this is an argument specifically for Mormonism. Serious Christians of all stripes have made a similar case in pleading with readers to be better Catholics, Lutherans, Mennonites, Baptists, Presbyterians, and Methodists.[13] When it comes to mounting an argument that sounds reasonable to modern believers, traditional Christians have the advantage over Mormons in that they've had a lot more time to tell their story. When you say something long enough and with enough power, it becomes real, no matter how outlandish it seems at the outset. The challenge of Mormonism to the modern mind is that its miraculous—and scandalous—stories are so tantalizingly within reach. Say that Noah built an ark and put two of every animal in it, and virtually no one will blink an eye. Hollywood will even make a blockbuster movie out of it. Say that a family of Jews left Jerusalem and built a boat and sailed to America six hundred years before Christ, and now you've got a punch line in a Broadway satire. Actually, the first story is more patently unbelievable than the second, but people have told that first story a lot longer, and they're used to it, so it doesn't draw so many laughs.

Of course, in the wake of Enlightenment rationality and scholarly biblical criticism, plenty of people have become dubious about the Bible's stories—not least that of Noah. But Mormons have a special burden because our stories—both the good ones and the bad ones—are not yet old and thus have not earned the reputable patina of myth or culture or tradition. Our miracles and our scandals are modern, and exceedingly well documented, and thus press upon us with particular urgency. We can no more hide behind the respectability of tradition than could the second- and third-century Christians who were literally being thrown to the lions.

In a thousand years, however, Mormonism will no longer be an upstart religion, with all the volatility and vulnerability of adolescence. People will no more leave Mormonism over the Mountain Meadows Massacre than modern Jews leave Judaism over biblical genocide. Mormon polygamy will be no more (and no less) vexing than ancient polygamy. The Book of Abraham will be no more textually troubling than the Bible's Deuteronomists or multiple Isaiahs. Multiple versions of Joseph Smith's first vision will be no more faith-shaking than varying accounts of Paul's conversion or the disharmony of the Gospels.

But we live now, not a thousand years from now. The scandals are real, and the doubt and pain they cause are real. To explain a problem and reconcile it in our minds is not to deny its existence or significance. Having spent my professional life working in an academy largely allergic to the extrarational claims of faith, and in a field of religious history where many colleagues are devoted evangelicals or Catholics, I know well that in the view of Enlightenment rationalism and scientism on the one hand and historic Christianity on the other, much of Mormonism appears foolish and scandalous. That the same can be said of every other religion hardly puts salve in the wound.

We are not called to abandon our natural reason; to do so would not only lead to fanaticism but also to reject one of our greatest divine inheritances. Yet to remain open to all the infinite possibilities of an inexplicable cosmos, we have to humbly acknowledge the limits of human rationality and accept complementary ways of knowing and being. We do not proceed merely on faith, but we do recognize that faith and trust are essential ingredients in a holistic approach to life. By definition, to have faith—in God, in Mormonism, in anything—is to act on claims that in the end can be neither proven nor disproven. To base one's life on unfalsifiable claims is not a sign of intellectual weakness or antirationality, but rather a perfectly normal human response to the uncertainty that is the lot of mortality. As LDS sociologist Armand Mauss has pointed out, "Even traditional American patriotism requires the acceptance of claims that are ultimately supernatural and just as unfalsifiable as religious truth claims." Indeed, the entire American experiment is based on the "self-evident" claim, written by Thomas Jefferson in the Declaration of Independence, that "all men are created equal, that they are endowed by their Creator with certain unalienable Rights." Mauss continues: "How would we test that claim? If it can't be tested, why should anyone believe in it? Yet millions do believe it and act on it. . . . The only difference with religious choices is that the outcomes for those choices occur in another world instead of in another decade."[14]

While remaining profoundly open to reason and all the light and truth discerned through rational processes, on this side of the veil Mormonism does demand a willingness to appear the fool in the face of exclusivist rationalism. It also requires us to think about religion in ways more commensurate with the restoration than with Christian tradition, however much we can and should learn from the latter. Our modern Zion, like the yet-imperfect Zions of all ages, furthermore necessitates a certain tolerance for snares, stumbling blocks, and offenses rooted dually in human fallibility and divine mystery. In this, our religion asks no more and no less than Paul asked of the first-century believers in

Christ. Being true to the faith means accepting the fact that we will never fully counter the critiques of the New Atheists and others committed to an unrelenting hyperrationalism; neither will the peculiarities of our theology, our history, and our way of life satisfy those rooted in another.

The call to live by faith is a call to vulnerability, trial, and trust. When the Lord said, "I will try the faith of my people" (3 Nephi 26:11), apparently he meant it.

4

Unicorns and Rhinoceroses

IN THE YEAR 1271, seventeen-year-old Marco Polo joined his father and uncle on a trip to the East. By the time they returned to their native Venice twenty-four years and some 15,000 miles later, they had acquired not only immense wealth but also incredible stories from their travels in lands far from home. In 1292, on their sea voyage home from China, they landed on the island of Sumatra, in modern-day Indonesia. In his diary Marco recorded seeing monkeys, elephants, and "plenty of unicorns":

> [The unicorns] are scarcely smaller than elephants. They have the hair of a buffalo and feet like an elephant's. They have a single large, black horn in the middle of the forehead. . . . When they want to do any harm to anyone they first crush him by kneeling upon him and then lacerate him with their tongues. They have a head like a wild boar's and always carry it stooped towards the ground. They spend their time by preference wallowing in mud and slime. They are very ugly brutes to look at. They are not at all such as we describe them.[1]

You and I recognize that what Marco Polo saw was not a unicorn at all but rather a rhinoceros. However, Polo did not know that there was such a thing as a rhinoceros, so he had to make sense of what he experienced in terms of what he knew, in the language that was available to him. The irony is that Polo's reality of stunning white unicorns was a fantasy all along. The rhinoceros was hairier, dirtier, uglier, and more brutish than fantasy—but it did have the singular advantage of being real. Polo's misidentification of the rhinoceros stemmed from two competing but simultaneous errors: an excess of imagination, supposing that certain things (like unicorns) are real when they are not; and a lack of imagination, failing to realize that the world may contain things (like rhinoceroses) that are outside of our inherently limited experience.

Most of us approach history a little (or a lot) like Marco Polo approached the Sumatra rhino. We have certain things fixed in our mind's eye about the way the world was. After all, we have read about the past in books or, more likely, seen it on TV or in the movies. We feel we understand the Holocaust because we saw *Schindler's List*, or World War I because we read *All Quiet on the Western Front*, or the Willie Handcart Company because we watched *17 Miracles*. When we imagine God speaking to Moses on the mountain, we have in our mind's eye a picture of Charlton Heston. And who can doubt but that *Downton Abbey* is a faithful rendering of life on an early twentieth-century English estate, with all its upstairs-downstairs drama?

It's only natural for us to try to make things intelligible. So we use metaphor to achieve better understanding. Your family isn't really a tree, but it helps to think about our connection to our ancestors that way. One's heart does not really break when jilted by a lover, but it feels like it. America is not really a melting pot—that would not be an enjoyable place to live—but it is a country where different people and cultures mix together. We take things that are foreign to us, or difficult to grasp, and put them in terms that we can make sense of. There is absolutely nothing wrong with this; it's simply what our brains do to keep from exploding. (By the way, brains don't actually explode—or at least they very rarely do.) Perception and comprehension are invariably acts of interpretation and translation.

Our minds are constantly translating the unfamiliar into familiar terms—turning rhinoceroses into unicorns. It takes conscious effort to stop or at least slow down the process long enough to acknowledge that "the other"—that which is alien or divergent from ourselves or from accepted norms—is, in fact, really and genuinely other, not just a variation on something we already know. Earlier generations of historians thought they could absolutely get to know their past subjects, essentially transcending time and space to put themselves into the mind of Cleopatra or Charlemagne. Modern historians are not so sure. They agree that it is crucial to do everything possible to bring forth that which has been lost to the passing of time. Masterworks of history such as Laurel Thatcher Ulrich's *A Midwife's Tale* are so artful in re-creating and repopulating past worlds and people as to make them seem almost tangible. But only almost. Ulrich's brilliant efforts notwithstanding, Martha Ballard and her neighbors remain just beyond our grasp, shrouded not only by the passage of time but also by the divide between their mental universe and ours.[2]

The previous chapters reflected on what it means to be a religious person, and specifically a Latter-day Saint, in the modern world. This and the following chapter look backward, offering suggestions on how we might relate to our collective past in a historically responsible but still constructive and faithful manner. We don't need to be professional historians to be saints. But Mormonism is a religion, like most others, that draws strength from and finds deep meaning in its past. We turn to it for instructive and inspirational stories, for heroines and role models, for a sense of belonging and rootedness in a fast-changing world. If we are not careful, however, we run the risk of actually silencing our ancestors by turning their rich and textured lives into simple, two-dimensional fables that offer either uplifting morality tales or the grist for our own contentions with the church. The past is just as morally complex as the present, and we disrespect the real people who have gone before by reducing them to mythological figments of our imagination. Learning to think like a historian won't save you or your kin, but it may help you relate to church history in new and sometimes surprisingly redemptive ways.

Traveling through space and time

It's a tricky business to recognize and honor difference without making it the grounds for contempt. In the popular BBC show *Doctor Who*, the Doctor and his companions travel throughout space and time. In their visits—whether to alien planets or to various points in Earth's past, present, and future—they form friendships with the staggeringly diverse range of people (loosely defined) they encounter. Yet no matter how profound the connection and how sophisticated the translation technology that allows them to communicate, the underlying fact is that they are different. They may visit ancient Rome or meet alien races such as the Sontarans, but they will never be Roman or Sontaran. Naturally, the first reaction of the Doctor's human companions when they meet members of an alien civilization is to be perplexed by their strangeness. After enough of those visits, however, they realize that things back home on Earth, when viewed from their newfound intergalactic perspective, are just as odd. Their prejudicial notions that one's own ways are the best or only ways are subverted. The very real differences between humans and aliens make it impossible to say glibly, "They're just like us," but the Doctor's fundamental ethic—and the lesson he has to teach over and over again—is to honor life in all its diversity. At the end of every episode or two, the Doctor and his friends, having saved the world or the universe from certain disaster, get back in their time-traveling police box and move on to the next adventure, having gained a little more understanding, and—this is the crux of the matter—a little more compassion. Traveling across time and space is certainly disconcerting, but it should also enhance our charity toward others.

Historians don't have the technological advantages afforded to the Doctor, but the underlying premise of their work is not altogether different. In large part, the work of history is to see strangeness and to grapple with unfamiliarity without surrendering to the notion that people in the past are utterly unknowable and thus unrelatable. Historians try to achieve enough escape velocity to get away from the twin gravitational pulls of both prejudice and presentism (anachronistically introducing present-day perspectives and concerns into our understanding of the past). As Richard White, an award-winning historian of the American West, observed, "Any good history begins in strangeness. The past should not be comfortable. The past should not be a familiar echo of the present, for if it is familiar why revisit it? The past should be so strange that you wonder how you and people you know and love could come from such a time." Another award-winning historian, Robert Darnton, asserts: "Other people are other. They do not think the way we do. And if we want to understand their way of thinking we should set out with the idea of capturing otherness. . . . We constantly need to be shaken out of a false sense of familiarity with the past, to be administered doses of culture shock."[3]

Seasoned travelers abroad are not shocked by the dissimilarities they inevitably encounter, though they may be unsettled that the linguistic or cultural gap in a particular locale is greater than they had expected. In general we are too quick to leap from observing distinctions to disparaging them, forgetting that when we journey to a far-off place or immerse ourselves in the past it is we, not the people who live there, who are foreign. Upon encountering the exotic, we are quick to transform it into something more recognizable. Like Marco Polo, we think that we are merely rehearsing facts when we are actually rendering interpretations and judgments. We inescapably make meaning out of our observations, which are themselves colored by our past experience and the filters we have developed, consciously or not. Therefore, facts are rarely, if ever, self-evident. They are always subject to interpretation, and interpretation is always subject to debate.

Treasure seeking then and now

Discussions of Joseph Smith's prophethood are loaded with such debates, which are rarely disagreements over facts but are usually contests over interpretation. An example from the career of Richard Bushman, one of Mormonism's most distinguished historians, is illustrative.[4] In the 1970s, when he began work on his book *Joseph Smith and the Beginnings of Mormonism*, the number one criticism of Joseph Smith was that his family practiced magic in the search for buried treasure. It was incongruous to think of a prophet of God using strange symbols and incantations in the search for Spanish silver. Critical scholars at the time thought it obvious that Joseph was a treasure seeker and thus could not possibly have been a prophet, while apologetic scholars denied the charge of money digging categorically, implicitly admitting that it and true prophethood clashed. To both parties, magic and divine inspiration seemed totally antithetical.

Joseph's defenders made their case by claiming the evidence for money digging was untrustworthy. The problem with their defense was that a number of historical documents emerged to support the charge. Historians found accounts of Joseph Smith's 1826 trial for disturbing the peace by claiming to look for lost objects, otherwise known as "glass-looking." In addition, the affidavits collected in 1833 by Doctor Philastus Hurlbut from Joseph's former neighbors in Palmyra described many instances of the Smith family searching by night for treasure, sacrificing lambs, and drawing magic circles. Most obviously, Joseph himself admitted the particular charge of treasure seeking. In an article published in the May 1838 issue of the short-lived *Elders' Journal*, Joseph Smith answered various questions about Mormon beliefs and his own history. The tenth question read, "Was not Jo Smith a money digger[?]" His answer: "Yes, but it was never a very profitable job for him, as he only got fourteen dollars a month for it."[5] The evidence was there, but many defenders of the Prophet dismissed it out of hand. They argued that evidence for the 1826 trial was discovered fifty years after the event and was likely fabricated by Joseph's enemies who only pretended to have discovered it. The Hurlbut affidavits, they noted, were collected by a man who had been hired to gather damaging evidence and who detested Joseph Smith. How could statements assembled by a known enemy possibly be trusted? Mormon historians admitted Joseph's own statement but explained it away by saying he merely dabbled in treasure seeking while working for Josiah Stowell; they claimed it was simply a job, one that he had no taste for. The rest of the evidence, they believed, had no credibility.

Once Richard Bushman began his research, he realized that as a professional historian he could not simply dismiss the Hurlbut affidavits with a wave of the hand. They had to be evaluated like every other form of evidence. Moreover, while Bushman was writing, Wesley Walters, a relentless critical researcher, proved that the 1826 glass-looking trial had indeed taken place based on evidence from a contemporaneous court record. Furthermore, careful research in the archives revealed corroborating sources from friendly contemporaries as well, including Martin Harris, Joseph Knight, Oliver Cowdery, and Joseph's own mother, Lucy Mack Smith. Taking all the mounting evidence into account, Bushman decided that money digging and magic were indeed part of the Smith family culture. Perhaps the precise form of their activities was exaggerated or misshapen by the obvious disdain of their neighbors, but the charges were not all baseless.

Serendipitously, at the same time that Bushman was writing about Joseph Smith, other historians were publishing path-breaking scholarship on the subject of magic in early modern Europe and America. They demonstrated that magical practices played a large part in the religious lives of Christians well into the eighteenth century. This was often a sore spot with the clergy, who tried to purify the practices of the European populace; they, however, enjoyed only limited success, and some even participated. Magical practices were deeply engrained in English culture at all levels, not just among the poor and ignorant. Isaac Newton was an alchemist; members of Parliament used seer stones; even Puritans included astrological signs in their almanacs.[6] Other scholars demonstrated how magical practices crossed the Atlantic and persisted in American popular culture through the eighteenth and into the nineteenth centuries. Their research showed that the very areas the Smith family hailed from and lived in—Vermont and upstate New York—were among the hotbeds of American treasure-seeking culture.[7]

All this work shed new light on the Smith family's participation in magical practices. It came to appear much less toxic than it had earlier. As treasure seekers, they were not outliers caught up in a bizarre, marginal culture. They were indulging instead in practices that were commonplace among ordinary New Englanders and New Yorkers. The evidence in the Hurlbut affidavits themselves showed that others in the Smiths' neighborhood commonly pursued treasure seeking as well. Not everyone in America invoked spells and rituals to find buried treasure, but enough did to make it a familiar practice, certainly within the realm of the ordinary. By the Smiths' time, magic was questioned and even scorned by the enlightened upper classes, but it remained a part of the life of plain people.

Perhaps the most important revelation of all this scholarship was that for those who practiced it, magic did not replace Christianity; the two worked side by side as they had done for hundreds of years. In the early nineteenth century, a person could embrace Protestantism and magic simultaneously. The Smiths' participation did not indicate a rejection of religion. It was possible to be a Christian, even a Christian prophet, and still dabble in magic.

This newfound understanding allowed Bushman's thinking about the Prophet to transform. Previously he, like others, had been aware of the evidence of Joseph's treasure seeking but did not take it seriously. It seemed too far-fetched and incongruous with everything he thought he knew about Joseph. As he wrote, it was "like asking me to believe that my grandmother was a lifelong member of the Mafia." Other historians helped him realize that folk magic and deep religious belief were not contradictory in America and therefore did not have to be contradictory in Joseph Smith. That newfound perspective allowed Bushman to focus not on his preconceived notions about Joseph and what a prophet may or may not look like, but rather on the evidence. If reliable sources proved that Joseph Smith Sr. and his boys went looking for buried treasure with a hazel wand or a seer stone, then we should accept it. Their participation in this one element of their culture did not contradict the family's belief in Christianity and divine revelation.[8]

Over time, money digging steadily moved down the list of logical objections to Joseph Smith's prophetic claims. It once ranked up as high as the Book of Abraham and contradictions among the first vision accounts do today, but no longer. Three decades ago many people's faith was shaken by information about Joseph's treasure-seeking activities; today the issue barely registers. With greater perspective, we now interpret magic differently. It is less threatening. It appears like a relatively innocent—if naive—feature of the Smiths' family culture rather than an automatic disqualification for prophethood.[9]

From village seer to prophet

Not all the questions are settled. Debate continues about how deeply Joseph was involved in folk magic practices and how long they persisted. But thanks to careful research and new historical vistas opened up by the work of LDS and non-LDS scholars alike, we can make sense of certain aspects of Joseph's past that once seemed outlandish, if not scandalous. Joseph Smith's money digging has shaken the faith of some members of the church, largely because it is so foreign to our contemporary experience. But when we drop some of our preconceived notions, do a little research, and put God and God's work at the center of the story, then we might even find a redemptive narrative that is far more powerful than a denial of historical fact.

Not coincidentally, evidence suggests that the Smiths were putting treasure seeking behind them after 1826, just before Joseph was finally allowed by Moroni to retrieve the gold plates. In the 1826 trial at South Bainbridge, where Joseph was accused of being a "disorderly person" for his "glass-looking," a man named W. D. Purple recorded lengthy testimony about Joseph's seer stones and money digging. No friend of the Smith family or the Mormons, Purple came away particularly impressed with one statement made by Joseph Smith Sr. (who had accompanied his twenty-year-old son to the hearing). Joseph Sr. freely admitted that his son had used his seer stones to search for buried treasure but that now "both he and his son were mortified that this wonderful power which God had so miraculously given him should be used only in search of filthy lucre. . . . His constant prayer to his Heavenly Father was to manifest His will concerning this marvelous power." As Bushman observed, "Smith treasure-seeking did not end right away; but from that time on, the Prophet and his family were caught up more and more in translation, the organization of the Church, [and] the building up of the Kingdom. . . . Treasure-seeking slid into the background."[10]

Joseph Smith used his seer stones to search for Spanish silver and other buried treasure—without much success. With greater maturity and spiritual insight, he later used those same skills and stones to translate the Book of Mormon by the gift and power of God. He was transformed from a common village seer into a prophet. The evidence suggests that Joseph was not allowed by Moroni to retrieve the plates in 1823 because as soon as he saw the gold plates in the ground, this son of a poor farmer couldn't get his mind past the gold.[11] It was not until he purified his heart and disciplined himself to keep an eye single to the glory of God that the angel allowed him to take custody of the plates. By 1827, having been prepared by his engagement with searching for earthly treasures, he was then ready to turn his gifts over to the Lord. "This wonderful power which God had so miraculously given him" could be applied to the ephemeral or the eternal. Joseph was schooled in the former, but then consciously chose the latter. Looking in the stone for lost objects readied him to look in the stone for lost words. However paradoxically, magic may well have been a vital part of Joseph Smith's spiritual education.

History does not always lend itself to moralizing. But there is something instructive for us about the gradual development of Joseph's spiritual gift of seership into his calling as a full-fledged prophet. Each of us has been given gifts and talents. Many of us spend years honing those natural aptitudes into skills that pay the bills or otherwise garner attention and praise. It might be business acumen, academic learning, or artistic creativity. We rarely give these pursuits a second thought because they are so deeply engrained in our culture as good and useful things. But each of these contain the inherent temptation of self-absorption, turning our hearts away from love of God and neighbor and toward love of money, praise, beauty, or achievement. All of these pursuits are instrumental and beneficial parts of our shared culture. None of these are evils in themselves, and we all know people who excel in these endeavors and then live wonderfully Christian lives. Nevertheless, inherent in all these aspects of our culture lies a danger to true religion.

For Saints living in the world, necessarily balancing celestial ideals with more mundane terrestrial realities and aspirations, the call is not to abandon culture altogether so much as to consecrate it to God and to Zion. In this light, we can relate to and admire Joseph's seemingly circuitous route to prophethood through the pathway of his contemporary culture. Even more, as Bushman incisively notes, "Far from condemning him for his failure to cast off his culture decisively, we should look to ourselves, and ask if we are as effectively redirecting our lives and our culture to godly purposes. Are we doing as well as he did in turning our treasure-seeking into service to our Heavenly Father's children?"[12] With that frame of mind, a potentially troubling episode in church history becomes a poignant lesson that reveals something deeper about the way God works in the world to redeem his children. Furthermore, this approach to our history performs its own kind of redemption.

Learning to see facts

Joseph Smith's money digging also provides an example of how changing interpretations put facts in a new light. Nowadays few people would list treasure seeking among the leading criticisms of the Prophet. Led by Richard Bushman, Mormon historians have found a way to tell the Joseph Smith story that includes both money digging and divine inspiration; one version of that narrative is now posted on the official LDS church website, and another in a recent *Ensign*.[13] A few new facts contributed to this latest outlook, but they did not substantially revolutionize our understanding. We have hit upon a new interpretation that puts the facts in a different light. The money-digging story helps us recognize that even the most apparently damning facts can be understood in a new light as historical scholarship evolves. What is obvious at one point becomes less obvious at another. The interpretive mills grind on, and our understanding of the past takes new forms. That is why as a historian I am comfortable with shades of gray (or all colors of the rainbow) rather than insisting on just black and white. I think it is likely that apparent certainties, like the seeming incongruity between Joseph's magic practices and his calling as a prophet, will seem less destructive later on, even if the facts do not materially change.

Underlying this view is the realization that what we know is contingent upon human perception and interpretation. Facts are not facts until someone makes them such. Bits of information may exist that we don't recognize as facts until someone brings them to our attention. Interpretation precedes fact, not the other way around. The historian Jared Farmer's award-winning account of Mount Timpanogos in Utah is a case in point. When Mormon settlers first came to Utah Valley, they paid little attention to the mountain range lining the eastern edge of their settlement. What attracted their attention was the lake. It contained precious water and fish and was a means of easy transportation. The indigenous Utes had lived near the lake for generations, and the Mormons built their first outposts not far away—tragically, this soon led to competition, horrific violence, and ultimate expulsion of the land's native peoples. Only gradually over the course of the nineteenth century did Timpanogos emerge as a feature of the landscape worthy of the settlers' attention. It was Eastern tourists, local community boosters, and tour guides who really drew attention to this peak. It was eventually given a name and carefully measured and turned into an object that everyone noticed. But the eyes of both settlers and tourists had to be trained to see the mountain.[14]

The attention to Smith family treasure seeking followed much the same course. Recently reexamining the original sources more closely, Bushman realized that the Smiths' money digging was not a fact that jumped out at anyone living in Palmyra in 1830 as relevant to Joseph Smith's translation of the Book of Mormon. When his "gold bible" was reported in the Palmyra press beginning in June 1829, nothing was said about Smith family treasure seeking. The Book of Mormon was presented as an "imposition," a duplicitous attempt to foist the book off on the public as a way to make money. It was essentially seen as priestcraft—making money through religion. (Recall that Moroni had the same concern back in 1823.) For an entire year after this first newspaper notice, no one said anything in any of the news articles about the Smiths' involvement with folk magic. Someone had to interpret the facts to make them relevant. Not until the summer of 1830 did Abner Cole, a local newspaper editor, suggest the novel idea that Joseph Smith had been a member of a band of treasure seekers, a fact portrayed to impugn Joseph's character sufficiently so as to undermine his claims of prophethood and translation. Even so, for more than a year no one took Cole seriously or picked up on his story. Only after the Mormons started gathering in Kirtland and a local newspaperman named Eber D. Howe republished some of Cole's essays did the money-digging angle gain any traction. Once Cole had noticed and named it, treasure seeking seemed obviously important to everyone, although no one had said a word about it for a year after the book was published. Cole was the guide who put treasure seeking on everyone's tour of Smith family history.

Taking all the evidence into account, two things become apparent. The first is that the Smith family was definitely involved in treasure seeking. Disagreements remain about how enthusiastic a participant Joseph was, but there is little doubt of his involvement. Friendly scholars who once resisted this claim now accept it, as has the institutional church. Though treasure seeking is unlikely to become part of the missionary discussions anytime soon, those who prepare the church's various curricular materials are now taking steps to introduce this and other lesser-known aspects of Joseph Smith's history to the general membership.[15]

The second conclusion takes the form of a question: Did magic shape Joseph Smith's worldview? Looking at the documents produced by Joseph and his associates before 1830, magic and money digging do not play a prominent role. They turn up here and there, but the references are scattered, not central. At least in the written texts they left behind, Joseph and his friends talked only about religion. They spoke of the second coming, divine visions, and Christ. The first written revelation of Joseph Smith, recorded in July 1828 and now section 3 of the Doctrine and Covenants, is in the voice of the Judeo-Christian God, not some pagan deity. Joseph's 1829 correspondence with Oliver

Cowdery focused on religious themes with not a speck of magic in it.[16] And the Book of Mormon was, as the first commentators agreed, a "gold bible." It was God-centered, saturated with biblical language, and filled with Christian theology. Virtually everything we have from the earliest Mormons in their own words was religious, and indeed Christian.

Though folk magic was present in Joseph Smith's worldview, it was probably never dominant, and even less so after the translation of the Book of Mormon. Evidence to the contrary is simply too thin. His neighbors did not automatically think of him as a money digger until Abner Cole suggested that proposition. Smith's own prophetic words, beginning with the revelation he dictated in 1828, had the sound and feel of biblical language. Taken together, the low frequency of magical references plus the Palmyrans' failure to speak of Joseph as a magic trickster in the beginning belie claims that his mature worldview was ever essentially magical rather than Christian. The supposedly magic-obsessed Joseph Smith may well have been Abner Cole's creation, later taken up by some historians trying to explain a complex life that Joseph himself admitted he would not have believed had he not lived it.[17]

History as a construction zone

We must recognize that history is always a work in progress. It is not just there. In significant ways, in fact, the past is gone. Because of this, history is a construction zone, and we have to put on our hard hats when we enter. Our understanding of the past is constructed, fashioned both by participants and later historians, and is always subject to change. Long after events happen, they take on new form and meaning as fresh evidence and interpretations emerge. Facts do not compel us to believe one way or the other because the understanding of those facts will inevitably change. This does not mean that nothing is real, but it does mean that reality may not be quite as definitive as we think. Furthermore, it puts a burden on us: we cannot escape the responsibility of interpreting facts for ourselves. Some things become less recognizable with the passage of time; other things that were once hard to digest have a tendency of softening over the years as what seems self-evident at one point becomes a matter of interpretation at another.

It may seem paradoxical for a scholar to say this, but there is nothing more unstable than basing one's life and outlook purely on the latest scholarship, let alone one's casual perusal of it. What appears to be solid is actually quite transient. The entire modern academic enterprise is founded upon the notion that scholars will say something novel in their published writings. That means they either have to expand upon current understandings or argue with received wisdom. The system is remarkably good at doing what it intends to do: create new knowledge. Yet by definition, then, scholarship makes for a fairly wobbly foundation upon which to build one's profoundest commitments. I can't imagine a more maddening life than to rise each morning to consult the learned journals to see what one's position du jour is.[18] Of course, no one actually lives his life that way. Even the most skeptical rationalist finds something deeper and more existential to make satisfactory meaning of her life. We assimilate the fruits of intellectual inquiry into a broader set of values and relationships that define us as complex human beings.

Perhaps the only thing more foolish than limiting ourselves to current scholarship is to abandon it altogether. People ask why they should trust or even bother consulting experts when their expertise is contingent and bound to change. The answer is that we do so every day. Medical knowledge is constantly evolving, but that doesn't mean we stop going to the doctor. We all expect scientists to make new discoveries, but we don't wait for them to decipher all the secrets of the universe before sending our children to physics class. Some people have sworn off all diets because of the wildly divergent claims of diet books and experts, but the consensus of medical research plus common sense dictates that certain approaches are healthier than others. We should blindly trust historians no more than we blindly trust any other kinds of experts. There is a certain faith involved in relying on experts of any kind. Because no one can master all knowledge in our modern world, we hope that the rigorous standards of the various professional communities will prevent irresponsibly false claims from becoming mainstream positions. Wisdom dictates a course of seeking to understand what our best scholarly endeavors can tell us—what they can add to our overall human flourishing and what they simply cannot. We should expect neither more nor less of scholarship—and the human scholars who produce it—than it can feasibly deliver.

The faithful pursuit of church history

Some people choose simply to avoid the problems in church history. They like their narratives clean, simple, and unambiguously faith-promoting. There is a certain attractiveness to that, and it may serve some individuals well. But it does not seem to serve the body of the church well. In the Internet age, when information of all kinds is available with only a few keystrokes, burying our heads in the sand is no longer viable (if it ever was). Even if you don't particularly care about ambiguities in church history, chances are that someone in your family or ward or circle of friends will. Not everyone needs to be a scholar, but willful ignorance impedes our ability to minister to one another. Numerous church members have been exposed to the complexities in our past and have not only remained faithful but will say their commitment to the gospel and the church has only been strengthened by their willingness to look at the whole picture. Thousands of them attend the annual meeting of the Mormon History Association or read periodicals like *Dialogue: A Journal of Mormon Thought*. Most are not professional academics, but what they share in common is a desire to thoughtfully embrace a reasonable faith.

I am one of them. I grew up in a rather typical Mormon household, with parents who were faithful to church callings and assignments. I was active in the church my entire life, served a mission, and became well versed in the scriptures, gospel doctrine, and the standard-issue narrative of church history. My first exposure to an academic approach to church history came at BYU in a history course called "Mormonism in the American Experience." It was the first time that I had ever heard that Joseph Smith was a money digger. That was news to me. On my mission I had repeatedly been confronted with anti-Mormon literature making all kinds of claims about Joseph, including the money-digger charge. I vehemently denied it, on multiple occasions. Once I learned the facts in my BYU class, I realized that I had been bearing false witness all those times—not maliciously, but because I literally did not know any better. Although I did so with all sincerity and in all innocence, I still denied the facts. When I finally learned the truth, treasure seeking did not trouble me because I had the guidance of a wise professor who laid out the issues and helped me understand that the Smiths were simply participating in the culture of their time and place. That made sense to me and still does. That gave me confidence to explore other nettlesome issues. Some are harder than others for me to process, but my faith has been strengthened by my association with fellow scholars and Saints who are on their own journey of intellectual and spiritual discovery.

In Mormonism we are in the truth business. We're not afraid of the truth, even when it is inconvenient, even when it challenges what we think we know and understand. Indeed, if we know anything in this church, it's that God has more to teach us, so long as we don't plug our ears and think we already know it all. An 1833 revelation declared that "truth is knowledge of things as they are, and as they were, and as they are to come" (D&C 93:24). That might mean that truth never changes, and no doubt some facts—like the existence of God and the resurrection of Christ—are fixed in the cosmos. But at least in this historian's ear, the revelation also suggests something else—that truth consists of what we know, and worshipping a living God means that what we know will change over time.

Along the way we discover that some of our unicorns are actually rhinoceroses. They may not be what we expected, and on first impression they might seem a bit on the hairy, dirty, ugly, and brutish side. The difference is that unicorns are figments of our imagination. When God made one-horned beasts, he made rhinos.

5

A Principled Approach to Church History

THERE'S A DECENT CHANCE YOU HATED your high school history class. It was probably taught by the football coach who forced you to memorize a bunch of facts and names and dates. (Mine assigned us to memorize the school song.) If that was your experience, and it left a bad taste in your mouth, you're not alone. Henry Ford—one of those names you had to memorize—expressed his disdain for history by saying, "What do I care about Napoleon? What do we care what they did 500 or 1,000 years ago? History is more or less bunk. It's tradition. We don't want tradition. We want to live in the present."[1] In the modern age, where progress is the watchword, what value could the benighted times of yore possibly hold for us? Ford would have us believe that forward-thinking individuals cast off the old and devote themselves only to the new. With such a view of the irrelevance of the past for the present, no wonder the musician Sting sings, "Sooner or later we learn to throw the past away. . . . History will teach us nothing."[2]

With all due respect, Henry Ford and Sting are wrong. History is not an assemblage of arcane and inconsequential facts. It is not about clinging blindly to tradition. And it is not useless. We do the human experience a disservice when we assume that the complexity of our ancestors' lives can be reduced to "C" on a multiple-choice test. Latter-day Saints in particular know that we have a vested interest in the past. Moroni's first instructions to Joseph Smith included an invocation of

Malachi's prophecy, placing at the very heart of the restoration the promise that "the hearts of the children shall turn to their fathers" (D&C 2:3). Having internalized the message, years later Joseph taught that "the earth will be smitten with a curse unless there is a welding link of some kind or other between the fathers and the children." The living and the dead are inextricably and powerfully linked: "For we without them cannot be made perfect; neither can they without us be made perfect" (D&C 128:18). This understanding was the foundation for one of the most glorious doctrinal and ritual innovations of the restoration: the sealing together of the family of God.

Malachi, Moroni, and Joseph probably didn't mean that each of us must become a professional historian; if so, the earth would be "utterly wasted" indeed. Rather, the prophecy suggests that we—as individuals and a community—have an integral and intimate relationship to our history. Mormons resonate with William Faulkner's insight that "the past is never dead. It's not even past."[3] We believe the church is not a modern creation but rather the restoration of a primitive organization. In many stakes, our children reenact the westward trek of the handcart pioneers. In holy temples we dramatize and participate in Adam and Eve's heart-wrenching, but ultimately redemptive, saga. We dedicate countless hours literally redeeming our forebears from the annihilation of obscurity. We resurrect their lives in retelling and ritual. We keep Emma and Joseph and Eliza and Brigham present among us through the stories that we share. One of the constant refrains of scripture is simply to remember.

As a people we have been extraordinarily good at keeping the very first commandment given by the Lord to the newly organized Church of Christ in April 1830: "Behold, there shall be a record kept among you" (D&C 21:1). We write personal histories and family histories and church histories. In recent years efforts to capture the voices of living generations through oral history have deepened our collective commitment to the value of every voice.[4] I recently had lunch with a distinguished Catholic historian who is now writing about Mormon women. "In all my years of research I don't think I've ever read a single diary by a Catholic woman," she recounted. "But now I've read hundreds by Mormon women." Our church's commitment to family history is widely recognized and appreciated; perhaps we can also help our sisters and brothers beyond our faith keep their own histories as well so that future Catholic historians will have more to go on.[5] Every life is precious.

Our initial impulse in recording our lives and remembering the past is to emphasize the good, even the heroic. This is a great virtue and an act of charity toward ourselves and our forebears. It is an implicit testimony of the redemption of history through the atonement of Jesus Christ. We don't pretend that we or our ancestors are perfect, but we do highlight what is noble and worthy of emulation. We hope our record will have inspirational value for someone down the road who might encounter it and need a bit of uplift. Naturally, there's some aspect of vanity involved as well—we want others to see us at our best, and then to say flattering things about us. For the most part, however, our emphasis on the positive is appropriate and beneficial.

But there are always skeletons in the closet. Benjamin Franklin opined on the inevitability of death and taxes, but had he been more theologically inclined he might have also added sin to the list. One of the primary reasons why some members of the church have become disenchanted, disappointed, or even angry in recent years is because they were never taught to expect skeletons in the closet of church history and so are shocked when they find them. If their surprise (or yours) reveals a certain naïveté, we must charitably remember that it is a learned naïveté. Understandably, almost all of the stories of prophets and pioneers that we learn beginning in Primary are positive and openly faith-promoting. A person could conceivably attend a lifetime of three-hour Sunday blocks and never hear about the Mountain Meadows Massacre or discrepancies in Joseph Smith's accounts of the first vision.

Like any other institution that cares about its image, the church has been selective in presenting its history in materials produced for public consumption. One notable example of this sanitizing came in the first volume of the Teachings of the Presidents of the Church series, which focused on Brigham Young. If there is one thing that everyone knows about Brigham Young, it's that he was probably the most-married man in nineteenth-century America. Yet Brother Brigham's polygamy, which was not just a curious sociological fact but also central to his theology, received nary a word in the church manual. Furthermore, the compilers of that text, no doubt acting with good and sincere intent, even changed some of President Young's original references from "wives" to the singular "wife." If a person didn't know any better, after reading the manual one would think Brigham Young was the world's most committed monogamist.[6]

If somewhat understandable, this editorial decision was problematic in many ways. It was bad history, it was misleading, and it treated some of the church's most intrepid pioneer women and their faithful sacrifices as if they never existed. I am sympathetic to the probable reasons why the book was prepared the way it was. Given that the general public still associates Mormonism and polygamy, the church naturally wants to make clear that its members no longer practice plural marriage. The manual was compiled as a collection of teachings meant to be relevant to the daily lives of modern Mormons, not as a history textbook. Arguably, certain information, even if factually true, is simply not germane for lesson materials designed for a worldwide ministry to a membership made up mostly of converts.

These reasonable arguments notwithstanding, expunging formative elements of our past from our curricular materials is largely unnecessary. Fortunately we have already begun to improve on this score. More recent editions in the Teachings of the Presidents of the Church series have at least acknowledged the practice of plural marriage. Even more notably, a series of new essays on the official church website offer a forthright overview of plural marriage from its origins in Kirtland and Nauvoo, through its public practice in territorial Utah, until its prolonged and messy denouement following Wilford Woodruff's Manifesto.[7] These essays address even the thorniest issues, including polyandry in Nauvoo, Joseph Smith's marriage to a fourteen-year-old girl, and the disciplining of two members of the Twelve for continuing to perform unauthorized plural marriages in the early twentieth century. Church leaders overseeing the production of these essays have concluded that obscuring our history—even the parts that appropriately won't make it into the missionary discussions—can be far more damaging than owning it. Elder Steven E. Snow, a member of the First Quorum of the Seventy and church historian and recorder, explained: "My view is that being open about our history solves a whole lot more problems than it creates. We might not have all the answers, but if we are open (and we now have pretty remarkable transparency), then I think in the long run that will serve us well. I think in the past there was a tendency to keep a lot of the records closed or at least not give access to information. But the world has changed in the last generation—with the access to information on the Internet, we can't continue that pattern; I think we need to continue to be more open."[8]

In their effort to put the church's best foot forward and offer inspiration, hope, and guidance to the Saints, church leaders and teachers have usually steered clear of the more controversial aspects of our past. I am convinced this is not, as some have accused, part of a massive conspiratorial cover-up campaign. It has more often been undertaken as an act of ministry. There is enough trouble and strife in this world, and many people come to church simply to get a bit of peace, inspiration, and strength to carry on. When they attend a sacrament meeting or a Sunday School class, most are not looking for an academic history lecture, with its intricate arguments and counterarguments. Those who are disappointed that church meetings are not as intellectually stimulating or historically nuanced as university classes suffer from category confusion; they would surely not expect or appreciate a sermon from their college professor. We can and should expect that when the church and its leaders do talk about history, they do so responsibly and accurately. At the same time, we must remember that the church is primarily concerned with preaching the gospel of Christ, not adult history education. Of course, the church does sponsor many educational classes, and we should expect the materials presented therein to be rigorously accurate as well as inspirational. Fortunately, the church's seminary and institute program has recently initiated updates to its curriculum, including better coverage of some of these challenging issues.

The apostle Paul wrote, "When I was a child, I spake as a child, I understood as a child, I thought as a child: but when I became a man, I put away childish things" (1 Corinthians 13:11). In the church we foster certain kinds of belief for children, or for investigators and new converts. Much of our church literature and teaching, especially on Sundays, is devoted to a presentation of the gospel able to reach the widest spectrum of church membership. This is not only appropriate but beautiful and redemptive, as our ability to minister to "the least of these" is a crucial indicator of our collective Christian witness (Matthew 25:40). But as Paul says, we are not children forever. Sunday School answers we gave as teenagers aren't always sufficient for adult questions and problems.

(They might not even be sufficient for some teenage questions.) Grown-up questions require grown-up answers. The Primary answers—read, pray, go to church, be good—never cease being important, even foundational. But life becomes more complicated and morally complex as we grow up, so it is essential for our religion to mature with us.[9]

With its Gospel Topics essays, the church is recognizing the need to provide sophisticated answers to perennially challenging questions.[10] Yet however grateful we are for the information provided in these essays, we can't expect the church to do all the work for us. Just as we are accountable to "work out [our] own salvation" (Philippians 2:12), we have to take personal responsibility for how we will approach, process, and ultimately handle challenging issues in church history and doctrine. Learning how to make better sense of difficult problems is not simply an esoteric exercise for an intellectual elite. Given that so many people are struggling with their membership in the church because of some of these issues, finding better ways to think and talk about the issues is an act of compassion in the original sense of the word—"to suffer with." It is an act of Christian love to go to places, whether geographic or intellectual, that we might otherwise prefer not to visit so that we can "mourn with those that mourn" and "comfort those that stand in need of comfort" (Mosiah 18:9).

For those fearful that they will never know enough to answer other people's questions, it is important to remember that we don't belong to a church of experts. A newly called Relief Society president or bishop receives no training in marriage counseling or social services, but we trust that with their good judgment, compassionate hearts, guidance from church handbooks and leaders, assistance from their counselors and spouses, and most of all the help of the Spirit, they can deal with problems that they otherwise would feel quite inadequate to tackle. God has confidence that we can use our spiritual and rational faculties, conditioned by inspiration, to minister to one another. Gospel leadership and ministry are based on broadly applicable principles, not step-by-step troubleshooting guides, because each individual is wondrously unique. Joseph Smith is famously reported to have said, when asked how he was able to inspire and lead so many people, "I teach them correct principles, and they govern themselves."[11] We know this phrase and we often cite it. As with most things, however, it's easier said than done. My tendency as a parent is to teach my children correct principles and then to force them to govern themselves in pretty much the way I want; otherwise they go to time-out. Whether or not that's good parenting, we cannot parent other adults. Joseph's principled approach employs deep wisdom. It resonates with the way that God watches over the earth and his children.

In that spirit, I offer here five broad principles for thinking about church history, particularly its more nettlesome aspects. The next two chapters also follow in that spirit, in extended form. I have found these principles useful, not as ironclad rules but rather as potentially useful guides. They are most suitable to addressing challenges in church history, but they also have application to approaching doctrinal problems or contemporary issues. Keep in mind that these are principles, not mathematical (let alone magical) formulas or precise blueprints. Insofar as they are true and correct principles, I hope they will be beneficial to you, either directly or in your friendship and ministry to those you love.

1. Tell the truth

> We believe in being honest. (Articles of Faith 1:13)
>
> Thou shalt not bear false witness. (Exodus 20:16)
>
> I glory in plainness; I glory in truth. (2 Nephi 33:6)

Honesty is a central Christian virtue; no one disputes that. Sometimes it gets a little tricky in the execution. We wrestle with how to balance tact and truthfulness. Some things are best left unsaid. Some stories that are patently false are generally harmless and even have a kind of underlying truth to them (Santa Claus comes to mind). Ultimately, honesty is less about facts and more about relationships: the full commandment states, "Thou shalt not bear false witness against thy neighbor." Our words, and the meaning and intent behind them, matter because of how they impact our relationships with others. Telling a blatant lie in a cave where no one else is listening is not the same as telling it in a room full of people.

Some people have left the church because they feel that they have been lied to, as we saw in chapter 1. Betrayal and hurt become the primary feelings for many people who discover that the narrative of church history they were told growing up does not match what the actual record says on some matters. They are usually less bothered by the facts themselves than the feeling that they were deceived. Even if they acknowledge that there was nothing conspiratorial or malicious about the partial narrative presented by the church, the nagging question becomes, "What else haven't they told me?" Essentially, it's a matter of trust.

We can never know as much as we would like to know, and some aspects of the past are simply lost in the mists of time. But what we do know we should be able to talk about. Bringing troublesome matters out into the open rather than letting them fester in secret is a positive thing, especially if it is done with forethought, sensitivity, and care. Doing so reveals a confidence that we have nothing to hide and that there is no problem or question so utterly dangerous that we cannot handle it. When certain things are off limits—implicitly or explicitly— then some people will naturally suppose that the church cares more about public image than about truth and that the truth will somehow destabilize the very foundations of the church's claims. That is simply not the case, as attested by the many scholars who are deeply familiar with the hard issues but remain faithful nevertheless.

One of the most preeminent of these faithful scholars was Leonard Arrington. Known by many as the dean of Mormon history, Arrington was a nationally recognized scholar and founder of the Mormon History Association. For ten years (1972–1982) he was church historian, the only professional academic to have served in that capacity. It's fair to say that Arrington knew as much about the history of the church—good, bad, and ugly—as any person who has ever lived. All that knowledge only strengthened his testimony. I recently came across some letters Arrington wrote during his time as church historian in response to questions about whether the church could bear to have the full truth about its past available for public investigation. One of Arrington's friends, a history professor skeptical about some of the historical claims regarding Joseph Smith, asked him, "Do we really want to publish the truth about Church history?" Arrington's answer was a resounding yes: "Of course we want the truth in Church history, and those of us who have worked intimately with the documents during the past [several] years are confident that the truth is palatable and basically, if not completely, faith promoting;

and that is the way it should be, shouldn't it, if this really is the Lord's Church?" He concluded, "I see no conflict between my integrity as a scholar and my faith as a Latter-day Saint."[12] In another letter, this one to a mission president in Europe, Arrington wrote on behalf of himself and his colleagues in the Historical Department: "Though fully aware of anti-Mormon charges, [we] have the firmest testimony of the Gospel. This testimony is based not only on the testimony of the spirit to us but also on a full examination of the most intimate documents of the Church. That this is the Lord's church, we have no doubt whatsoever."[13]

My experience very much echoes Arrington's. I believe that the history of the church is "basically, if not completely, faith promoting." I have seen that people are not only resilient to learning the truth about church history but also strengthened by the ability to talk through their questions—especially when those they know and trust present, contextualize, and consider the information. During my graduate school years at Notre Dame, I regularly got together with a small group of other LDS graduate students. Sometimes we met in an institute class, but usually just in someone's home for dinner and discussion on a Saturday night. It was totally informal, and we could talk about anything, from football to theology. We debated and laughed and argued and yelled. And then we went to church the next morning and in various capacities served in a ward encompassing an economically depressed and racially diverse Rust Belt city. Frank discussion was part of our emergent full discipleship. Those conversations were transformative for all of us, less because of the propositional knowledge we gained and more because we fostered a community where we could talk through our honest questions and concerns and begin to think through what it all means. Not everyone who participated in those discussions—which continue in often-spirited email exchanges—has remained active in the church, but for me and many others the opportunity to talk freely helped us face up to hard questions without feeling switched off or squeezed out.

What should we do when someone says something factually untrue from the pulpit in sacrament meeting or in a Sunday School class? Is it our responsibility to always enlighten people with all our accumulated wisdom? This is a dilemma for everyone, but especially for LDS students and scholars who have acquired some kind of real expertise, whether in church history or scriptural studies. How do we balance our commitment to the truth with the virtues of generosity, harmony, and plain old good manners? On the one hand, we don't want untruths to go publicly unchallenged and therefore become at least tacitly accepted. On the other hand, we don't want to turn our church meetings into graduate school seminars or debates; it would defeat the entire purpose.

My experience is that when you are teaching a church class you can bring in all your hard-won knowledge about a particular topic (assuming it is relevant to the lesson), and people will generally be interested. People like to learn new things, and they appreciate having someone in the room who can really teach them. But your teaching must be done in the right spirit—and with the Spirit. If your aim is to shock people or to demonstrate superiority—to the people in the room or the set-apart leaders of the church—you will meet resistance and perhaps hostility. If you truly desire to enlarge their souls, enlighten their understanding, and strengthen their testimony of and commitment to Christ and his gospel, then most people will be open (see Alma 32:28; Moroni 7:16). The ability for truth to be heard depends not only on the openness of the hearer but perhaps even more so on whether the messenger is deemed trustworthy. When someone has helped you move in, faithfully served alongside you in a calling, or befriended and mentored your children, you're more liable to listen to what they have to say.

In a previous ward my wife and I used to have Sunday dinners almost every week with some dear friends. We did this for years. Normally our conversations were purely social, but we often talked about gospel topics as well. One evening the translation of the Book of Mormon came up. I carefully explained what the historical documents say about the actual process of translation, with much of it accomplished by Joseph Smith gazing into a stone at the bottom of a hat while the gold plates laid covered under a sheet.[14] My friends were surprised, but because we could talk about it openly and honestly and because they trusted me, they were not troubled. Fast forward a few months later, when I was at a Primary activity focusing on the Book of Mormon. The church was set up with different stations where the kids could have fun and educational activities. I had to smile when I visited the station on Book of Mormon translation, led by one of my friends from our dinners. The children listened raptly while he told them about the Prophet Joseph looking into a hat. None of the kids ran screaming from the room or even blinked an eye. In the future, when they read online about Joseph using a stone in a hat, they're far less likely to leave the church over it. Instead they'll say, "I know that—I learned it in Primary." They will be empowered by the truth we tell.

2. Do your homework

In late 1832 and early 1833, Joseph Smith received two of his most theologically profound revelations, now canonized as sections 88 and 93 of the Doctrine and Covenants. The revelations, worth quoting at length, connected the acquisition of knowledge with an increased capacity for discipleship and ministry:

> Teach ye diligently and my grace shall attend you, that you may be instructed more perfectly in theory, in principle, in doctrine, in the law of the gospel, in all things that pertain unto the kingdom of God, that are expedient for you to understand; of things both in heaven and in the earth, and under the earth; things which have been, things which are, things which must shortly come to pass; things which are at home, things which are abroad; the wars and the perplexities of the nations, and the judgments which are on the land; and a knowledge also of countries and of kingdoms—That ye may be prepared in all things when I shall send you again to magnify the calling whereunto I have called you, and the mission with which I have commissioned you. (D&C 88:78–80)

The early Saints learned that in order for them to fulfill the mission that God had given them, they would have to study not only the doctrines of the gospel but also topics such as astronomy, geology, history, political science, public policy, conflict resolution, law, and geography—in other words, the whole glorious spectrum of human knowledge. The Lord then commanded Joseph that he was to hasten the work of translating the Bible and at the same time to "obtain a knowledge of history, and of countries, and of kingdoms, and of laws of God and man, and all this for the salvation of Zion" (D&C 93:53). With this divine instruction in mind, no wonder the Prophet later taught the Saints, "A man is saved no faster than he gets knowledge."[15]

In the church we often talk about the importance of seeking learning "by study and also by faith"; the quotation is emblazoned prominently on a wall of the Harold B. Lee Library at Brigham Young University. The full verse is even more instructive: "And as all have not faith, seek ye diligently and teach one another words of wisdom; yea, seek ye out of the best books words of wisdom; seek learning, even by study and also by faith" (D&C 88:118). The purpose of learning is not to show off or even to capitalize our knowledge into a good salary and financial security. Rather, the Lord's commandment to seek learning is offered as a response to our modern predicament of doubt. God's own voice acknowledges that the modern church includes some, perhaps many, who "have not faith." That the Lord states this fact so casually, so matter-of-factly, suggests that perhaps we need to rethink doubt within the church. Are those who "have not faith" like a cancerous disease that demand quarantine or frenzied attempts at eradication?

The revelation takes a less harried approach. It exudes confidence that the Saints will benefit from more knowledge, not less. It does not treat doubt as a specter menacing the foundations of the church. It does not take evasive action. Nowhere in the section do we get some version of "forget your questions and do your home teaching." (Though, as an aside, yes, please do your home teaching.) The Lord's answer to those who "have not faith" and those who minister to them is disarmingly simple: *study*. Faithful study is a requirement, not an elective, for students in God's classroom. God trusts us to seek and learn and ask and dive deeply into the best books. The scriptures certainly rank as the best of books, but they do not exhaust the category.[16]

In seeking learning, the revelation counsels, we must do so "diligently." If we want answers to our questions, we have to put in the time. Research is hard work. If we have existential questions, we cannot be satisfied with blog-level answers. In this respect, the Internet has spoiled us. Simple keyword searches are excellent at delivering simple answers. But the range and depth of human wisdom on a given topic cannot be satisfied, or even skimmed, by a quick glance at Wikipedia or a cursory scan of the random thoughts of a blogger whose musings happen to come up on the first page of our Google search. There is respectable, evidence-driven, peer-reviewed scholarship available on almost every question—certainly on the ones that typically lead people to question their relationship to the church. (For a start, see the suggested reading selections at the end of this book.) More important than offering timeless or final answers, such work also models faithful, rigorous, and variable ways of authentically engaging questions about our history and belief.

If you think you might have cancer, you don't begin and end your search for answers by consulting WebMD. You probably won't even stop by seeing just one doctor. If your life is at stake, and serious treatments are being suggested, you will probably want to receive multiple expert opinions. You don't rely on just the good news or listen only to the people who tell you what you want to hear. It's perfectly reasonable to search out contrary opinions and weigh the worst-case scenario with the best. Once you have identified a treatment regimen that you believe will help, you are willing to spend however many hours, weeks, months, or even years it takes in order to return to health. If one course of treatment makes you worse or otherwise doesn't work, you try another one. You approach the issue with utmost seriousness, not as a casual hobby.

For people who have dedicated themselves to the church and have built their lives around it, discovering something incongruous in church history can be just as destabilizing as receiving a troubling medical diagnosis. But not all conditions are terminal. You certainly don't throw away your health, your relationships, and the things you love simply because you get bad news from the doctor. Your body may have temporarily betrayed you, but that doesn't mean you lose hope for a resolution. This metaphor breaks down, of course, because physical life comes to an end for all of us, while spiritual life will be nurtured into the eternities. The lesson is that when your life is on the line— whether physically, spiritually, emotionally, or relationally—you put in the necessary time and effort and diligence to save it. Consult experts. Go deep. Critically weigh evidence. Think for yourself. Don't make the first thing you read the last. Give the issue the attention and care it deserves. As Richard E. Turley Jr., an assistant church historian and recorder, is fond of saying, "Don't study Church history too little."[17] Do your homework not only by study, but also by faith—which includes the elements of prayer, fasting, scripture study, repentance, hope, humility, perseverance, charity, and grace.

3. The past is a foreign country

Historians are fond of quoting the opening line from L. P. Hartley's 1953 novel *The Go-Between*: "The past is a foreign country: they do things differently there."[18] It's easy for us to forget this and become inhospitable and rude in our sojourn to the past. We can easily assume many of the characteristics of the stereotypical "ugly American" traveling abroad. This person assumes his own culture's superiority: if it's not my way, it's the wrong way. He criticizes the strange customs and beliefs held by the natives—or worse, makes light of and even desecrates what local people hold sacred. He shouts slowly and loudly to "foreigners" who don't speak English, as if they are the problem. And when things get a little hot and sticky outside, he prefers to view the world from the comfort and safety of the air-conditioned tour bus rather than getting out and actually interacting with the locals.

As detailed in chapter 4, delving into history should be disorienting. We are, after all, peering in on a completely different time and place, where norms and values may be quite divergent from our own. We can appreciate certain commonalities, safely assuming for instance that virtually all humans love their children.[19] But good history should always remind us not to carry those assumptions of essential similarity too far. As the award-winning Italian historian and author Carlo Ginzburg wrote, "The historian's task is just the opposite of what most of us were taught to believe. He must destroy our false sense of proximity to people of the past because they come from societies very different from our own. The more we discover about these people's mental universes, the more we should be shocked by the cultural distance that separates us from them."[20]

We may be tempted to think that the world of early Mormonism was merely a more rustic version of our own contemporary culture. After all, early Mormons' written English is readable, they were citizens of countries we still locate on the map today, and we are all members of the same church. But in fact, a century and a half makes a big difference, especially in modern times when technological and social change occurs so rapidly. Consider some of the cultural differences between the world of the first generation of Mormons and those of today. In 1830 slavery was still legal and widely accepted; abolitionists were generally considered cranks and troublemakers—and many of them held racist beliefs, by our contemporary standards.[21] Women did not have the right to vote. Not only that, but "coverture" was still the dominant legal doctrine, meaning that upon marriage, a woman's legal rights were entirely subsumed under those of her husband. Married women could not legally own property or represent themselves in court because the husband and wife were considered one person before the law, and the husband fully represented that one person. Extralegal violence—including lynching—was common, and commonly accepted, as a necessary means of supplementing or correcting an inadequate legal and law enforcement system. The federal government had almost nothing to do with most private citizens; there was no IRS, no FBI, and no CIA. Evolutionary theory, Marxism, and Freudian psychology did not exist. There was no electricity or air conditioning or, in most places, running water and indoor plumbing.

Not just the external culture would be foreign. The church itself was rather different as well. My favorite description of this comes from Jan Shipps, the distinguished non-LDS scholar of Mormonism, who muses what it would be like for contemporary Latter-day Saints to travel back in time to the Mormonism of 1880:

> If these Saints, by chance, should step from their time machine out into the land of Zion on the morning of the first Sunday of the month, they would find families unabashedly eating hearty breakfasts. Disoriented as much by the discovery that the day was not being treated as a day of fasting as by time-machine lag, the latter-day visitors would, most probably, seek out a ward meeting place. . . .
>
> The visitors would learn that sacrament meeting was held only in the tabernacle located in the center of town. This would cause them to expect to join in with all the Saints in the area in a large-scale worship service, but that would likewise lead to disappointment, since at the appointed hour the tabernacle would still seem virtually empty. In time disorientation would give way to dismay: a brother with a tobacco habit could well be seated on the stand; another brother's shirt might be so marked with coffee stains that the visitors would certainly know that he indulged in that forbidden beverage;

still another, conceivably a bishop's counselor, might from the stand be sending the telltale aroma of a recently consumed toddy wafting across the front rows in the building. . . .

Moreover, modern Mormons are accustomed to participating in flawlessly orchestrated conference sessions via television [and now Internet]. If these interlopers from the future had dropped in at conference time instead of visiting on an ordinary Sunday, their disorientation level would surely have reached the crisis stage. It is very possible that—upon hearing one of the many variations on John Henry Smith's opening statement in his 1885 annual conference address, "What the Lord may have for me to say to you I cannot imagine"—the visitors would simply have left, fleeing forward to their familiar [twenty-first-century] Mormon world as fast as their time machine could carry them.[22]

The key thing to remember is that when we step out of that time machine, it is we, not the people whom we encounter, who are out of place. Disoriented though we may be, our first responsibility is to get to know them on their own terms. However, that does not mean we can never pass judgment. The violent displacement of Native Americans from Utah Valley can be better understood by making sense of nineteenth-century views of race and Manifest Destiny, but the sin remains. To explain is not to excuse. Nevertheless, generosity, fairness, and human solidarity require us to make our best efforts to understand and empathize with our brothers and sisters in the past, recognizing that some aspects of their lives and culture will never be fully comprehensible for us. And it should also make us pause to think what future generations will condemn us for. All cultures and historical eras have their blind spots. The Saints in the nineteenth century had theirs, and we certainly have ours. For the Christian, the recurring dilemma of the mysteriousness of the other is best met with charity, the perfect passport for entry into the foreign past.

4. There is none good but God

> And when he was gone forth into the way, there came one running, and kneeled to him, and asked him, Good Master, what shall I do that I may inherit eternal life? And Jesus said unto him, Why callest thou me good? there is none good but one, that is, God. (Mark 10:17–18)

> For all have sinned, and come short of the glory of God. (Romans 3:23)

This principle is pretty straightforward. We're all sinners. If during his mortal ministry Jesus resisted being called good—having not yet completely fulfilled his appointed mission—then the rest of us can hardly claim or expect ourselves, or our brothers and sisters, to be fully good. The prominent twentieth-century Protestant theologian Reinhold Niebuhr expressed it this way: "The doctrine of original sin is the only empirically verifiable doctrine of the Christian faith."[23] We can't empirically prove core Christian doctrines like the existence of God, the resurrection of Christ, or the miracles of scripture, but we can demonstrate convincingly that people are sinners. Mormons don't accept the doctrine of original sin per se, but we do acknowledge, with the apostle Paul, that we all fall short of God's glory, meaning that even if sin isn't original to us at our birth, it is the common denominator of the human experience.

This doesn't mean we have to constantly fret about human depravity. Calvinist theology—which was embraced by many early American colonists, most notably the Puritans—held that because of the taint of original sin, all humans are so utterly and inherently wicked that they can literally do no good thing of their own accord. It is literally impossible for us to choose righteousness, because our very inclinations, desires, and thoughts are wicked through and through. On our own, we are thoroughly wretched, corrupt, and loathsome creatures, and that puts us in a relationship of complete enmity with God. Only the grace of God working in us empowers us to think or say or do anything remotely godly. No one expressed this notion of human depravity more powerfully than Jonathan Edwards, America's pre-eminent eighteenth-century theologian:

> The God that holds you over the pit of hell, much as one holds a spider, or some loathsome insect, over the fire, abhors you, and is dreadfully provoked; his wrath towards you burns like fire; he looks upon you as worthy of nothing else, but to be cast into the fire; he is of purer eyes than to bear to have you in his sight; you are ten thousand times so abominable in his eyes as the most hateful venomous serpent is in ours.[24]

This is not Mormon belief. Mormons are not Calvinists. Nor are we evangelical Protestants, many of whom resonate with Edwards's theology, even if they shudder at his imagery. We do not use words like depravity. We are never abhorrent or abominable in God's sight—though some of our behaviors may be.

The singularly brilliant insight of Mormon theology is that God and humans are of the same species and that humans are coeternal with God. If that was Joseph Smith's only statement about the human condition and our place in the cosmos, it would rank him as one of the most important and innovative theological contributors of the modern age. We are not mere creatures. We are eternal spirits, children of God, goddesses and gods in development. When we act out of harmony with God's commandments, it's not so much that we have broken the arbitrary rules of a stern taskmaster but that we have departed from our own true nature and destiny and are in need of a course correction we call repentance. Obviously, we come up short—most of us every day, some of us quite spectacularly. The heart of the gospel—the good news—is that we are redeemed and saved from our sin through the atonement of Jesus Christ. We are never cast out. Christ's "arms of mercy are extended towards" all people, and there is no expiration date on his invitation (Alma 5:33). God's love is the fundamental reality of the universe. And because we are his children, we are the primary objects of that love.

When we see sin in others, it should focus our attention on exactly two things: our own personal need for redemption and our call to minister compassionately to others who are struggling. When we encounter sin in others, past or present, we are presented with a test: Will we apply the Golden Rule? Would we want others to focus exclusively on our many sins?

We take our cue from the One whom we can truly call good (despite his erstwhile protestations):

> Do not judge, so that you may not be judged. For with the judgment you make you will be judged, and the measure you give will be the measure you get. Why do you see the speck in your neighbor's eye, but do not notice the log in your own eye? Or how can you say to your neighbor, "Let me take the speck out of your eye," while the log is in your own eye? You hypocrite, first take the log out of your own eye, and then you will see clearly to take the speck out of your neighbor's eye. (Matthew 7:1–5 NRSV)

5. Learn the lessons of history

"History repeats itself."

"Those who don't remember history are doomed to repeat it."

No doubt you've heard slogans like this, probably from a historian trying to convince you that her book or class is essential for you to be a complete person. Personally, I'm dubious of such claims. In fact, history never repeats itself. While there are obvious constants in the human predicament—our species' propensity for violence, for instance, hasn't changed much over the millennia—every moment is completely new and unique, open to a range of choices that are not fully contingent on what has happened before. We call that agency. While learning about past human choices can give us wisdom in approaching our own challenges, we are never condemned by our historical ignorance. People make plenty of wise decisions completely oblivious of past precedent. By the same token, simply remembering the past is no guarantee of learning moral lessons from it; past atrocities are often invoked to justify current ones.

The other problem with such slogans is that they make historians out to be some superior class of moral being. The implicit message is that historians have special access to the unique wisdom of the ages that will guide us to a golden age of the future. This is simply not true. I have interacted with lots of historians over the years, and while they are usually smart and interesting people, they have no corner on sagacity or ethical behavior. As a class of professionals, we can be just as petty, biased, and intolerant as anyone, and plenty of historians over the years have gotten mixed up in putting their work to use in some rather unsavory ways.

I am not suggesting that we should rely on a certain group of professional historians for absolute moral direction, nor do I believe that knowledge of certain propositional truths will itself solve our problems. However, certain habits of mind and perspectives are often cultivated through historical inquiry. Over the years I have watched many friends and colleagues successfully navigate complicated questions of history and faith. Though every person is different, I've seen that those who make peace with the difficult elements in our past generally share some commonalities, which can serve as a pattern for others.

First, we become comfortable with complexity and nuance. We know that in our present lives things are rarely black-and-white, and so we expect the same of the past. Situations are almost always more complex than they first appear. We may not be able to solve all problems to our full satisfaction, but we learn that problems often recede in importance with time and perspective.

Second, we also get comfortable with the human side of church experience. We come to see church members and leaders, past and present, less as cardboard superhero cutouts—larger than life but two-dimensional—and more like real people. For many of us, this humanizing view of past Saints, including the prophets, actually makes them more compelling in our journey, not less. Instead of unreachable icons of piety or spirituality, they become more relatable in their humanity and therefore more suitable as actual examples of faith. People are not all good or all bad. Basically decent people make poor choices with tragic consequences, and scoundrels sometimes help old ladies across the street without stealing their purse. A particularly eloquent expression of this principle came from Elder Jeffrey R. Holland, who encouraged us to "be kind regarding human frailty—your own as well as that of those who serve with you in a Church led by volunteer, mortal men and women. Except in the case of His only perfect Begotten Son, imperfect people are all God has ever had to work with. That must be terribly frustrating to Him, but He deals with it. So should we."[25]

Third, we come to think differently about history itself. We become accustomed to the idea of change over time—in fact, we come to expect it. We come to see cultural and political and social context as mattering a great deal, often more than we think. We get comfortable with what history can and can't tell us. We suspend final judgments and are content with preliminary hypotheses when the evidence is incomplete. We realize that because the past is in many ways unavailable to us in the present, studying history is less like an exact science and more a matter of argument and interpretation. We conclude, in fact, that matters as fundamentally spiritual as the prophetic calling of Joseph Smith cannot be arbitrated by history alone—"especially since much of what is needed" to have a truly complete historical picture, as Elder D. Todd Christofferson reminded us, "is either lost or never existed."[26]

Perhaps most importantly, many of us who have made peace with troubling episodes in Latter-day Saint history have come to see ourselves as seekers, not unlike Joseph Smith himself, as President Dieter F. Uchtdorf suggested:

> Brothers and sisters, as good as our previous experience may be, if we stop asking questions, stop thinking, stop pondering, we can thwart the revelations of the Spirit. Remember, it was the questions young Joseph asked that opened the door for the restoration of all things. We can block the growth and knowledge our Heavenly Father intends for us. How often has the Holy Spirit tried to tell us something we needed to know but couldn't get past the massive iron gate of what we thought we already knew?[27]

We see the pursuit of truth as a lifelong endeavor. Spiritual certainty often comes piecemeal and only incrementally. We patiently gather the facts and are open to being surprised by what we find. Because the evidence is often incomplete or contradictory, we are willing to put things on the shelf for a time. Camilla Eyring Kimball, a woman with an insatiable intellect and voracious appetite for reading, beautifully articulated the seeker's approach:

> I've always had an inquiring mind. I'm not satisfied just to accept things. I like to follow through and study things out. I learned early to put aside those gospel questions that I couldn't answer. I had a shelf of things I didn't understand, but as I've grown older and studied and prayed and thought about each problem, one by one I've been able to better understand them. [At the age of 81] I still have some questions on that shelf, but I've come to understand so many other things in my life that I'm willing to bide my time for the rest of the answers.[28]

And so we strive to find balance between patience and diligent inquiry. We try to hedge the natural human conceit that we know all that we need to know—that if we don't know it, it's not worth knowing.

Yet in our search for knowledge, we also want to learn from established wisdom, thus avoiding the ancient Athenians' trap of spending our time "in nothing else, but either to tell, or to hear some new thing" (Acts 17:21). Rather than abandoning the accumulated wisdom already gained by ourselves or our people, we resonate with Elder Jeffrey R. Holland's advice to "hold fast to what you already know and stand strong until additional knowledge comes."[29] We allow what we do not know to coexist alongside what we do know rather than to immediately overwhelm it. We strive to find the right balance between the different components of the ninth Article of Faith, seeking truth among "all that God has revealed, all that He does now reveal, and . . . [all] that He will yet reveal." In the face of our incomplete understanding, we seek further light and knowledge from God and his servants, acknowledging that our view will always be limited. We trust that just because your "knowledge is perfect in [one] thing" (Alma 32:24) does not mean your journey of faith is at an end. There is no shame in not knowing yet. The mere "desire to believe" (Alma 32:27) qualifies you for a place at the Lord's table.

Taken together, these five principles—tell the truth, do your homework, the past is a foreign country, there is none good but God, and learn the lessons of history—help us to approach the past more like historians do. Thinking like a historian isn't always the best approach—you don't want a historian to build a bridge or diagnose that pain in your chest—but when it comes to reckoning with the endless complexities of the past, it helps. More importantly, however, these principles help us approach history and the people who live there in more Christian terms. God does not ask us to suspend our critical faculties, but he does require us to enhance them with humility, generosity, and most of all charity.

6

In All Patience and Faith

I HAD A GREAT MISSION. I worked hard, learned a lot, and strengthened my testimony of and commitment to the gospel. But I do wish a few things went differently. I wish I could have learned a foreign language. I wish my youthful zeal had been tempered by a bit more charity. Maybe most of all, I wish Greg and Lynnette had been baptized.

I did a lot of door-to-door tracting and came to rather enjoy the conversations I had with people on their doorsteps. Rarely did those conversations actually turn into solid teaching opportunities, which made Greg and Lynnette and their two adorable children, whom I met on the porch of their trailer home, so special. We hit it off immediately. Lynnette had a vaguely Christian background; Greg was initially skeptical about organized religion and even the existence of God. It was a powerful experience to watch them plant and nurture the seeds of faith over the course of several weeks. The transformation not only in their spiritual life but also in their marriage and family was palpable and real. It was because I loved—and liked—them so much that it was such a joy when they started coming to church and befriending members of the ward. Here was the dream: an entire nuclear family joining the church together. Their fledging conversion to the gospel was changing their lives for the better, and no one knew it better than they did—which made it all the more devastating when the wheels came off.

It started innocently enough. To help Greg and Lynnette in their Book of Mormon reading, both for themselves and with their children, I gave them the standard-issue illustrated *Book of Mormon Stories*, the same one that I had grown up with. They loved it—that is, until they got to the part where Lehi dies and the Lamanites are cursed for refusing to follow Nephi. The book graphically illustrates the Lamanites' "skin of blackness" (which in the pictures looks more reddish-brownish) and general state of being "loathsome" (2 Nephi 5:21–22). Lynnette, who had been getting pushback and anti-Mormon literature from some of her friends and family, was bothered. The illustrations seemed to reinforce what people had told her about Mormons being racist based on the pre-1978 priesthood-temple ban. The next time we visited, she and Greg—who were, by the way, working-class whites—tentatively broached the topic. It just didn't fit with everything else they had learned from us about the gospel of Jesus Christ or with the good people they had met at church. No one *seemed* racist, but here it was in our scriptures, our history, and the pictures we showed our children.

I did my nineteen-year-old best to answer their honest questions. I've never subscribed to the sorry theology that blacks were somehow "less valiant in the preexistence," so I can take comfort that at least I didn't offer them that line. I can't remember now what exactly I did tell them, but ultimately it came down to the fact that the policy started with prophets, and prophets had maintained it, and then revelation to prophets had ended it. The matter was laid bare by a series of innocent but perceptive questions from Greg, who was still figuring out whether he believed in and trusted God at all. (This was the same guy who had the single most memorable line I've ever heard about the Word of Wisdom: "Obviously God has never had a double-tall latte if he made a rule against it.") Greg asked whether God loves everyone. Yes. Does God love white people more than black people? No. Does God want everyone to follow the gospel and receive all the ordinances of the church? Yes. Does God lead his church through prophets? Yes. Then why did God either inspire prophets to create a policy, or at the very least allow prophets to perpetuate a policy, that barred blacks from full participation in the church? And even if the policy had originated in something other than direct revelation, why didn't God intervene until 1978—almost a quarter century after the Montgomery Bus Boycott? Shouldn't prophets be a step ahead, not a step behind?

I had no answer.

At first, the issue didn't seem like a deal breaker. We kept meeting with Greg and Lynnette. They even came to church a few more times. But you could see it in their eyes—the fire was gone, extinguished by legitimate doubts about whether true prophets called by God would really establish or maintain policies that discriminated against people based on the color of their skin. I was transferred out of the area, and we kept in touch for a while. They started looking at other churches, never really finding one. The last time I saw Greg, he and Lynnette had divorced. I don't know if joining the church would have saved their marriage, but they did tell me that while they were immersing themselves in the gospel their family life was happier and more harmonious. I wish for their sake that somehow they had been able to find a way to carve out some space for honest doubt or disagreement in the context of an otherwise life-changing conversion. I know the church would have been a great place for them and their children, and they would have added a lot to the ward. But in the end they couldn't square the priesthood-temple ban with everything else I had taught them about God's love, the importance of prophets, and brotherhood and sisterhood in the church. Honestly, I can't say I blame them. If there is blame to be had, it's that as a duly ordained minister of the gospel I didn't have answers for them—or rather, the answers I gave them simply weren't good enough.

Because of that experience and others, when I got back to BYU I read everything I could on the topic of the priesthood-temple ban. Like so many readers, I was transfixed by Lester Bush's courageous and pioneering 1973 essay, "Mormonism's Negro Doctrine: An Historical Overview." Bush convincingly demonstrated that contrary to later pioneer reminiscences, African-American men were in fact ordained to the priesthood during Joseph Smith's day and that the policy changed once the Saints arrived in Utah.[1] Scholars like Armand Mauss and Newell Bringhurst helped me first to learn the historical facts and then to begin to make sense of them.[2] I discovered the stories of stalwart Saints like Darius Gray, who as a spiritual and proud African-American man joined the church before 1978 because the Spirit told him to, despite his feeling of betrayal when he learned that he could not hold the priesthood. And I learned of Jane Manning James, who walked to Nauvoo on bleeding feet, worked as a servant in Joseph Smith's family, and innocently declined the offer to be ritually adopted by him before emigrating to

Utah with the Saints. She became a pillar of faith and despite never being allowed to enter the temple to be endowed or sealed was eulogized in the Tabernacle by President Joseph F. Smith. And Elijah Abel, an early black convert who was ordained to the Melchizedek Priesthood (first as an elder, then a seventy) served several missions for the church, including one at the age of 76 that taxed his health and likely contributed to his death.[3]

I'll never forget the fireside organized by Eugene England that I attended in London on a Sunday evening in the summer of 1998. England was one of late twentieth-century Mormonism's great intellectuals and champions for justice. England brought together dozens of black members of the church—the most black Mormons I had ever seen in the same room—to talk about their experiences and how they made sense of the priesthood-temple ban. There were tears and pain and grief that evening but also healing and testimony and reconciliation. Those Saints were in the church because they knew that God loved them and wanted them there, no matter what had happened in the organization's past (or present). Darius, Jane, Elijah, and the people at the London fireside are among my spiritual heroes.

Admiring the faith and courage of these black Saints, however, does not take away the basic theological dilemma that Greg posed. How could the ban happen in a church that worships a God who "doeth that which is good among the children of men . . . and he inviteth them all to come unto him and partake of his goodness; and he denieth none that come unto him, black and white, bond and free, male and female" (2 Nephi 26:33)? Assuming that God does not consider skin color to be a marker of worthiness or favor—and knowing that I could not rightly worship a God who did—how could a church led by his chosen prophets continue in that way for over 125 years? Why didn't God inspire at least one of the prophets—there were ten in that span, from Brigham Young up until Spencer W. Kimball—to make a change on such a momentous issue?

Especially in light of the good research we have on the subject, Greg and Lynnette were basically correct in their analysis: the problem with the priesthood-temple ban is, at root, theological. Simply getting our history right doesn't make the problem go away. We know the basic facts; the question is to determine what the facts mean. This strikes right at the heart of what it means for members of The Church of Jesus Christ of Latter-day Saints to claim that God calls prophets in modern times and leads the church through them. This is true of many of the individual subjects that have troubled people's faith, whether it is polygamy or the Book of Abraham or Proposition 8.

Prophetic fallibility

Many of our problems stem from the fact that in the church we have developed an erroneous cultural notion of prophetic infallibility that has its foundation neither in scripture nor in the teachings of the modern prophets themselves.[4] This isn't the place to trace where this notion came from, but it suffices to say that even Joseph Smith's most ardent followers never considered him infallible. President Lorenzo Snow's rumination on the topic is instructive: "I saw Joseph Smith the Prophet do things which I did not approve of; and yet . . . I thanked God that He would put upon a man who had these imperfections the power and authority which He placed upon him . . . for I knew I myself had weaknesses and I thought there was a chance for me. . . . I thanked God I saw these imperfections."[5]

Indeed, perhaps in this respect the members of the nineteenth-century frontier church had an advantage over those of us living in the twenty-first-century global church. Nowadays most of us encounter the prophets and apostles only via general conference and the official publications of the church. This makes it easier to put them on a pedestal as unapproachable icons of saintliness. When the church was much smaller, however, members personally interacted with the prophets and apostles on a more regular basis and thus experienced them as ordinary humans, albeit with a godly calling. However it happened, my sense is that church members today are less comfortable with admitting the prophets' human limitations than were our pioneer ancestors. I don't know who came up with the following saying, but it gets at the heart of the matter: "Catholics teach that the pope is infallible, but nobody believes it. Mormons teach that the prophet is fallible, but nobody believes it."

How liberating it is to relieve ourselves and our leaders of the burden of perfection. Even a casual perusal of scripture and history reminds us that the prophets that God calls to act as his mouthpieces are quite human. They are liable to sin and error not only before their prophetic calling (which we can all readily admit) but also during their prophetic ministry (a somewhat tougher pill to swallow). This fallibility makes it all the more important for us to sustain, or bear with and support, them much like we need to be sustained and borne with in spite of our errors.

The scriptures contain their fair share of judgments against the Gentile nations, but God's calls to repentance are mostly directed toward the covenant people and oftentimes toward the duly appointed religious leaders and even prophets of Israel. Jonah is the most obvious example. His prophetic calling is undisputed, and he may well have had some great years that we don't know about. But what we do read leaves us less than impressed: we don't typically think of prophets who "flee . . . from the presence of the Lord," or who are "very angry" when the people they preach to actually listen to them and repent (Jonah 1:3; 4:1). The Jonah story has been applied in many fruitful ways. Jesus deployed it as a type to prophesy about his own resurrection (Matthew 12:40). The *VeggieTales* version—which inspired my son, then three years old, to approach people saying "I bring you a message from the Lord"—teaches children the virtues of compassion and mercy. The Gospel Doctrine lesson covering the book of Jonah wants class members to learn that "the Lord loves all his children"—even the Ninevites—"and that we, as latter-day Israel, have the great responsibility to share his love and the truths of the gospel with all people." That same lesson also includes an intriguing question to be posed by the instructor: "How did the Lord show mercy and help Jonah repent?"[6] In other words, the official Sunday School curriculum of the church teaches that prophets, like the rest of us, are in need of repentance and the Lord's mercy. Most departures from the divine will not be as notable as were Jonah's—or have quite the same dramatic consequences—but they are nevertheless real.

This principle is powerfully taught by one of the great prophets of scripture, Moroni. As he finishes his father's book, believing that these will be the final words he writes, Moroni offers a kind of last will and testament for future readers to consider. Moroni testifies of the truthfulness and importance of the words etched into the plates. Then he asks readers to "condemn me not because of mine imperfection, neither my father, because of his imperfection, neither them who have written before him." In other words, Moroni tells us point-blank that he, his father Mormon, and all the other inspired prophets who wrote the Book of Mormon were in fact imperfect. The beautiful thing about Moroni's admission is he does not use it as an excuse but rather as a lesson in grace, charity, and Christ-centered moral improvement. He begs for our forgiveness and remarkably asks us to "give thanks unto God that he hath made manifest unto you our imperfections." Pause to appreciate this phrase: Moroni says that we should be *grateful* to know that God's prophets are imperfect. Why? "That ye may learn to be more wise than we have been" (Mormon 9:31). God's prophets never set themselves up as *the* light but rather stand on the mountain pointing people to the true Light. Prophets instruct people to learn from their teachings and from their lives, which include many wonderful acts of righteousness as well as the sin and error that are the lot of all humanity. In that way prophets doubly fulfill their calling to encourage all in the sound of their voice to become perfected in and through the atonement of Jesus Christ. Prophets are not called to save us; they are called to lead us to the Savior.

Somehow we have conflated claims of truth with expectations of moral perfection, or a close approximation to it. In doing so we are setting the bar too high and acting uncharitably toward leaders (from the General Authorities, to our branch, ward, and stake leaders) who are themselves participating in the plan of salvation. My own hunch is that Mormons began to paint ourselves into the difficult corner of equating truth with superior moral virtue when the early members of the church responded so vehemently, and in many ways appropriately and understandably, to various slanders on the character of Joseph Smith issued by his earliest critics. One of the first lines of argument undercutting Joseph's prophetic claims was that he was all too human. Critics of the church, including Eber Howe and (the wonderfully named) Doctor Philastus Hurlbut, used interviews and affidavits from the Smith family's neighbors in New York to show that Joseph Smith was just an ordinary farm boy, with all the foibles common to his day and time. Even if we discount some of the accounts as prejudiced or exaggerated, the general weight of evidence confirms Joseph's own self-assessment (canonized, by the way, in LDS scripture) that he sometimes engaged in associations and behaviors "not consistent with that character which ought to be maintained by one who was called of God as I had been" (Joseph Smith—History 1:28).[7] This line of attack, identifying flaws in Joseph's character and personal conduct as evidences against the very possibility of his prophethood, continued throughout his life. If he was anything less (or more) than a stock hero, then of course he could not be a true prophet of God.

This line of critique has an attractive logic to it, but only if we are to assume that prophets of God are either superhuman by nature or upon being called are mystically transformed into flawless puppets of the divine will. Of course, neither is the case. The requirement for prophets to be faultless, or even morally superior, is fundamentally inconsistent with the precedent set in scripture where the Lord repeatedly demonstrates his power and grace precisely by calling as his servants people who are just as flawed as their neighbors. However, the early Saints took the bait. They could have offered a rebuttal to Joseph's critics based on God's own pronouncement that he accomplishes his will via "the weak things of the world" (D&C 1:18). This may have helped them (and us) develop a theology of what it means for God to choose and work through a truly human prophet—as if there is any other kind. Instead, they did what friends often do: they defended Joseph's character even when it could not be or did not need to be defended. Much of this continues today. It is honorable to defend someone's character against slander and charitable to highlight the positive aspects of a person's character rather than dwelling only on the inevitable warts and flaws. This is all the more understandable for people covenanted not to speak ill of the Lord's anointed. As Elder Boyd K. Packer instructed, it is not necessary for us to dwell on the human limitations of a particular prophet in order to "convince everyone that the *prophet* was a *man*. We knew that already. All of the prophets and all of the Apostles have been men." In our study of history, Packer advises, it is "more worthwhile" for faithful Saints to highlight those aspects convincing us "that the *man* was a *prophet*, a fact quite as true as the fact that he was a man."[8]

In our admirable desire to guard the individual and collective reputation of our latter-day prophets, however, we have sometimes forgotten Elder Packer's commonsensical reminder that they have always been men. It's natural to expect a strong correlation between personal virtue and being called as one of God's servants. And indeed, those who personally associated most closely with Joseph Smith and all his successors have testified to the basic goodness of their intentions, conduct, and leadership. They are men touched by God and ordained to his work who are doing their best to fulfill their unique and heavy calling. But in our well-intentioned, and in many ways honorable, defense of Joseph Smith's (and Brigham Young's and Thomas S. Monson's) good name, we sometimes fall into the trap—laid by Joseph's critics—that the central issue at stake in determining the validity of the restoration's salvific message is the personal character of the prophets who are its messengers. Unintentionally adopting the false argument of the church's opponents, we have occasionally confused and conflated the quality of messenger and message. But to expect prophets to be perfect, to be troubled by anything that falls short of what we perceive as a celestial paradigm, and to make it an ironclad requirement that prophets be 100 percent right 100 percent of the time supposes that God's call overrides human agency. That is not only bad history but also bad theology. As one of those prophets, David O. McKay, taught, "When God makes the prophet, He does not unmake the man."[9] To require God's work to go forward exclusively under the supervision of incorruptible paragons of virtue whose every word comes straight like lightning from heaven and whose every action is godly in both purpose and execution is unrealistic, unscriptural, and frankly, borderline idolatrous.

President Dieter F. Uchtdorf provided wise guidance along these lines when he taught:

> Some struggle with unanswered questions about things that have been done or said in the past. We openly acknowledge that in nearly 200 years of Church history—along with an uninterrupted line of inspired, honorable, and divine events— there have been some things said and done that could cause people to question. . . .
>
> And, to be perfectly frank, there have been times when members or leaders in the Church have simply made mistakes. There may have been things said or done that were not in harmony with our values, principles, or doctrine.
>
> I suppose the Church would be perfect only if it were run by perfect beings. God is perfect, and His doctrine is pure. But

> He works through us—His imperfect children—and imperfect
> people make mistakes.[10]

President Uchtdorf helpfully acknowledges human error within the church, and even within its leadership, without giving up on the basic truthfulness of the gospel or the centrality of the church for fostering discipleship.

Saying that the church and its prophets are not perfect is *not* the same as saying they are not true.[11] Just the opposite is, in fact, the case according to our understanding of our Heavenly Father's plan. The prophets *cannot* be required to be perfect because that would foil the whole purpose of the plan, which is for human beings (including church leaders) to exercise moral agency. In this life we learn through our experience to distinguish good from evil and choose truth over error. If God were to dictate every decision and forcibly instigate every policy, if he refused to allow his church leaders, from prophets to Primary presidents, to ever make mistakes or commit sin, he would be defeating his own purpose: to help us learn to use our moral agency to develop our divine nature and become like he is. God treats the church very much like he treats individuals. As we strive to follow him, he intervenes occasionally to provide us with guidance, to warn us from danger, or to admonish us to change direction. Much of the time, however, even for those blessed with the gift of the Holy Ghost or the mantle of prophethood, he teaches us correct principles and allows us to govern ourselves.

Patience, faith, and trust

In the very first revelation that the Lord gave to the organized Church of Christ in this dispensation, he spoke of what it means for us to follow a living, human prophet: "Wherefore, meaning the church, thou shalt give heed unto all his [the prophet's] words and commandments which he shall give unto you as he receiveth them, walking in all holiness before me; For his word ye shall receive, as if from mine own mouth, *in all patience and faith*" (D&C 21:4–5, emphasis mine). As a church we have generally emphasized following the prophet in faith. But what does it mean for us to follow the Lord's counsel to be patient with our prophets?

The Lord has called prophets and apostles in modern times who are watchmen on the tower and are reliable guides for a life of faith in an age of doubt. I am pleased that one of my children's favorite Primary songs is "Follow the Prophet" (although I must confess it makes me squirm a little when they march around singing it when my non-LDS in-laws are in the room). They are learning, if only implicitly, that they are not the center of the universe, nor are their finite minds and undeveloped moral consciences the final arbiters of all that is right and true and good. I have confidence that my children's boisterous utterance that they should follow the prophet because "he knows the way" will be complemented in the church and at home by reminders that we follow the prophets insofar as they "know the Way"—Jesus Christ—and direct us to him. In time their youthful innocence will be replaced by a more mature understanding that giving heed to a prophet's words is not always easy, convenient, or comfortable—and certainly not as much fun as it seemed in sharing time.

Following a prophet forces us to use our agency to sacrifice some of our precious individual autonomy. In an age of iPads and iPhones, we are constantly tempted to become "iProphets"—or in the Lord's own description of the modern age, "They seek not the Lord to establish his righteousness, but every man walketh in his own way, and after the image of his own god" (D&C 1:16). In such a context, the covenant to sustain living, fallible men as prophets and apostles is one of the most countercultural and arguably difficult aspects of Mormonism. The Lord calls us to walk the harder way situated between the easier paths of blind obedience and blanket rejection. At the same time, he mercifully reminds us that it takes not only faith to follow the words of a human prophet but also patience. He knows he is asking us to do a hard thing.

Revisiting the priesthood-temple ban is instructive here. It is a genuine theological dilemma—how and why could prophets initiate and then maintain the ban? The problem has come to a head recently with the publication of the essay "Race and the Priesthood" on the church's official Gospel Topics website. The statement explains that when Brigham Young initiated the priesthood ban in 1852, he broke from the precedent established under Joseph Smith of ordaining black men to the priesthood. The essay goes on to say, "Over time, Church leaders and members advanced many theories to explain the priesthood and temple restrictions. None of these explanations is accepted today as the official doctrine of the Church." However we assess the motivations of Brigham Young and his successors, contemporary LDS teaching is clear: "Today, the Church disavows the theories advanced in the past that black skin is a sign of divine disfavor or curse, or that it reflects unrighteous actions in a premortal life; that mixed-race marriages are a sin; or that blacks or people of any other race or ethnicity are inferior in any way to anyone else. Church leaders today unequivocally condemn all racism, past and present, in any form."[12] The church's current position is unequivocal. Church members have more work to do going forward to implement the ideals outlined in this statement, as well as in scriptures like 2 Nephi 26:33, which declare that "all are alike unto God." But the past still poses questions for us. What are faithful Mormons to do with the clear discrepancy between Brigham Young's policy and modern church teaching and practice? It is one thing to say that prophets from Joseph Smith to the present are subject to human error, but it gets difficult, and to some even painful and disorienting, when we consider the multigenerational impact of prophets withholding temple blessings and the priesthood from blacks without a clear understanding as to why.

This gets to one of the central elements of Mormonism as a lived religion. Can we believe that fallible human beings can also be conduits for the Lord's will? Can a prophet be inspired and in error, even on the same day or in the same sermon? Do we believe our bishops and stake presidents can be trusted to carry out the Lord's will in their jurisdictions, which our theology states is just as significant and sacred as the prophet's stewardship over the entire church? Can we ourselves, with all our flaws, filters, and prejudices, nonetheless be genuinely inspired of the Lord? Do we really believe that the "weak things of the world" can be agents of God (1 Corinthians 1:27; D&C 1:19; 35:13)? It is a daring assertion, but it is a crucial element of our religion. Part of the essence of Mormonism is trusting the revelation of other fallible human beings. In a secular age already suffering from a deficit of trust, this is perhaps one of our greatest collective challenges. Our leaders, like ourselves, have made and will continue to make mistakes, sometimes grave ones. We can only hope that we will all learn to correct our transgressions—to repent—and go on, still confident that God is with us if not with our sins.

President Spencer W. Kimball, the prophet who finally wrestled with God until he received the revelation that overturned the priesthood-temple ban, provides a poignant lesson. Looking back on the revelation and the process leading up to it, he candidly described his struggle as an internal one:

> Day after day, and especially on Saturdays and Sundays when there were no [sessions] in the temple, I went there when I could be alone. . . .
>
> I was very humble. I was searching for this. I wanted to be sure. . . .
>
> I had a great deal to fight . . . myself, largely, because I had grown up with this thought that Negroes should not have the priesthood and I was prepared to go all the rest of my life until my death and fight for it and defend it as it was.
>
> But this revelation and assurance came to me so clearly that there was no question about it.[13]

Before the restriction was lifted, President Kimball recognized that it may have been based in error and that the Lord could extend forgiveness if needed: "I know the Lord could change his policy and release the ban and forgive the possible error which brought about the deprivation."[14] This humble acknowledgment of human fallenness and the joyful recognition of the necessity and genuine possibility of forgiveness is the very essence of the good news of Jesus Christ.

President Kimball was born only eighteen years after Brigham Young's death. He grew up in a church culture in which the priesthood-temple ban was simply a given. Although there were clearly external pressures on the church in the 1970s to reverse its position, Kimball was determined to defend the policy to his death if that's what he felt was right. But God, who had prepared his humble servant, pricked his heart enough to get him to ask the question. Still that was not enough. It took months, and even years. Kimball had to struggle and fight—mostly, he admitted, against himself, and against the prejudices natural to a white man born in America in 1895. Some assume that for many decades prophets had patiently waited on God to reveal if and when the policy should change. Based on Kimball's self-assessment, perhaps it was the case that God was patiently waiting on his prophets.

Grace and forgiveness

Our doctrine that humans are coeternal with God means that we believe in and worship a Heavenly Father who is perfected but not fully sovereign. God can do many wondrous things, but he cannot control our wills. Martin Luther King Jr., in his brilliant "Letter from a Birmingham Jail," wrote that "Human progress never rolls in on wheels of inevitability; it comes through the tireless efforts of men [and women] willing to be co-workers with God."[15] In Mormonism we have a robust sense that we are cocreators and coworkers with God. This incredibly optimistic view of humanity and our divine potential—what theologians would call a "high anthropology"—is one of the most beautiful and profound truths of the restored gospel.

In placing so much cosmic meaning and responsibility on the shoulders of fallen humans, we are set up for both spectacular success and colossal failure, and everything in between. Collectively and individually, "we have learned by sad experience that it is the nature and disposition of almost all men, as soon as they get a little authority, as they suppose, they will immediately begin to exercise unrighteous dominion." We may not always be fully conscious of it, but too often we use whatever scraps of authority and privilege we gain "to cover our sins, or to gratify our pride, our vain ambition, or to exercise control or dominion or compulsion upon the souls of the children of men" (D&C 121:37–39). Joseph Smith penned this devastatingly incisive description of human nature as a characterization not of the degenerate outside world—which he may well otherwise have done, given that he wrote it while unjustly imprisoned in Liberty Jail—but rather of Zion, and even more specifically of the holders of the priesthood.

In that marvelous prison letter, the Prophet Joseph, inspired by the Lord, provided not only a perceptive diagnosis of the human condition but also the divinely proposed cure: "The powers of heaven cannot be controlled nor handled," he wrote, "only upon the principles of righteousness." Godly power is never coercive, impatient, arrogant, spiteful, mean, ignorant, or deceitful. It only operates upon principles of persuasion, patience, gentleness, humility, kindness, pure knowledge, authenticity, and love (D&C 121:36, 41–42).

We are often quick to point out where prophets and other church leaders have acted either according to or against these principles; the most superficial study of the scriptures or church history, or our personal experience in our own wards and branches, makes this an embarrassingly easy exercise. If we take the Sermon on the Mount seriously, however, our first impulse as Christians should be to look inward and consider how this reflects upon and even tests our own discipleship. God's calling of generally virtuous but nevertheless imperfect prophets, some of whom have said or done things that perhaps should have landed them in the belly of a whale, is uniquely designed to help us learn and practice grace. We learn grace when we divorce personal character or qualifications from the divine call and allow God to lead us through human vessels whose flaws are altogether obvious. We practice grace when we are patient and when we forgive. Indeed, one of our modern prophets, Elder Jeffrey R. Holland, reminded us that when dealing with "finite [human] vessels" that "can't quite contain" all of God's glory and perfection, our best response is to "be patient and kind and forgiving."[16] In saying this, Elder Holland is simply reiterating what the Lord told the church on the day of its birth: following a prophet takes faith, and it also takes patience.

Choice and accountability

The historical facts regarding the fallibility of church members and leaders, including prophets and apostles, are rarely in doubt. The theological implications are profound and admittedly still require some working out by the membership and leadership of the church. In the meantime, individual believers are faced with a choice. In one sense, it is a matter of faith: can I believe that God leads the church through flawed prophets? But in another, perhaps more important sense, that question is only ancillary to the more significant issue laid before the Christian disciple: can I forgive prophets for their faults, even their occasionally severe ones, and be patient with my brothers? If I personally believe that Brigham Young erred when he instituted the priesthood ban in 1852, can I forgive him? If I believe that certain actions by ancient or latter-day prophets, leaders, or other church members seem contrary to my sense of acceptable moral behavior, can I forgive them?

If I find any particular current teachings or actions of the prophets and apostles hard to accept—not simply because of my personal preferences or politics but because of my deeply felt commitment to my understanding of the gospel of Jesus Christ—can I exercise patience and faith? Just as important, am I simultaneously and authentically open to the possibility that I might be wrong and they might be right? Can I be long-suffering, meek, kind, guileless, and loving toward the prophets, as the revelation dictates, or do I only require those virtues to be exercised by the prophets on my behalf?

To be clear, this does not mean prophets are not accountable for their teachings and behavior, nor does it require us to abdicate our own agency or personal responsibility on matters of moral conscience. Rather, it recognizes that I am no more the prophets' ultimate judge than they are mine. In the church we frequently cite the revelation given, with some cosmic irony or perhaps foreshadowing, on September 11, 1831—the same day as the Mountain Meadows Massacre twenty-six years later and the attacks on the World Trade Center and Pentagon 180 years later: "I, the Lord, will forgive whom I will forgive, but of you it is required to forgive all men." We rarely consider the context for this commandment given only three verses earlier, where God straightforwardly announces to the entire church that Joseph Smith "has sinned." (If Joseph Smith had ever been inclined to promote a doctrine of prophetic infallibility, he might have left out the parts where the Lord calls him to repentance repeatedly throughout the canonized revelations in the Doctrine and Covenants.) The Lord is not casual about sin, but he seems far more ready to pardon us than we sometimes are. The solution to Joseph Smith's sins was simple and no different from ours: "I, the Lord, forgive sins unto those who confess their sins before me and ask forgiveness." And to the rest of us not-so-innocent bystanders? "Wherefore, I say unto you, that ye ought to forgive one another; for he that forgiveth not his brother his trespasses standeth condemned before the Lord; for there remaineth in him the greater sin" (D&C 64:7–10). It seems that God's position on prophetic fallibility is stunningly, perhaps scandalously, uncomplicated: it exists. It can and should be forgiven, and he, not we, will decide whether sufficient confession and repentance has occurred.

Remember Nephi's broken-bow incident, when the veteran com-plainers Laman and Lemuel were joined by the prophet Lehi, who "began to murmur against the Lord his God." Nephi, as was his habit, delivered a lecture to his brothers, but from the record it seems he was silent toward his father-prophet regarding his lack of trust in the Lord. Instead, Nephi plowed ahead, fashioning a new bow out of exist-ing materials, and then, in a remarkable gesture of patient faith in the prophet, went to his father to ask for his inspiration on where he should hunt for food. When the humbled prophet turned back (liter-ally, repented) to the Lord, "the voice of the Lord came . . . and [Lehi] was truly chastened because of his murmuring against the Lord, inso-much that he was brought down into the depths of sorrow" (1 Nephi 16:20–25). The prophet was not let off easy for his temporary lapse, but Nephi astutely discerned that the divine calling had not been removed from his father at the first sign of mortal failing—in modern parlance, he sustained him. The fallible prophet was still a prophet, and when he returned to the Lord, the voice of the Lord returned to him. The story gets better. Because God is incomprehensibly good and forgiving, he immediately overcompensated the chastised prophet and his family with the miraculous gift of the Liahona. A prophet's misstep provided Nephi with an opportunity to learn and practice grace. Then God showed what true grace is.

Of course, Lehi's temporary lapse isn't equivalent to the denial of priesthood and temple blessings based on race, nor did his murmuring have the long-standing and painful impact of the corresponding racist theories that weakened the body of Christ for generations. Our faith, patience, and forgiveness will require spiritual exertions proportionate to the scale of the offense. To forgive is not to be willfully ignorant in the face of human fallenness; it is rather to stare sin in the eye and declare that it will not triumph, no matter the suffering it has caused. The greater the sin, the more difficult the forgiveness. It does not come easily, and it rarely comes immediately. The scars may never heal; as far as we know, Jesus's still haven't.

If I could go back in time, back to my mission to meet again with Greg and Lynnette, that is the message I would give them. I would stop trying to explain and start teaching and practicing forgiveness and grace. I would add that following a prophet is never a blind or robotic act. Choosing to trust another person's calling and revelation does not negate the underlying fact that we are each "free forever, knowing good from evil; to act for [ourselves] and not to be acted upon" (2 Nephi 2:26). We can and should never relinquish our agency. What happens when we disagree with a prophet, not out of convenience or whim but out of deep-seated and gospel-inspired moral conviction? Sustaining another fallible human being as a coworker with God will sometimes be in creative tension with following our own inner light and personal revelation. There are no rules for what to do in every case, only principles to apply with the assistance of the Spirit. We find ways to balance faith, patience, grace, forgiveness, integrity, conscience, community, and covenant.

The prophets are painfully aware that they do not speak or act with either infallibility or impunity. Joseph Smith, who was quick to publicly admit his "inability" and "weakness," knew he had to tread lightly, "remembering that the eyes of my maker are upon me and that to him I am accountable for every word I say."[17] I don't have to justify Brigham Young for his words and deeds—"It is God that justifieth" (Romans 8:33). Sound moral judgment leads me to grieve the consequences of human frailty and sin, regardless of who exhibited it. And yet on this side of the veil, where I "see through a glass, darkly," and only "know in part," I am compelled toward charity (1 Corinthians 13:12–13). Christ has faithfully delivered his church and his prophets before, and he will do so again in the future: "He who rescued us from so deadly a peril will continue to rescue us; on him we have set our hope that he will rescue us again" (2 Corinthians 1:10 NRSV). Following the apostles and prophets has brought me thus far to Christ, so I will continue to walk the path with them.

7

Abide in the Vine

IN RECENT YEARS, MUCH INK HAS BEEN SPILLED, and many hackles raised, regarding the question, are Mormons Christian? Although superficially significant, the debate is mostly a silly and tiresome one. The matter comes down to a disagreement over definitions. Is a Christian someone who exercises faith in and devotion to Jesus of Nazareth as Son of God and Savior of humanity via his atonement? Or to be a Christian must a person subscribe to specific beliefs and adhere to certain traditions that descend from a particular historical-theological religious genealogy— namely the early church councils at Nicaea, Constantinople, Ephesus, and Chalcedon? It suffices to say that Mormons certainly qualify under the first definition but not under the second; after all, one of the main points of the restoration inaugurated with Joseph Smith was to reestablish a latter-day Church of Christ not beholden to the historic creeds.

Mormons don't need non-Mormons to validate their relationship to Christ, but outside perspectives do help clarify the matter. In his recent study of Mormonism, philosopher Stephen Webb has been awestruck by our religion's unabashed focus on Christ. "In affirming the divinity of Jesus, Mormons are Christians who do not know where to stop," Webb writes. "Mormon rhetoric is guided by the conviction that the only way to say enough about Christ is to say too much. . . . Mormon theology is Christology unbound."[1] When historian John Turner, who has written an award-winning biography of Brigham Young and taught several courses on Mormonism, decided to sit down and read the Book of Mormon, he was surprised by how Christ-saturated it was: "It's even more Christocentric than I presumed. It's overwhelmingly Christocentric. Detailed prophecies about Jesus all the time. I find the [Book of Mormon] to be persistent and exuberant in its insistence upon the divinity of Jesus Christ."[2] Richard Mouw, a prominent theologian, former president of Fuller Seminary, and leader in evangelical-Mormon dialogue (for which he has taken considerable heat in his own religious community), understands and articulates the distinction between Mormons and traditional Christians well. From his perspective, he believes that Latter-day Saints "have a defective theology about Christ" because we embrace unique doctrines revealed through the Prophet Joseph Smith which depart from certain key creedal formulations. Despite his suspicions about certain aspects of Mormon theology, however, Mouw has no doubt that many if not most Mormons genuinely place "their trust in the true Christ."[3]

Latter-day Saints know that the true Christ in whom they trust is the Prince of Peace. When our confidence is shaken and all else fails, he is the one to whom we can turn to find peace and refuge. By far the most important principle in navigating our relationship to the church, especially when we encounter issues that trouble our hearts, is to rely "wholly upon the merits of him who is mighty to save" (2 Nephi 31:19). Emma Lou Thayne's hymn speaks deeply to the distress of faith crisis, with all its swirling feelings of betrayal, hurt, emptiness, and anger:

> Where can I turn for peace?
> Where is my solace
> When other sources cease to make me whole?
> When with a wounded heart, anger, or malice,
> I draw myself apart,
> Searching my soul?
> Where, when my aching grows,
> Where, when I languish,
> Where, in my need to know, where can I run?
> Where is the quiet hand to calm my anguish?
> Who, who can understand?
> He, only One.[4]

The message of this chapter is simple. Christ is "the founder of peace" (Mosiah 15:18). If we are ever to find peace in the church, we can only do so by finding Christ in it.

The fundamental principle

From its earliest days, The Church of Jesus Christ of Latter-day Saints has always had its fair share of internal as well as external conflict. Diversity makes disagreement natural. Compounded with human fallibility, a certain amount of discord is inevitable. Making our way through this conflict, and finding a way to invite peace into the house we share, requires us to focus on the One who can bring this peace and not to be unduly distracted by the maelstrom. Can we, both individually and as a people, construct our narratives of church history and discipleship with Christ truly at the center? No doubt there are many other interesting and important things to concern ourselves about, but we risk losing sight of the forest when we zero in on certain trees.

This church, its prophets, its history, its doctrines, and its practices are beneficiaries of the redemption of Jesus Christ as surely as are you and I. "Remember, remember," the Book of Mormon teaches, "that it is upon the rock of our Redeemer, who is Christ, the Son of God, that ye must build your foundation" (Helaman 5:12). In the garden and on the cross, Jesus broke the bonds of sin for me, for you, for the church, and for the world. For the Christian, all of human history is framed by a grand narrative of sin and redemption in which Christ's atoning work is not only the major plot point but in fact constitutes the entire stage upon which we act. "I am the vine, you are the branches," Jesus taught. "Those who abide in me and I in them bear much fruit, because apart from me you can do nothing" (John 15:5). When we abide in Christ, our history, our theology, and our ministry will bear fruit. Conversely, any story that we tell that is disconnected from the narrative of sin and redemption in Christ is bound to be lifeless.[5] However, I fear that in too many of our stories we have treated the branches—historical figures and incidents or points of doctrine—in isolation from the Vine that gives them life and constant nourishment. Both active members of the church and its critics have been guilty of this.

When we abide in the True Vine, the various individual branches—whether it is Joseph Smith's character, the method of his translation of the Book of Mormon, Brigham Young's teachings about blood atonement, or even continuing patriarchy in the church—can be viewed in broader perspective and not bear so much moral weight. As Joseph

Smith declared: "The fundamental principles of our religion is [*sic*] the testimony of the apostles and prophets concerning Jesus Christ, 'that he died, was buried, and rose again the third day, and ascended up into heaven'; and all other things are only appendages to these, which pertain to our religion."[6] Appendages matter—I rather enjoy having the use of my arms and legs, thank you very much—but they are not the main story, and we can live (and even thrive) without them. A Christ-centered approach helps us to distinguish between appendages and fundamental principles.

Placing Christ at the center of our stories does not mean we give misdeeds a pass. Christ's doctrine is exalting and exacting. Jesus was no relativist during his mortal ministry. Along with his frequent extensions of forgiveness was an acknowledgment of underlying sin that required repentance. He does not reinforce our values—he demands that we accept his. As he told Joseph Smith and the church in the earliest days of the restoration, he will lift us out of our afflictions, counsel us, and deliver us from our enemies and the powers of darkness. But, he admonished the Prophet, "thou art not excusable in thy transgressions." To the individual disciple and to the church, Christ's encouragement to "go thy way" is always accompanied by the corollary of "sin no more" (D&C 24:1–2; John 8:11). Applying the redemption of Christ as our principal lens on history and culture will therefore shine a penetrating, sometimes fierce, light on human sin, while at the same time offering grace toward its perpetrators.

Revisiting Mountain Meadows

Let me offer one example of how we can retell one story from church history by focusing on the vine rather than on the branches. On September 11, 1857, Mormon settlers in southern Utah, marshaled by men who were simultaneously their church, civic, and military leaders, and joined by some local Indians they had recruited, slaughtered some 120 emigrant men, women, and children in cold blood. We know this as the Mountain Meadows Massacre.[7] For decades the official church position was that it was an Indian massacre. Although church leaders, including Brigham Young, knew the general contours of what happened relatively soon after the events unfolded, they covered up the extent of Mormon involvement both internally and publicly. From a political perspective, the denials and cover-up seemed prudent, particularly in an era in which the leadership was scrambling to literally save the church from federal prosecution. For a century and a half, the main LDS narrative of Mountain Meadows was concerned primarily with damage control— denying responsibility, blaming others, and refusing to acknowledge the pain that members and leaders of our church had caused. These obfuscations both reflected and perpetuated myths that God's chosen people could never commit such an atrocity, that church leaders invariably speak truth and stand for justice, and that some things that are true are not very useful in spreading God's kingdom throughout the earth. This was a narrative that focused on the branch—the church and its reputation—rather than on the vine of Christ and his gospel of repentance, peace, and reconciliation.

The irony is that our story never convinced anyone but ourselves. Murderous Mormons became a common trope in journalistic accounts, exposés, and dime novels throughout the period. Sherlock Holmes's first case, written by Sir Arthur Conan Doyle three decades after Mountain Meadows, involved the "Avenging Angels" of Utah.[8] Missionaries in the Southern States Mission in the late nineteenth century complained that when they took questions from a crowd, "it is Polygamy first," but as soon as "they dry up on that subject [they] fly to the Mountain Meadow [sic] Massacre."[9] The massacre became one of a long list of atrocities and heresies laid at the feet of the church by its critics.

Members of the church, on the other hand, by and large believed the story of Mormon innocence and reacted viscerally to the mere suggestion that their noble pioneer leaders or ancestors could possibly be guilty of such a horrific crime.[10] It has only been in this century that the church has fully acknowledged the Latter-day Saint role in the massacre through careful scholarship as well as official statements. At a ceremony on the massacre's 150th anniversary held at the site, Elder Henry B. Eyring, shortly before becoming a member of the First Presidency, expressed "profound regret" to the victims, their descendants, and the Paiute people for the sinful behavior of the nineteenth-century Saints: "What was done here long ago by members of our church represents a terrible and inexcusable departure from Christian teaching and conduct. We cannot change what happened, but we can remember and honor those who were killed here."[11] Only after many decades were we able to take collective accountability for the actions of our forebears. Honest confession and sincere regret on the part of the church has in turn paved the way for further acts of personal reconciliation, such as two "friendship quilts" made by descendants of both the perpetrators and victims of the massacre. Messages on the quilts' squares include expressions such as, "We honor the memory of those who died and express profoundest condolences to all affected," and simply, "Jesus wept."[12] Fidelity to the faith of our fathers means worshipping our ancestors' God, not our ancestors.

The Mountain Meadows Massacre and its subsequent cover-up together represent one of Mormonism's lowest points. It is a classic story of human sinfulness, seemingly ripped from the pages of the Old Testament. Otherwise godly people—real pioneer heroes—lost their way and fell into a spiral of greed, lying, blame, murder, and hiding from God (not to mention federal marshals). For generations, focusing our moral imagination and energy on protecting the integrity of the branch kept us from truth telling, reconciliation, and peace. It separated us from the vine. It was only when we reckoned with the full brunt of the massacre that we could find healing—even atonement—in our own time. When faced with courage, honesty, and grace, Mountain Meadows is a scandal that leads us to Christ and, through him, to reconciliation with our neighbors. It reminds us that even dedicated Saints can descend into depravity when their moral reckoning departs from the basic teachings and example of Jesus. Our darkest day as a people thus becomes a means by which we can turn back to Christ and enhance our discipleship, even though of course it would have been better for the sin to remain undone and those precious lives saved. Those of us looking back on past misdeeds do so neither to justify sin nor to consider ourselves superior by comparison.[13] We put ourselves in our ancestors' shoes, while acknowledging the tragedy in their moral choices. Both individually and collectively, we can learn from the past and move forward in Christ, resolved to be perfected in him and not to return to the error of our previous ways.

The virtue of hope

True repentance allows us not to be constantly wringing our hands about the past. Mormonism is an optimistic, forward-looking faith. A non-LDS friend recently joked to me that we Mormons smile too much. Whether or not that's true, our cheerfulness comes precisely because we are so confident in Christ's redemption. In his vision of the tree of life—representing Christ's atonement, the purest and most expansive expression of the love of God—Father Lehi saw a river of water that was interpreted as "filthiness." Yet he hardly gave it any notice, "so much was his mind swallowed up in other things" (1 Nephi 15:27), particularly the fruit of the tree and his desire for his family to also partake of it. A Christocentric worldview is not naive toward the world's (and the church's) moral complexities, conundrums, and compromises—neither does it surrender to them, animated and anchored as it is by hope in Christ.

The three great Christian virtues are faith, hope, and charity. The first and the third receive significant attention, but hope—like many middle children—sometimes gets lost in the shuffle. Hope is often relegated to the status of a flimsy wish, like what we hope to get for Christmas. But true hope is no more passing fancy than true love is fleeting infatuation. Martin Luther King Jr.—whose dream of a more just and inclusive society literally changed the course of history—offered one of the most articulate meditations of the nature of hope in his frequent assertion that "the arc of the moral universe is long but it bends toward justice."[14] America's heroic civil rights struggle was predicated on the deep hope that the universe, in its truest sense, is a moral order, and that justice eventually prevails because of the very nature of God and reality. This was the hope that propelled the movement's activists despite repeated setbacks, constant privation and suffering, and even martyrdom.[15] It constitutes a poignant critique of the modern world's nihilism. Hope is emboldening and liberating. Hope orients and anchors us in the midst of chaos.

Latter-day Saints are also a people well acquainted with hope. The Mormon pioneers are the very personification of the virtue, but we have other examples as well. One of my heroes is Helmuth Hübener, who was a paragon of hope in a time of hopelessness. As a sixteen-year-old boy living in Hamburg during World War II, Hübener knew enough, based on his own moral intuitions and knowledge of gospel principles, that something was rotten in the state of Germany. After surreptitiously listening to BBC radio broadcasts, he decided he had to do something to get the truth out to his fellow Germans, so he began printing and then distributing leaflets exposing the Nazis' lies and crimes. He recruited three friends to help him—two of them also Latter-day Saints—and together they constituted one of the youngest resistance groups to Hitler's regime. The Gestapo caught them and sentenced Hübener, still a minor, to death by guillotine. His own priesthood leaders, some of whom were members of the Nazi Party, turned their backs on him and even excommunicated him, presumably to save the rest of the members of their German branch and the church from the regime's wrath. (His membership was posthumously restored.)[16]

Yet even in the face of death, Hübener understood implicitly, like Martin Luther King, that the arc of the moral universe bends toward justice. Because of his faith in the resurrection, he knew that the Nazis could kill his body but not his soul. One of the three final letters his executioners allowed him to write concluded: "My Father in Heaven knows that I have done nothing wrong. . . . I know that God lives and He will be the proper judge of this matter. Until our happy reunion in that better world I remain, your friend and brother in the Gospel, Helmuth."[17] In short, Helmuth Hübener had hope. He exemplified Moroni's teaching that "whoso believeth in God might with surety hope for a better world, yea, even a place at the right hand of God, which hope cometh of faith, maketh an anchor to the souls of men, which would make them sure and steadfast, always abounding in good works, being led to glorify God" (Ether 12:4).

Mercifully, Nazi prisons and torture are inconceivably distant from most of our everyday lives. Our need for and exercise of Christian virtues is less dramatic, typically, than was Helmuth Hübener's. Yet when our experiences lead to a crisis of faith, hope is often one of the chief casualties. How can we place our hope in a church whose leaders, members, history, and practices fall short—not Nazi short, but short nevertheless? How is it possible to witness or endure infelicities within an institution that claims to be God's true church? How can God expect us to follow prophets "in all patience and faith" (D&C 21:5) when he knows full well that they not only preach the gospel of Jesus Christ and administer saving priesthood ordinances but also institute priesthood bans and cover up massacres? How can we possibly place our hope in imperfect human vessels such as Joseph Smith, Brigham Young, and the current President of the church, not to mention our bishops and stake presidents?

Hope of Israel

The answer, of course, is that we do not. We do not place our ultimate hope in prophets and priesthood leaders. We do not place our ultimate hope in the church. We place our ultimate hope in Christ and his atonement. The prophets and priests of Israel, both anciently and today, enliven our hope by directing us toward the Hope of Israel. God points us to prophets and the church not because they can save or redeem us, but because they are the temporal means by which he orients us to our Savior and Redeemer.

Christ is not only the Redeemer of Israel and redeemer of our souls but also the redeemer of history. The resurrection of Jesus Christ changes everything. It extends the timeline for the achievement of justice, righteousness, and peace, allowing for the arc to stretch well beyond any person's mortal sojourn. No part of scripture more powerfully testifies of this than the final book of the Bible. Reading Revelation can be intimidating when we focus on all the vivid but vexing details. Yet there is a reason that Joseph Smith stated that "the book of Revelation is one of the plainest books God ever caused to be written."[18] No doubt the Prophet had special insight into scripture that most of us do not share, but I think he was speaking straightforwardly.

Taken as a whole, Revelation is easy to understand because the message is simple: Christ wins. In John's vision we see that the resurrected Christ—transformed from the Suffering Servant of Isaiah to the "Lord of lords, and King of kings" (Revelation 17:14)—has already assured a conclusive and definitive victory over not only death and sin, but also all the fruits of the fall, including conquest, war, famine, and pestilence (Revelation 6:1–8). The reality of the resurrection assures that in the end Christ "shall have subdued all enemies under his feet, and shall have perfected his work" (D&C 76:106). That means that God's work on the earth is not yet perfected, but also that disciples should not be overly troubled by present conditions. To use a sports analogy, the outcome of the game has already been decided, with Christ as captain, star, and coach of the winning team. Nevertheless, the losing team remains on the field desperately trying to score a few meaningless points and injure players from the winning team until time runs out. In the meantime, we put our faith in Christ and stay on the field because we've already seen the game highlights on SportsCenter, and therefore we know in hope that his team is victorious. It feels a little like cheating to know the final outcome while the game is still being played—making Christians the envy of Las Vegas oddsmakers—but actually it is the essence of Christian hope.

We have hope that Christ has redeemed humanity and human history because he entered into it. This is the central Christian doctrine of the Incarnation, or as Mormons more typically call it, following Nephi, "the condescension of God" (1 Nephi 11:16). King Benjamin would later prophesy about "the Lord Omnipotent" who would "come down from heaven among the children of men, and shall dwell in a tabernacle of clay, and shall go forth amongst men, working mighty miracles. . . . He shall suffer temptations, and pain of body, hunger, thirst, and fatigue" (Mosiah 3:5–7). According to Mormon theology, human mortality was not something Christ went through simply to show sympathy for us but because it was a crucial experience in his divine formation. The flesh is sanctified by the Son of God's entry into it. Similarly, the stuff of human history—from high politics to wedding feasts—is imbued with a sacred quality after being touched by the presence of Christ.

His walk among us reminds us that everyday life—with its mustard seeds and lost coins and prodigal sons—may feel mundane but is fundamentally sacred. Faith and discipleship occur in history rather than apart from it. What we previously thought was a secular story separate from God's work of salvation among individuals now takes on a new cast, with greater purpose and meaning. The church has a central role in the drama. In the words of Christian scholar Charles Mathewes, "This is how the Christian churches offer a richer and more fruitful perspective, by telling the story of God's dealings with humanity from alpha to omega, from Israel through the story of Christ. And yet this is not escapist, because God is going to redeem *all* of history, not just a selective part of it—and God is going to redeem history through the work of the churches."[19] Mormonism both confirms and expands upon this insight by noting that Christ's work continued anciently with his visits to the Americas and other unnamed locales and then again in modern times beginning with Joseph Smith's first vision. Nor is God's entry into history limited to remarkable visions and visitations. Since every person possesses the light of Christ, and the Holy Spirit moves among all the nations, God is and has always been intimately at work among us.

The redeeming work of Immanuel—"God with us"—both culminated in and was most powerfully displayed in the atonement, which was "finished," as Jesus said, on the cross of Calvary (John 19:30). Jesus was not a passive or accidental victim on that fateful Friday. He deliberately oriented his life toward the cross so that from that literal platform he could reveal the true nature of God. Once resurrected, Christ emphasized this positive power of the cross when he declared to the Nephites: "my Father sent me that I might be lifted up upon the cross; and after that I had been lifted up upon the cross, that I might draw all men unto me" (3 Nephi 27:14). With his public crucifixion, Jesus offered a public revelation not just for a chosen few prophets but for the whole world: here was the Son of God lifted up for all to see, for all time. What we witness when we gaze upon the crucified Christ is a God who is suffering and vulnerable, a God who has subjected himself to the corrupt judgment and depraved violence of humanity, a God who at once chastens those who have lost affection but who is ultimately merciful and forgiving, indiscriminate in his love and grace. In his very vulnerability, mercy, and love, Christ draws us to him. We can hardly help but be touched—shaken to our very core—by his suffering, born out of unspeakable compassion for us and our fallen world. Our hearts are swollen with anguish at his innocent torment, for which we feel somewhat culpable, both individually and collectively. Through his suffering, and the sympathy born of it, he binds our hearts to his. We are willing to follow his call and obey his words and live in and build his kingdom because we are drawn in by the power of his devotion to us. Through his atoning work, culminating in the everlasting victory of the resurrection, Christ has transformed everything we thought we knew, and powered the moral universe through love.

The good news

This is the good news that Christ has entrusted to his church to preserve and to share. Mormonism hardly has a monopoly on this news—in the early twenty-first century there are literally a billion-plus of our sisters and brothers on this earth who similarly exercise hope in Christ. But the preponderance of latter-day revelation through and about Christ puts Mormons in a uniquely strong position to be evangelists, or messengers of the gospel. Like the earliest disciples, "we preach Christ crucified" (1 Corinthians 1:23), knowing in whom we place our trust. If we ever deviate from that message, or fail to locate it at the core of our preaching, then we are trading the vine for the branches.

As church leaders and members review church policies, practices, and teachings, past and present, certain branches or appendages will seem to be of questionable worth. Through the course of our history we have lopped off entire branches that once had been considered as central. Polygamy immediately comes to mind. How do we reconcile the formal cessation of plural marriage—recognizing that it continues, in a way, with the sealing of a widower to a second wife—with the emphatic, consistent teachings of Brigham Young, John Taylor, Joseph F. Smith, Orson Pratt, George Q. Cannon, and many other prophets and apostles that the belief in and willingness to practice "the Principle" was essential to our exaltation? Were they all wrong, or did God change the entrance requirements to the celestial kingdom around 1890? Mormon theology actually allows for either option: prophets can be wrong, and God's revelation today can trump his revelation yesterday. This mutability in church history and doctrine can perplex individual believers who are trying to walk the straight and narrow path—the course of which doesn't always seem particularly straight. Beyond fundamental principles such as faith and repentance, what God requires of his children has clearly changed over time, and the promises he has offered to one person have not always matched those offered to another. John's fate was to tarry in his ministry until Christ's return, never to experience death; Peter's was to minister until being crucified like his Master. As my seven-year-old would exclaim, "That's not fair!" Christ didn't apologize to Peter for the difference or even explain it. He simply asked of his disciple, "What is that to thee? Follow thou me" (John 21:22).

There are certain inequities, iniquities, and injustices in this world that no amount of historicizing, contextualizing, or theologizing will satisfy. Some are so devastating that they challenge our faith in humanity and sometimes our faith in the church and even in God. As we ponder on certain controversies and conundrums, sometimes we are simply left without a good answer, either for ourselves or for those we love. These are the moments that test our hope. In our pain and disorientation, we are forced to plumb the depths of our faith, our hope, and our love—the very foundations of our Christian discipleship. At times the church itself may be both the source and the site of our struggles. More will be said in chapters 8 and 9 about how and why the church can be the place where we find Christ even as the church itself tries our souls. But at the heart of that proposition is the indispensable truth that we must find Christ and abide in him.

Christian discipleship has always been beset by internal and external crises that have shaken the faithful. It was true in the early Christian church; it is true today. Then as now we need the encouragement of those who have come through the crucible with their resolve strengthened. Some of these tested Saints we call apostles. Few were more acquainted with the challenges awaiting those faithfully seeking God than was the tentmaker from Tarsus, who as Saul the persecutor had been the source of many such vexations and as Paul the apostle had both precipitated and experienced his share of conflicts—inside and outside the church. Paul was confident that Christ's atonement redeemed not only individual souls but also the church and all of history. So it is appropriate for him to offer a benediction for us, in the form of his eloquent and reassuring message of hope to those who are trying to abide in the Vine:

> If God is for us, who can be against us!
> God hasn't held anything back. He sacrificed his own Son and gave him up to death. Why, then, wouldn't God give us every grace? And who has the right to accuse us when God has claimed us? God himself has sealed us and set us right. Jesus, our rescuer—Jesus who died and yet now lives—sits on God's right hand and prays on our behalf!

What could divide us from such love? Hard times, or heart-break, or prejudice, or hunger, or old age, or sickness, or war? No! God's love will conquer all these things. Nothing can resist his grace. I know in my bones that neither life nor death, nor angels, nor rulers, nor the present, nor the past, nor the future, nor powers, nor height, nor depth, nor anything in all creation can divorce us from the love God displayed in Jesus.[20]

A Meditation on "Doubting" Thomas

HIS VERY NAME HAS COME to be associated with faithlessness and doubt. The story is familiar but worth retelling:

> Thomas (who was called the Twin), one of the twelve, was not with them when Jesus came. So the other disciples told him, "We have seen the Lord." But he said to them, "Unless I see the mark of the nails in his hands, and put my finger in the mark of the nails and my hand in his side, I will not believe."
>
> A week later his disciples were again in the house, and Thomas was with them. Although the doors were shut, Jesus came and stood among them and said, "Peace be with you." Then he said to Thomas, "Put your finger here and see my hands. Reach out your hand and put it in my side. Do not doubt but believe." Thomas answered him, "My Lord and my God!" Jesus said to him, "Have you believed because you have seen me? Blessed are those who have not seen and yet have come to believe." (John 20:24–29 NRSV)

Thomas had every reason to doubt and to leave. His professed messiah was executed as an enemy of the state. His fellow disciples had spent the previous days quibbling over who would get the chief seats in the kingdom of heaven and then had disappeared into thin air when their master was taken. The vaunted "kingdom of God" consisted of a few hundred people, max, and now even that number seemed laughable.

But had Thomas set off on his own on Good Friday, when things looked so bleak and Jesus's broken and bloodied body was being interred in the cold, hopeless tomb, had he separated himself from the company of his fellow apostles—most of whom were also more full of doubt than belief in those days—then he would never have witnessed the miraculous manifestation of the risen Christ.

In the moment of his greatest crisis, when he had absolutely no reason to believe and even less to stay, when it looked like everything he had lived and sacrificed for over the past three years was a complete sham, Thomas encountered Jesus, and he did so in communion with the apostles. He came to believe, spiritually, because he came, physically, to believe. It was the church, for all its early faithlessness and imperfections, which was Thomas's salvation and ultimately the agent of God's grace in his life and in the world.

8

The Church Is True

THOUGH OFTEN EXPERIENCED SOLITARILY, belief is in fact never separate from belonging. The remainder of this book will consider our membership not only in the metaphorical body of Christ, but also in the actual, concrete, day-to-day Church of Jesus Christ. What does it mean to pursue a life of faith, with all its challenges, in the context of a community?

In the next chapter I will address some of the challenges attendant to being a member of the church, especially for people who feel that they don't fit the prevailing culture. Before considering the travails of church membership, however, I want to linger a bit on the goodness of Mormonism, and specifically of the church. I don't want to sound Pollyannaish or naive about the issues and difficulties that we face together, and I am not ignorant of the fact that for some people those three hours of church on Sunday are among the most alienating and frustrating times of their week. But Mormonism cannot be fully lived outside of community. A person can believe in the doctrines of the gospel in solitude, but she cannot fully be a Mormon in seclusion. Mormonism is by definition a social religion. It is meaningless outside the web of human connections that bind us together, in this life and the next.

In this chapter I will rely on the wisdom of four Latter-day Saints—Claudia Bushman, Richard Bushman, Lowell Bennion, and Eugene England—who together have more than three hundred years of life experience in the church. I won't recount their full biographies here, but it's enough to say that they have each experienced their fair share of both triumphs and difficulties in their relationship to the church, its leaders, and its members. What unites them is their persistence and the wisdom gained from many decades of faithful service and reflection. Their collective conviction, and my own, is that the church is true, and the church is good—not simply because of some metaphysical essence but also because it is one of the most important means we have for developing Christlike character. The church achieves its aims not in spite of its many evident imperfections but often precisely as a result of them.

The loving village

Claudia Bushman is a lifelong member of the church. Her very first church story comes from when she was still a newborn. Her father was the bishop at the time. Shortly after Claudia's birth, another woman was holding her at church, and her father complimented the woman on her beautiful child. The woman said that if he didn't recognize his own daughter, he was working too hard and was away from home too much.

Claudia grew up in San Francisco as a proud California Mormon. Unlike today, when there are over three-quarters of a million members of the church in the state, then Mormons were the tiniest of minorities. Still, she was secure growing up in a warm, loving ward where she learned many valuable life lessons and skills, including how to organize things, how to speak in public, how to act and sing and dance, how to be part of a community—lessons she has used every day of her life.

Happy to defer to a woman with more than eight decades of church experience (and still going strong), let me quote a bit from Claudia herself, as it sounds better in first person:

> I think it is a great opportunity and pleasure to be part of such a huge, fertile, evolving body with so much energy, so many aspects, such a rich culture, an organization that promises a community wherever you go. I love the church for its variety, richness, and way of life. I love the people. I love their devotion, their diversity. I love the wisdom, the craziness, the willingness, the openness of my people.
>
> I love the opportunities that the Church gives to its people. The Church serves as an arena for developing our skills and talents and provides willing people to help us carry out our ideas. That has been a tremendous benefit for me, all my life.

Working together in the Church makes us friends and more than friends—brothers and sisters. I cannot tell you how much I value that.

Church provides the loving village that young people need to grow up in. I certainly admit that some of these villages are more nurturing than others. These village experiences give us skills in speaking, organizing, singing, teaching, working together, that enrich our whole lives and make us more valuable citizens of the world.

Mormon people vary widely in style. Mormon belief is broad, wide, and flexible. A wide spectrum of beliefs is permitted on many topics. People see things differently. What I see in us is a big melting pot, each congregation being stirred around by a great spoon, all of us just trying to be part of the big soup, just trying and learning how to get along together, each adding our bit of flavor to the general whole, accepting the lumps that don't mix in easily, working together to live out our planned community. We belong to something bigger that works to further a general aim while developing the skills of the individuals.

The church described by Claudia is not a final product delivered straight from heaven to earth. It is a process, a work of constant creation. It is vibrant, active, alive. It is inseparable from, and defined by, the lives and actions of its members. Every one of us is an integral ingredient in the great soup of Mormonism, with each person retaining his or her own unique character while also contributing to and flavoring the whole. Significantly, religion is a communal exercise. It only happens in the collective—"where two or three are gathered in my name" (Matthew 18:12). One of the Latin roots for the English word *religion* is *religare*, which means "to bind together." This should resonate for Latter-day Saints, as our scriptures describe heaven's eternal glory with words like *sealing* and *sociality*.[1] Another Latin root for religion is *religio*, which means obligation. Religion is thus what binds us together in a common striving for the good and the sacred. It consists of our obligations not only to the divine but also to one another. It unites us together as a group of believers and strivers and gives us opportunities to serve and be served. The holy can be encountered by a fourteen-year-old boy alone in a grove of trees, but religion only happens when he gets together with his friends and family.

The all-encompassing Mormon village of Claudia's youth has changed much as a result of church correlation, growth outside the western United States (which means less geographic concentration of members), and conscious efforts to limit church meetings and activities so as to not take people away from their homes too much. Nevertheless, the church still remains a rich site of cultural training where individuals develop important basic life skills as part of the normal rhythms of community life. Mormons may not be the most dynamic public speakers in the world, but by the time they reach adulthood they have far more experience in front of an audience than do most other people. Furthermore, Mormons learn how to blend personal initiative with the ability to work together to get things done. If church activities often look and feel like amateur hour, that's precisely the point. In the Mormon village we value energy, effort, and commitment more than polish and style. Voluntarism is one of the hallmarks of a healthy society, and Mormonism has it in spades. And it's by working together, serving together, and playing together that we best learn to love one another—even the "lumps that don't mix in easily."

The house that we live in

After thousands of hours of assiduous research, Richard Bushman has learned more about early church history, and especially the life of Joseph Smith, than almost anyone.[2] That hard-won knowledge has both complicated and buttressed the faith he inherited from his parents, nurtured throughout his youth, and preserved during his education at Harvard and throughout his illustrious academic career. Yet Richard readily admits that all the information swirling around in his head is not the most meaningful part of what makes him a Mormon. I'll quote directly from him:

> What it comes down to is that I believe in the founding events [of Joseph Smith's visions and the inspired translation of the Book of Mormon]. I think of them as the foundation of my faith. But they are the foundation, and I do not live in the

cellar. I live in the rooms built on these events—the way of life, the attitudes, the institutions, the relationships, the experiences they support.

This is what I meant when I spoke to Anselm Min, the Catholic theologian at Claremont Graduate University where Claudia and I taught for three years. Anselm took me to lunch soon after we arrived at Claremont. No sooner had we ordered our food when he bluntly asked me how I could believe in Joseph Smith. My immediate, unplanned response was that when I lived in the Mormon way I became the kind of man I wanted to be.

Those words summed up a lot—my sense of having God's spirit when I needed it, the salutary discipline of Mormon life, the friendships and commonalities of a Mormon ward, the requirement of unselfish service, the valuation of family, the tempering of pride and fear—a host of things. Like many people, I wrestle with demons. I frequently feel inadequate to my responsibilities. At the same time, I know I can be better, and when I live the Mormon way, I am lifted up. I see things more clearly. I can figure out how I really feel. I know how to relate to my wife and children and colleagues. I am temperate, incisive, generous, and focused. On bad days, Claudia and I often say we are out of sync with the universe. Over the many years I have been in the Church, I find that following the Mormon path puts me back in sync. I don't use the word "know" a lot, but I do know I am a better person for being a Mormon.

What I believe is not distinct from what I am as a person. I feel an obligation to try to live my best. I feel I owe it to my children, my wife, my students, and my fellow citizens—to live life well. That is what I value most. And the fact of the matter is I live life better when I am supported by the spirit of God.

That is the core of my belief. And while I do not diminish the importance of rationality and facing up to every challenge and doubt, I feel a prior obligation to be a good man. I cannot wait for the scholars to settle all the issues that arise before I decide, especially when as a historian I know these issues come and go. I have to go on living. I can't afford to ground my life in transient concerns. My first concern is to be a good and useful person. Mormonism helps me to live that way.

All of us, Mormon or not, have foundational beliefs upon which we build our lives. These might be theological propositions, historical certainties, political ideologies, or other "self-evident" truths. But life is not lived merely in the world of ideas and beliefs. Life is gritty, mundane, and messy. It often fails to correspond to our ideals—at least until we force it to. Even for those of us who have built our house upon a rock, the sturdy foundation is largely invisible to the daily workings of dwelling and working and playing in the house.

Richard's statement that "What I believe is not distinct from what I am" recalls the proverb, "For as he thinketh in his heart, so is he" (Proverbs 23:7). A life of integrity is predicated on a general correspondence between the values we hold and the values we embody. Though none of us live up to our highest ideals—a daily reminder of the need for reconciliation and atonement—the life of the Christian disciple is based on the ethical imperative of love and care for the other, which cannot be accomplished in the abstract.[3] Creeds, confessions, articles of faith, and other elements of orthodoxy, or right belief, are significant only insofar as they orient our minds and hearts toward orthopraxis, or right living.

Mormonism is superb at providing not only the blueprint but also the scaffolding whereby individuals, families, and communities can construct houses of exemplary, faithful living by building upon the rock of Christ and his revelation to the modern church. Simply put, Mormonism produces good and useful people—people who are kind, generous, devoted, talented, compassionate, courteous, mindful, and accomplished. To be sure, Mormons have a monopoly on none of these commendable qualities; mine is not an argument that an ethical life cannot be pursued outside the church. I am simply affirming Richard's modest proposition that living the Mormon way produces good fruits. This affirmation is implicitly supported by the recurrent suspicion from outsiders that Mormon individuals and families are "too good to be true"—a backhanded compliment that at the heart of Mormon life lies an essential, and admirable, goodness.

A life predicated on good works always has its dangers. The pursuit of righteousness is separated from hypocrisy and pharisaism by only a hair's width. Ritual displays, checked boxes, and achieved goals, however worthy, can easily obscure "the weightier matters of the law, judgment, mercy, and faith" (Matthew 23:23). Because we live in a community and often know our neighbors' foibles and perhaps even their sins, their white shirts can easily appear as "whited sepulchers" (Matthew 23:27). Patience and forgiveness thus become two of the house of faith's load-bearing walls.

In the meantime, we live in houses in a gated community that paradoxically swings open its gate for all to enter. Yet like many intentional communities, ours has a set of neighborhood covenants that delineate the terms of life within and that shape the quality of the shared experience to make it meaningful for those who enter. Among the chief descriptors of our community life is the shared aspiration toward "being honest, true, chaste, benevolent, virtuous, and in doing good to all men." At the same time, recognizing that the neighborhood is still far from perfect, ours is an association of seekers and strivers after the true, the good, and the beautiful: "If there is anything virtuous, lovely, or of good report or praiseworthy, we seek after these things" (Articles of Faith 1:13). Along with faith, hope, charity, and all the other Christian virtues, the pursuit of "these things" means that when we live the Mormon way, in Richard's words, we become the kind of people we want to be.

The Latter-day Saint concept of church

In a secular age when it is increasingly in vogue to be "spiritual but not religious," the very notion of being a member of a church—any church, let alone the LDS Church—is seriously in question. There is a growing body of literature demonstrating that not only individuals but even entire communities can be "good without God."[4] So how do Latter-day Saints best make the argument, both internally and externally, for why it matters to be a member of a church and especially *this* church? A typical answer is that only in the LDS Church is found the divine priesthood authority to perform required ordinances for salvation and exaltation. This reply is doctrinally sound but also insufficient, given that one of the glorious aspects of the restoration is its universalizing impulse of providing church membership and saving ordinances to all of God's children (subject to each spirit's individual approval), regardless of whether or not they joined the church in this life.

The doctrinal argument for the necessity of the church is complemented by other reasons, many of which were articulated by Lowell Bennion and Eugene England, two of twentieth-century Mormonism's great intellectuals, teachers, and Christian disciples. Together, they help us further make the case for why the church is both true and good.

Lowell Bennion changed countless lives both inside and outside the church during his career first as director and teacher at the LDS Institute of Religion at the University of Utah from 1934 to 1962, then as dean of students and professor of sociology at the University of Utah for a decade, finally as leader of Salt Lake Valley's Community Services Council until he was past eighty.[5] Bennion authored over thirty books and hundreds of essays and lectures, many of which were commissioned as official church manuals or lesson materials. One of these, *The Religion of the Latter-day Saints*, was published by the church and used as an institute manual for more than twenty years.[6] In his chapter "The Latter-day Saint Concept of Church," Bennion considers the relationship of theology, religion, and the church and argues for the essential purpose of the institutionalized church in the life of followers of Christ.

Bennion, like the early apostle James, was a great believer in practical theology and lived religion. On its own, he wrote, theology too easily becomes "theoretical and abstract" and thus is "sterile and ineffectual when considered apart from religion." At the same time, true religion needs "an intelligent theology" for grounding and direction, so the two operate hand in hand. Both are necessary, but they remain distinct. Bennion compares it to the relationship of science and medicine, the former being more theoretical and the latter more applied. "Religion is to theology," he writes, "what the art of medicine is to certain of the sciences. Religion is the art of living. Theology is the theoretical background which enriches the art."[7]

The church is distinct from both religion and theology. Church can be defined in many ways, but ultimately it is "a social institution." One could presumably have a theology or even a religion in isolation, but one cannot meaningfully have a church without the company of others. Significantly, Bennion notes, "The Church is not an end in itself." He cites Elder John A. Widtsoe, who paraphrased Jesus in teaching that "man was not made for religion (or the church), but religion (or the church) was made for man. When the church or any part of it does not function for the good of man, it fails to function properly, and corrective measures should be undertaken." But to say that the church is a means to an end, and not an end in itself, does not render it inconsequential: "The air we breathe is only a means to life," Bennion reminds us, "but try to live without it." Insofar as the church fulfills the purpose for which it was established—assisting God in his work of developing intelligent personalities into gods—it cannot be ignored or discarded.[8]

Because of its commitment to human progression, the modern church cares about the whole person. However, it accepts its own limitations and gratefully acknowledges that other institutions can more effectively provide for basic human needs such as health care, economic development, criminal justice, secular education, and political government. The church does not yield its interest in those matters, but recognizes that it does not need to directly provide for all things.

Yet there are certain functions and obligations that only the church can provide and that it therefore specializes in. In Bennion's words, the church "has the obligation to discover and to conserve that which is sacred and of value to mankind." That which is sacred and therefore valuable is preserved in the scriptures, history, traditions, and practices of the church, but also in music, painting, architecture, and literature produced by church members and nonmembers alike. Another of the church's essential and unique purposes is to encourage and assist people in the worship and service of God, including the administration of sacred priesthood ordinances. Significantly, "No other human institution exists primarily for this purpose," and so the church necessarily and appropriately dedicates substantial time and resources to accomplishing this grand aim that cannot be performed by government, markets, or civil society. The church actively cultivates godliness—"the desire and ability to live in harmony with the will of God." Tremendous exertions are made to encourage people in the moral and ethical life. Bennion observes, "Men cannot be happy in this world without social justice, peace, and a good measure of brotherhood. The Church has the teachings, universal scope, purpose, and means to lead men to right living, to do the will of a good and just God." It does so in large part by creating "an environment in which the Christian life is lived."[9]

The church always exists in culture. That means it will constantly change to respond to contemporary issues, concerns, and conditions.

To expect the church to remain static in the face of historical and cultural change is to call for its irrelevance and eventual demise. But in order to fulfill its prophetic purpose, the church cannot simply mirror society or be captive to culture. Instead, "The church is to be a moral critic of society and other social institutions and an exemplar of right behavior." Because it is ultimately concerned with neither the profit motive nor the acquisition and maintenance of political power, the church can and must always act as a gadfly to the powers that be in a secular society that functions according to a quite different logic than that of the kingdom of God. With our theology of the inherent, inestimable, and eternal worth of souls, the church is, in principle, more committed to human dignity and equality than any earthbound institution. Mormon theology thus translates into a "fight for social and political justice—for those policies which lead to freedom, peace, and human brotherhood. The Church has a right to condemn corruptness in the body politic and selfishness and unfair play in men's economic relations." Though it does not and seeks not to control society, the church "ought to serve as a leaven in human society which would permeate the whole and lift it to a higher plane of social and moral life." At its best, it avoids partisanship or political entanglements, but does not eschew the deep questions that animate politics. Ideally, the church and its members consider pressing social and moral issues in the light of the gospel before they become divisive partisan debates, thus offering insights that are proactive and spiritually informed rather than reactive and politically driven. While respecting local diversity and human creativity, the church should be able to speak with confidence and revealed insight about the principles that make for good government, economics, education, and social relationships.[10]

Of course, due to its inherent human limitations, the church, like all other social institutions, sometimes fails to live up to its own best ideals and throughout the course of its history has even promoted views or engaged in practices that have undermined its principal purposes. Nevertheless, Bennion notes, institutionalized religion remains vital in the spiritual progress of God's children not only because the church can "achieve certain things better than other types of social institutions," but also because the whole is greater than the sum of its parts. Public worship, teaching, service, and welfare for the underprivileged are all better accomplished together than apart. The Church provides necessary fellowship for striving Saints and "lends comfort, courage, and moral support to its members. Our lay organization gives every willing person social status and recognition, an opportunity for self-expression, service, and achievement." One of the little-recognized but inestimably valuable aspects of the church is that it "helps people to grow old gracefully and happily." It gives senior members, women and men alike, meaningful things to do, rather than putting them out to pasture upon reaching a certain age.[11]

The church thus serves any number of invaluable functions in promoting individual welfare, social cohesion, and communal uplift. Yet the church is not and cannot be reduced to a mere social organization, however effective. What ultimately gives the church vitality and strength is its divine origin and purpose as well as the Spirit of God that animates the lives of its members. We recognize that the work we do at church has a certain quality that distinguishes it from the indispensible work we do with the PTA, professional societies, political parties, and other community organizations. Bennion puts it simply, if audaciously: "The Church is the Kingdom of God because it is the work of Christ." We do not believe that the current church is the fully realized kingdom, but it is "in the making."[12] This echoes President Dieter F. Uchtdorf's teaching that "in reality, the Restoration is an ongoing process; we are living in it right now."[13] The church may be "built upon the foundation of the apostles and prophets, Jesus Christ himself being the chief corner stone," but it is the consecrated work of the members who are "fellowcitizens" that transforms the church from another social institution into "the household of God . . . an holy temple in the Lord" (Ephesians 2:19–21).

Why the church is as true as the gospel

Eugene England was a professor at BYU and then Utah Valley State College (now Utah Valley University), a prolific author and essayist, and a dedicated church member and leader until his untimely death in 2001. The cofounder of the first independent academic Mormon studies journal, *Dialogue: A Journal of Mormon Thought,* and recipient of some of BYU's most prestigious teaching awards, England inspired countless Latter-day Saints to more fully live the gospel of Jesus Christ and to combine their intellectual and professional vocations with deep discipleship. I have already mentioned, in chapter 6, how profoundly touched I was by the fireside he sponsored for black members of the church in London in summer 1998, only a couple years before he was diagnosed with terminal brain cancer.

Because he took outspoken, principled positions on various controversial subjects, England was often painted as a liberal, and various church leaders were troubled by some of his writings. Yet in an era in which a number of other Mormon intellectuals were disciplined and even excommunicated, England's devotion to the church was so apparent that his membership was never in question, though he was famously admonished by one apostle and eventually dismissed from the BYU faculty.[14] In the wake of such stinging disappointments, it would have been easy, and no doubt was at times tempting, for England to separate the perfect, true, and elegant gospel of Jesus Christ from the evidently earthbound, flawed, and sometimes clunky Church of Jesus Christ. But he steadfastly refused to do so. To the contrary, in 1986 he published (and in 1999 republished) an essay called "Why the Church Is as True as the Gospel," which some have called his "love letter to the Church."[15]

England's classic essay begins with boredom—specifically, the boredom he regularly experienced as a child attending stake conference. During one of those seemingly interminable meetings, twelve-year-old Eugene was teasing his sister and not paying any attention to the talks when suddenly he felt a "burning at the center of [his] heart and bones." He sat up to hear an apostolic blessing being delivered to the congregation by visiting apostle Harold B. Lee. The young man was transfixed by "the presence of the Holy Ghost and the special witness of Jesus Christ." In the essay he reflected:

> How many boring stake conferences would I attend to be even once in the presence of such grace? Thousands—all there are. That pearl is without price. And because I have since learned better what to look for and find there—not doctrinal revelation so much as understanding of and experience with the members of the Church—the conferences are no longer boring.

Thus, one of the earliest and most important pillars of my faith came not through some great insight into the gospel but through an experience I could only have had because I was doing my duty in the Church, however immaturely.

That experience, and countless others, convinced England that "the Church is as 'true,' as effective, as sure an instrument of salvation as the system of doctrines we call the gospel." This is not in spite of the church's manifest weaknesses and stumblings, but "in good part because of the very flaws, human exasperations, and historical problems that occasionally give us all some anguish."

Citing the German Reformer Martin Luther, who proclaimed that "marriage is the school of love," England affirmed that so too "any good church is a school of love"—The Church of Jesus Christ of Latter-day Saints most of all, not just because of the doctrines it teaches or the priesthood it wields, but "because the Church provides the best context for struggling with, working through, enduring, and being redeemed by those paradoxes and oppositions that give energy and meaning to the universe." In other words, "The Church is true because it is concrete, not theoretical." It is the place where we not only talk about Christian discipleship but exercise it, however awkwardly at times. "In the life of the true Church," England writes, "there are constant opportunities for *all* to serve," not just an elite few, "especially to learn to serve people we would not normally choose to serve—or possibly even associate with—and thus opportunities to learn to love unconditionally."

The organization of the church into strictly enforced geographic units compels us to love our neighbors as we find them, not to choose the congregation that we feel best fits our personal tastes. The church thus caters to our needs far more than our wants. We are subjected to other people who don't always think like we do and who sometimes publicly offer misinformed and prejudicial notions as authoritative fact. We are asked to follow leaders who are untrained amateurs, who occasionally make bad decisions and say or do things that are hurtful and possibly even constitute unrighteous dominion. (Of course, our *own* statements and decisions are always entirely reasonable and justified, and any offense taken is the result of other people failing to recognize our good intentions and wisdom.) We are asked to visit people whose opinions, grooming habits, childrearing techniques, or wall décor are odious to our tastes. In turn we are visited by other people, often at inopportune times, who endlessly recount their latest in a string of unpleasant medical maladies or their judgment about the state of our souls—or in a really efficient visit, both.

All of this unpleasantness is precisely the stuff of discipleship. As England observes, "Church involvement teaches us compassion and patience as well as courage and discipline. It makes us responsible for the personal and marital, physical, and spiritual welfare of people we may not already love (or may even heartily dislike), and thus we learn to love them. It stretches and challenges us, though disappointed and exasperated, in ways we would not otherwise choose to be—and thus gives us a chance to be made better than we might choose to be, but ultimately need and want to be."

I have a friend who holds a chaired professorship at a prestigious liberal arts college. He is also the bishop of his ward, which includes both a fairly wealthy area and a chunk of one of the poorest and most crime-ridden cities in the region. His academic colleagues know he is a Latter-day Saint and that he is the volunteer leader of his congregation. They don't talk with him about religion much, but when they do, they make comments about how nice it must be for him to leave the Mormon bubble and come to campus where he can engage the real world. He chuckled to me that they have it exactly backward. To be sure, his research and teaching include great debates over pressing international political and economic matters. But he is the first to admit that he opines from the comfort and security of a lavishly endowed institution catering primarily to the children of elite parents. His college is in many ways the very definition of a bubble, characterized by first-world luxury and a certain degree of intellectual aloofness. He encounters the real world when he steps off campus and into his calling as bishop. It is there that he encounters broken marriages, drug and alcohol addiction, multigenerational poverty, homelessness, mental illness, spiritual crises, teenage stupidity, interpersonal conflicts, sickness and death, and hopelessness and despair. As bishop he spends more time in trailer parks than gated communities. Nobody cares about his academic pedigree or his peer-reviewed research. They just want someone who can offer a listening ear, a few words of inspired counsel, a priesthood blessing, or spiritual companionship on the hard, lonely path to personal repentance. In which of these two places—at work or in church—is my friend more likely to encounter the face of God?

Our modern culture is unrelentingly oriented toward the self; the most common photograph taken these days is not a family photo or a nature shot but a "selfie." In this context, the church—like marriage and family—sticks out like a sore thumb. As England writes, it "assaults . . . our lonely egos" and imposes upon us "bonds and responsibilities." Through its buffet of unchosen associations, the church pushes us "toward new kinds of being in a way we most deeply want and need to be pushed." The church is a classroom where we do not necessarily choose either the content of our lessons or how or when they will be presented to us. Citing a statement by President David O. McKay, England observes that the learning we need and the grace we receive comes "as a natural sequence to the performance of duty" within the church, the home, and in the faithful pursuance of our other daily obligations.[16] And as Jesus taught, we find ourselves only through the loss of self-importance, self-centeredness, and self-satisfaction.[17] We must constantly remember, in England's wise words, that "the Church is not a place to go for comfort, to get our own prejudices validated, but a place to comfort others, even to be afflicted by them." The path of ease, recognition, and casual sameness is not the way of the cross Christ calls us to bear.

So yes, the church is "a repository of redemptive truths and of the authority to perform saving ordinances." That makes it crucial in our spiritual journey and eternal progression, as well as in the salvation history of the world. But in addition, England affirms, "The Church is the instrument provided by a loving God to help us become like him. It gives us schooling and experiences with each other that can bind us in an honest but loving community, which is the essential nurturing place for salvation." We cannot engage, let alone live, the gospel independently of the body of Christ. As a man who endured his share of challenges within the church and who published considerable scholarship on Mormon history and theology, England concludes: "If we cannot accept the Church and the challenges it offers with the openness and courage and humility they require, then I believe our historical studies and our theological enterprises are mainly a waste of time and possibly destructive."

The standard of the church's divinity is not its perfection but its ability to serve as a schoolmaster for gods in embryo. The things that may be most frustrating and perplexing may be the very means by which God is teaching us what it's like to be him. The church is not something we merely tolerate while striving to live the true gospel or anticipating the coming kingdom of God. The kingdom of God is among us. The good news is that as we gather together in Christ's name, however imperfectly, he is with us.

With England, I believe that the church is as true as the gospel. I have pondered on this when sitting in a church meeting and hearing perfectly sincere people say outrageous things about women or gays or liberals or intellectuals or immigrants or Utah Mormons or what blacks did or didn't do in the premortal existence. I believe that religion is meant to comfort the afflicted and afflict the comfortable—and that Mormonism is exceptionally good at both.[18] Full participation in the church invites, even compels, me to have not just grudging tolerance for my fellow humans but to develop deep empathy and genuine charity for them, all while shining a light on my own flaws and hoping that others will forgive my many trespasses against them. I fully acknowledge the great store of goodness and truth that resides outside the church. But for me, like Richard Bushman, I know I am a better person—and a better disciple of Christ—for being a Mormon, and I believe that's true of most of my fellow Saints as well.

The church is not only a repository of true doctrine and ordinances but is also a laboratory of love, where we discover and encounter Christ through fellowship with and service to our sisters and brothers. In this lab, God gives us really dangerous chemicals to work with and clear instructions on how to handle them, but ultimately we have almost complete freedom to do with them what we will. Like any other laboratory, on occasion we blow things up. The explosions are real, and they hurt people, sometimes badly, and we wonder why God gave such powerful chemicals to students like us who obviously have so little clue what we're actually doing. His chosen teaching assistants seem to have a better handle on things, and following their lead generally keeps us safe, but upon closer inspection it's clear their lab coats aren't spotless either—they are, after all, still in graduate school themselves. Some of the students have gotten so disillusioned or hurt that they've left the lab altogether. But God's answer is to stay in the lab, to clean up the mess—whether it was made by us or by others—to keep experimenting and gaining experience until we get it right and do something really amazing with the materials and tools he gave us.

Most individuals who have ever spent time in the church can cite any number of positive things it has done for them and others. But there are other, less congenial moments as well. Along the way many of us will have our doubts, our conflicts, our moments of exasperation, and genuine crises of integrity when we seem to be at our limit with this imperfect organization and its less-than-celestial leadership, membership, and history. Believing that the church is true and that it transforms me in ways that I sincerely doubt would happen in any other way doesn't make it much easier—and in fact may make it harder when I expect more and better from an institution I know has done so much to bring me to Christ. In the next chapter I offer some reflections addressing the basic reality that for many people, the fact that church is hard can sometimes overwhelm their original conviction that it is true.

9

When Church Is Hard

I'VE BEEN AN ACTIVE MEMBER of the church my entire life. I don't recall ever missing church meetings on a Sunday simply because I didn't feel like going. This is not to claim any heroic or saintly virtue on my part— since childhood, going to church has simply been part of my weekly rhythm. My father summed up his attitude about both parenting and church service with one simple phrase: "Just show up." I've tried to follow that advice, and by virtue of regularly showing up have had lots of different church callings. Those callings have given me the chance to meet and associate with people and practice my professed Christianity in ways I surely wouldn't have otherwise. For about a decade I lived in a ward in South Bend, Indiana, where active members were at something of a premium. I served in all kinds of callings, including some that I was definitely not good at. (One particularly memorable slip was when as ward activities chair I made one of my committee members break down in tears because I insisted, with so much righteous zeal, that there would be no Santa for her kids at the ward Christmas party.) My many missteps notwithstanding, in most of my wards I've typically been regarded as one of the "go-to" guys.

Which made it quite strange a few years ago when we moved into a new ward and I didn't receive a calling. Weeks passed by, then months. My wife got a calling. We showed up to church every week and to virtually every ward activity. I did what Mormons are culturally supposed to do: I wore a white shirt to church, stayed clean shaven, did my home teaching (more or less), tried to keep my kids reverent in sacrament meeting (more or less), and smiled and talked to people in the hall. Occasionally I was asked to substitute teach this or that class, but still no calling. Finally, about half a year after we moved in, the elders quorum president called me to be an instructor. In the course of the conversation he let slip (and then immediately regretted it) that the bishopric had really struggled with what to do with me because "they were worried that you would bring your politics into church."

My head started spinning. In my mind, I reviewed the past few months wondering what I had done that made me so suspect. It was an election year, and there was a certain LDS candidate for president. Naturally, at ward parties and other gatherings people talked politics, and so did I. It just so happened that my political preferences didn't match most of theirs, but I wasn't combative about it, and neither were they. I had scrupulously avoided talking partisan politics during the three-hour block—I believe we're there to discuss more important things, and it's not the time or place to have those kinds of disagreements, however friendly. Even so, I thought, plenty of other people bring up their politics at church without anyone blinking an eye. I can't count how many times I have had to endure sacrament meeting talks or Sunday School or elders quorum lessons that sounded like they were taken from a certain party platform more than from the scriptures. If those were my politics too, I guessed, the bishopric wouldn't have thought twice about issuing me a calling.

On the cosmic scale of injustices, this one hardly registers. And for many people, the idea of several months without a calling is hardly something to complain about. For me, it wasn't so much about the calling per se, as I found other ways to serve and keep busy. What troubled me was that the very men who had signed my temple recommend also apparently doubted my fitness for service in the kingdom. I was hurt and left with a feeling I never had before—the impression that this was not really my church. If it didn't want me, then why did I want it?

I made peace with the situation by drawing upon my reservoir of positive experiences in the church, my core conviction of why I went to church in the first place, and my understanding of the simultaneous sincerity and fallibility of my fellow church members. How many times in my own leadership callings had I overlooked someone's capacity to serve because of some arbitrary set of criteria that said more about me than about them? The words of Christ, which the church had taught me, became an important guide: Would I remain "angry with [my] brother," or could I forgive another's trespasses at the same time that I sought forgiveness for my own (3 Nephi 12:22; 13:14)?[1] Could I, to paraphrase Gordon B. Hinckley's father, forget myself and go to work?[2]

Being anxiously engaged

In many cases, people begin to feel disconnected from church activity due to practical experiences with real people. But thinking theologically about these issues can help us situate these experiences within a Latter-day Saint worldview, thereby simultaneously reshaping their meaning for us and empowering us to cope. Central to Mormon theology is the understanding that at our core we are each intelligences coeternal with God, possessing agency to act and decide for ourselves. Of course that agency is buffeted and constrained in a million different ways, sometimes to the point that it's hard to see what meaningful agency remains. Even choosing our attitude in a given situation is not a clear-cut proposition, as our decisions are conditioned by a host of emotional and psychological factors, many embedded in our own body chemistry and DNA, that are out of our conscious control. Nevertheless, Mormonism preserves the notion that our moral character and destiny are ultimately tied to the freewill decisions that we each make within our given contexts. The Lord revealed to the modern Saints that they "should be anxiously engaged in a good cause, and do many things of their own free will, and bring to pass much righteousness; For the power is in them, wherein they are agents unto themselves" (D&C 58:27–28). The Book of Mormon's greatest discourse on agency urges the children of God "to act for themselves and not to be acted upon" (2 Nephi 2:26). Similarly, God's presentation of his law to the children of Israel culminated in a simple set of alternatives: "See, I have set before thee this day life and good, and death and evil. . . . Therefore choose life, that both thou and thy seed may live" (Deuteronomy 30:15, 19). The call of true religion is always to choose life, specifically the abundant life offered through Christ and his gospel, and to proactively bring greater righteousness into the world (see John 10:10).

It can be easy to feel overwhelmed by membership in the church. Christ's yoke may be easy and his burden light, but life in the church is sometimes anything but. There is so much to do, so many ways to fall short, so many people to disappoint and offend us, so many people for us to offend and disappoint, and so much that is clearly human. When members of the church or its leaders fail to live up to the values they espouse, it's easy to question the value of maintaining our association with them. If Zion is the ideal society, then it's immediately apparent that our local wards, and therefore the church as a whole, fall woefully short. Previous chapters have offered a theological rationale for why this arrangement is not only inevitable (due to human sin) but also redemptive (due to its unique capacity to help us develop Christian character). That understanding may give us perspective and hope, but it doesn't change the fact that staying in the boat and holding on is hard, often straining us to our very limits.[3] Sometimes we need more concrete coping strategies.

The following section is less explicitly theological and more expressly practical than the rest of the book.[4] However, the advice here is not offered as the religious equivalent of "take two and call me in the morning." There is no magic formula for remaining in the church when doing so is difficult. The prescriptions here may or may not work for you or the people you love. Your ability to communicate directly with God and be guided by your own experience and revelation will be a surer guide than anything offered here. But perhaps these suggestions will serve as a useful prompt as you ponder your own situation and your own inspired way forward, whether in your own faith journey or in your ministry to those you love.

Simplify. The church is such a big institution—so complex, so varied, so all-encompassing, with so many possible activities and rules—that to some, it seems impossibly hard to keep up. For some, church life can even seem oppressive and judgmental. Sometimes it's just too much.

Since you can't do it all, don't try. Simplify. Pick out a favorite scripture and live by that. It might be the Lord's Prayer, the 23rd Psalm, the Articles of Faith, or the Ten Commandments. Even then, there are so many rules. So if it's all you can do, pick just one to focus on. Say to yourself, "Okay, I'm not going to kill anybody today"—beginning with your children or coworkers. That's enough. Then you'll start to think about not killing other people's spirits, ambitions, or hopes. You'll become more kind and compassionate. And that will be enough.

It might help to refrain from thinking of church life as a massive to-do list that one can never exhaust. Rather, it might be that the church's many meetings, programs, and classes form a rich inventory of possibilities. It falls to every individual, every family, to wisely choose the "better part" (Luke 10:42 NRSV)—that combination of the most pressing priorities for their particular time, place, and situation. Not long ago, the church's official *Handbook* added directions for adjusting its institutional particulars in places where the church is small.[5] That kind of flexibility has long characterized how God deals with his children. It's true that some of us can treat the church or the gospel too much like a buffet where we self-servingly avoid what's best for us. Even so, since we literally can't hope to do it all, the spiritually taxing work of hearing God's call for what's most important *now* forms the sometimes lonely path of every disciple. New bishops are routinely overwhelmed by the *Handbook*'s oft-repeated phrase "Bishops ensure . . ." They quickly learn that church work is never done. Rather, their spiritual survival and ours depends on seeing each day as a set of possibilities for doing good, not an endless set of ways to fall short. For all of us, realizing that there is no way to do everything, especially all at once, is a simultaneously freeing and stretching stroke of insight. If I could do only one thing well today, what should it be?

Claudia Bushman has told me that the sacrament prayers are her anchors. She tries to listen to and live by them—but over the decades she has heard them so often that they frequently pass unnoticed, with the wail of a child or her upcoming Sunday School lesson crowding her thoughts. But when she can really concentrate and listen, and refer back to those words during the day and the week, she finds clear direction. For her, those few words say it all, and she knows that is all she has to do. Keeping those aims in mind, everything else falls into place.

I like Micah 6:8, which reads, "[God] hath shewed thee, O man, what is good; and what doth the Lord require of thee, but to do justly, and to love mercy, and to walk humbly with thy God?" I can ask myself at the end of the day, Have I been just? Have I been merciful (or at least loved mercy if I didn't always show it)? Have I been humble? Have I tried to walk with God? If so, it's been a good, successful day—at home, at work, at church, or wherever life took me. And that's enough.

Creatively work it out. If there is something in the church that bothers us, we work it out the best we can. We can't solve problems by doing the same thing over and over and expecting different results. We have to be creative and proactive—"anxiously engaged." The church may sometimes feel or appear static, but in fact there is always movement of some kind, and new practices are always underway. An important recent development has been the elevation of ward councils, restoring female leaders to a more central position in ward leadership. In those meetings each female leader is told to represent not just her own organization or even just the sisters, but the whole ward. New leadership positions for sister missionaries have accompanied the surge of women responding to the call to serve.[6] Wider female leadership is being phased in.

Naturally and inevitably, there are problems in every quorum, every Relief Society, every ward, and every other level of the church. We identify the problems and then work to solve them. We find compromises that work for us. But we don't just impose our ideas on everyone else, any more than we enjoy being imposed upon. We act in ways that show sensitivity and compassion for our people, rather than being limited by inflexible practices.

The church is made up of its members—in many significant respects, we *are* the church, and we determine its course and future. A few years ago a leading Mormon feminist scholar visited my classroom. When a student asked her why she chose to remain in the church, she responded simply, "Why should I leave? It's my church too."

Create spaces of inclusion. At some point, someone thought up the idea of ring ceremonies so that family members and friends who could not attend temple sealings would not be entirely left out.[7] Some church leaders aren't crazy about ring ceremonies, and in practice they can still be awkward and not quite a suitable replacement. But the ceremonies are important as an effort to create inclusion where it is otherwise not possible. We want to be in the business of creating additional space for exceptions to long-held rules, many of which are important but nevertheless have unintended consequences that we want to try to avoid.

In the early 2000s, when the church was still new in Eastern Europe, a particular branch was thriving. There was a palpable sense of excitement, as high school and college-aged students especially were flocking to the branch. The young people's enthusiasm was sustained not only by the spiritual encounters they had in church on Sunday but also by the many branch activities held during the week. Especially meaningful was the family home evening held on Monday evenings at the branch building, attended primarily by investigators and converts to the church who were the only members in their family. When a letter came from Salt Lake City saying that there should not be church activities on Monday nights so that families could be at home together, the branch president obediently declared that the building would be locked on Mondays. No doubt the policy provided a welcome respite for him, as he had a young family and could now spend that evening at home with them. But for many other members of the branch, the locked building took away one of their main sites of fellowship and connection to the church. The branch lost energy and momentum and now has dwindled significantly in numbers. Many other factors have contributed to the branch's decline in membership, but at least one factor was a centralized policy, faithfully applied, that had unintended consequences for those who did not have ideal LDS nuclear families to gather with on Monday nights. (Why they didn't just get together on a different weeknight is unclear to me.) A more flexible interpretation and application of the policy might have pursued a "both-and" approach, allowing nuclear families to stay at home while the single members of the branch gathered together at the branch building with their newly adopted church family.

Some women in the church are hurt by being excluded from the blessing of their babies in sacrament meeting. This has been an area where people have found creative solutions to be more inclusive. For instance, some women have offered their own prayers for a new child at home. They invite their female friends over and ask everyone to wear their best clothes and bring fancy food for the special occasion. They make it a festive celebration of new life. They write out inspired blessings for the baby and save them in the family record as part of his or her heritage. They pray over the baby, acting well within the confines of current church policy; this is a mother's prayer, not a Melchizedek Priesthood ordinance. For families who choose to have their children blessed by their mother at home and their father at church, this represents a both-and solution rather than an either-or dilemma. It is done out of love and concern for the baby's life and well-being, not as a political statement. This particular approach may not be a perfect solution for everyone, but the key is that it is a meaningful and inclusive spiritual practice that creates a space for women to participate in activities important to them.

Another question is how to get more young women in front of the ward, similar to the presence of the young men who bless and pass the sacrament every week. The young women can participate in various ways—they can run errands for the bishop or serve as ushers. They can be in charge of the music and can play or lead in sacrament meeting. With a little practice, the girls can do just as well as the adults in most wards. Young women can give at least their equal share of the youth talks. We can honor those who earn the Young Womanhood Recognition Award just as prominently as we do the recipients of the Eagle Scout award, perhaps with its own ceremony rather than merely a perfunctory nod at the podium. Innumerable possibilities for raising the visibility, recognition, and respect of our young women abound—it's simply a matter of thinking creatively. Undoubtedly Mormons love their daughters as much as their sons, so the question is how to show we value them publicly and not just privately.[8]

We have to think about what we value most. As a blogger recently put it, "If your ultimate goal is less competition for parking when you are running late for sacrament meeting," then policies that exclude are appropriate. "But if your goal is to find a way for people who struggle with these issues to remain in the church," then we need to make church a place where all types of people want to be and where they feel genuinely valued when they are there.[9]

Make a place for yourself. In Micah's vision of the millennial era of peace, he saw that people "shall all sit under their own vines and under their own fig trees, and no one shall make them afraid" (Micah 4:4 NRSV). We don't have to go off and start our own churches, but we do have to find our own vine and fig tree to rest under within the church. Although wards can be insular and people can be parochial, the church is capacious enough that almost anyone who wants to can make a place for herself in our congregations.

When Richard and Claudia Bushman were teaching in southern California, one of their LDS graduate students was a strong-minded single woman in her forties. She had been the absolute center of her singles ward in Washington, D.C., but upon moving to California, she found herself in a family ward with lots of young families and old families but no singles. She decided that she would be part of things. At church she vowed to herself, "When I leave this place, they're going to miss me." She talked to the Sunday School, Primary, and Young Women's leaders, offering to substitute anytime they needed it. She told them that she loved kids and loved to teach and would always be available. She told the women in Relief Society that she was going to the temple regularly on Tuesday afternoons, that she had room in her car for four others, and that she would be glad to drive them. She initiated conversations with people in the hall. She volunteered for things. After a while people began to invite her to baby showers or to call her for information about one thing or another because she was active and in the know. At that point, she really felt she had arrived. And when she left, people did miss her.

Use the church to accomplish good things. One of the notable features of Mormon culture is that when people are asked directly to help with a worthy cause, they will typically say yes. Some of these projects will be official assignments from a stake leader, Primary president, or bishop, while others will be our own ideas, completed with or without formal approval. When we lived in Indiana my wife Melissa directed the children's programs at the local Center for the Homeless. When she needed help with some project at work that would bless the lives of the mothers or children she worked with, she approached our fellow ward members and got them to pitch in. The youth assembled back-to-school kits; the Relief Society sisters knitted hats for babies and scarves for children; families went together to do after-school tutoring. In the process, ward members became more connected to one another, to their community, and to an ethic of Christian service. If we see something that we should be doing in the church, we can do it, and we can recruit people to help us. We have more power than we think we have. We do not need to be directed in all things—in fact, it's those who constantly require formal direction before acting who are called "slothful" in the revelations (D&C 58:26–29).

Of course, the very Mormon impulse to do more and to be more anxiously engaged is often in tension with the deeply felt need to simplify. The objective is to seek balance, not to run faster than we have strength (see Mosiah 4:27). Sometimes the best way to use the church is to allow others to serve us in the best way they know how.

Work with church leaders. Jesus told his disciples to be "wise as serpents, and harmless as doves" (Matthew 10:16). In simplifying, working creatively, making spaces of inclusion for ourselves and others, and working through the church to accomplish good, it is far more effective to work with church leaders than against them. Direct confrontation with leaders forces them to take stands that they would rather avoid or puts them in a position in which they must respond immediately without time to ponder and pray about the situation. Remember that today they may be a bishop, Relief Society president, or stake president, but just a few months or years ago they were each just an ordinary member like you, and in time they will be again. Even the General Authorities and officers of the church came up through the ranks with no special training other than the school of hard knocks provided in their wards and stakes. We are providentially stuck with one another, and we have to live with one another. We are neighbors, fellow laborers in God's vineyard, sisters and brothers—not enemies.

Consider the example of Maxine Hanks. In the 1980s she became disenchanted with gender inequities she saw in the church, while at the same time being inspired by the nineteenth-century LDS women who gave blessings, engaged in political activism, and referred to their Relief Society leaders with titles such as "priestess" and "presidentess."[10] In 1992 Hanks compiled and edited the book *Women and Authority: Re-emerging Mormon Feminism.*[11] For her outspoken views directly challenging church authority, she became one of six LDS intellectuals and feminists excommunicated in September 1993.

Almost twenty years later, in February 2012, Hanks was rebaptized as a member of the church in full fellowship. The following year she spoke at the annual FairMormon Conference about her experiences as a Mormon feminist.[12] With composure and frankness, she admitted that despite the firmness of her belief in the principles she espoused two decades earlier, her approach was wrong. At the time, she confessed, she did not love and respect the men in the leadership of the church, both locally and on a general level. She thought she had to fight them and that they were obstacles in the way of progress. During the intervening years, self-reflection led Hanks to realize that she had been just as stubborn and obstinate as her leaders had been and that she had not extended the same charity and tolerance toward them as she expected them to extend toward her. She decided that she could accomplish more by working *with* church leaders than by working against them. In her interviews preparatory to rebaptism, she did not recant her feminist views or apologize for her book—nor was she required to. She simply accepted the leaders of the church as her brothers whom God has called at this time and as fellow Saints that she could labor alongside in cooperatively building Zion. That was enough—for Hanks and for the church, which is so much stronger for having her back on the inside.[13]

Two foundational principles of Mormonism are agency and obedience. These principles are in tension with another, creating a kind of paradox for life within the church. But it is precisely at the place where two seemingly disparate values come into contact with one another that creative tension is born. The friction between obedience to church authority and the personal agency belonging to eternal intelligences creates sparks that give energy and vitality to Mormon theology and life. Terryl Givens has rightly identified this tension between authority and freedom as perhaps the chief paradox of Mormon theology and culture.[14] Only three weeks before his death, Joseph Smith suggested that working in and through paradox was not antithetical to the pursuit of truth but was the very definition of it: "By proving contraries," he wrote, "truth is made manifest."[15] A half century earlier, William Blake had similarly observed, "Without contraries is no progression," and warned, "Whoever tries to reconcile [the contraries] seeks to destroy existence."[16] Father Lehi had taught his sons the same principle, "that there is an opposition in all things," and that inherent opposition was necessary for God "to bring about his eternal purposes" in exalting his children (2 Nephi 2:11, 15). Acting within the zone of paradox and discerning the way forward in a world of contraries can be disconcerting and disorienting, but it is the only path that entails the moral progress necessary to become like God.[17] Balancing our individual freedom with sustaining and following our church leaders gives us opportunities to prove contraries and thereby encounter truth.

Of course, none of the suggestions above do anything to change the church *Handbook*, a resistant church leader, persistent structural differences between men and women in the church, or instances in church history that make us uncomfortable. To create a church where people's legitimate concerns can be heard and their experiences honored, we have to build the confidence that members and leaders of the church can work together and listen to one another. So much disillusionment comes because we feel we can't trust one another, and that it's us against them (whoever "we" and "they" might be). We must find a way to have healthy, mature conversations about difficult and complex matters—if not always in public church settings, then at least behind closed doors in private conversations and always as fellow Saints who are at least trying to love one another and be like Jesus.

One of the greatest hindrances to faith and discipleship is cynicism. Not every problem can or will be solved immediately. But when we foreclose constructive dialogue or disallow critiques based in love and genuine concern, then cynicism naturally sets in as people become frustrated, feeling that they are not valued and that things will never get better. By the same token, those naturally inclined to be cynical must learn to temper their feelings by cultivating trust, openness, and generosity toward others. Paul provides good advice when he counsels, "Let your conversation be always full of grace," because only in that space of grace we will "know how to answer everyone" in godly fashion (Colossians 4:6 NIV). At the beginning and end of the day, the Christian virtues of mercy, patience, tolerance, and forgiveness must govern our interactions and conversations with one another. If we cannot do that, the body of Christ will be neither healthy nor whole.

Gravity

If I learned one thing from Alfonso Cuarón's beautiful 2013 film *Gravity*, it's that for all its allure, outer space is an utterly terrifying place. The view is magnificent, the feeling of weightlessness is no doubt exhilarating, and space walks and jet packs look like an adrenaline junkie's dream. But when the space debris hits and the astronauts are cut off from the tethers connecting them to their ship, things get really bad really fast. Beyond its stunning visual effects and fine performances,

I saw the movie primarily as a parable about human connectedness. Even when we're hurting and our relationships have been less than ideal, as is the case for the main character played by Sandra Bullock, what we still want and need as human beings is connection.

Since the beginning of the church, people have left, and many have found other communities that have given them meaning and purpose. Because of their experiences, some people come to feel that they have no choice but to leave, that the only option with any integrity is to drop out altogether from church activity and perhaps church association of any kind. For some people the church feels toxic, and they can't bear to be present. For others it is not so clear. They are still attracted to many of Mormonism's virtues, even while witnessing or experiencing some of its shortcomings. They genuinely agonize about whether to stay or leave.

From the remoteness of the printed page, I am severely limited in the empathy I can demonstrate for those who face such difficulties. As a general rule, however, I am saddened when people give up their rich church culture, a culture that they are an integral part of. Those of us who are American don't always like what our elected leaders do in Washington, but not many of us choose to leave the country. We don't always like how our family members act, but we are not going to disown them. We don't always like our coworkers, but we don't usually quit our jobs over that. We don't always like all our teachers or what they teach us, but we typically stay in school until we earn our diploma. In short, we regularly recognize the limitations and flaws in the many institutions of which we are a part, but except in the case of egregious abuses we normally stay and try to make things better rather than washing our hands and walking away. While acknowledging that our church community is far from perfect, I for one have my doubts about whether there is anything much better, not only in terms of doctrinal truth and priesthood authority but also in terms of providing personal purpose, meaning, and opportunities to develop Christlike character. I don't question for a second that those who leave the church have their reasons, and they may be exceedingly good ones. But I hope if you feel you must step away for a time that you think deeply about your decision, that you have somewhere to *go to* rather than just *flee from*, that you remain connected to the good people and godly principles you have encountered in Mormonism, and that you keep the door open to come back someday.[18]

It is possible to live within the church even while racked with doubts, questions, and feelings of alienation. When you run into trouble, exiting the church is not the only option. There are many benefits of staying within the community even if you are distressed by one or more of its aspects, and even if you have to renegotiate some terms. In most cases, issues can be best worked through in the company of other Saints rather than by leaving them and the church behind.

As suggested throughout this book, the intellectual problems may not be as bad as you think. Not everyone who runs across these challenges feels that they have to leave, and many come out stronger on the other side after having grappled with the issues. Perspectives vary on even the most difficult problems. Those who have decided against the church can offer their arguments, but in the spirit of honest inquiry it is good to keep your mind open to those who still believe and can offer a faithful narrative that counters some of the more critical interpretations. Multiple perspectives and as much information as possible should be sought in order to gain a fully balanced picture. Don't assume things are certain that are in fact open for debate—nor that things that have been spiritually confirmed to you are completely up in the air. If you cut yourself off from faithful narratives you are more likely to hear only things that confirm your decision to leave. That is not really fair to you as a seeker of truth. Keep an open mind that God and the church just might pleasantly surprise you.

Staying in the orbit of the church also helps avoid familial conflicts that frequently arise when a person experiences and acts upon serious doubts. Though many couples find ways to recalibrate the nature of their relationship, marriages can become strained to the limit when one spouse leaves the church. The doubter's spouse often feels betrayed, not getting what he or she expected upon entering the marriage, especially if the couple was sealed in the temple. The loyal spouse often tries to mobilize all possible resources to try to stop the departure. This can make the doubter feel ganged up on more than genuinely heard or understood. On the other hand, the doubter often feels obligated to bring the spouse along, and may even browbeat or ridicule the loyal spouse for continuing to exercise faith, similar to how the doubting spouse felt browbeaten or ridiculed by some in the church for having doubts. There are disagreements over how to raise the children.

And extended family gatherings with active members of the church, especially parents or siblings, easily become contentious. Marital and familial relationships may not be sufficient to keep a person with severe doubts in the church, but neither should those doubts become the impetus to discard otherwise healthy relationships. In Mormon culture and theology, church, family, and community are so inextricably intertwined that it sometimes seems to be an all-or-nothing proposition. Persistent doubt may force the lines of certain relationships and social arrangements to be redrawn, but it does not have to mean cutting the ties that bind.

Because of the epistemological crisis that often accompanies a faith crisis, individuals may be tempted to shed everything once associated with belief, including the church's prescribed moral standards. Some abandon the Word of Wisdom or feel free to transgress the bounds of sexual morality, all in the name of personal liberation. Even if engaging in these behaviors was not part of the original cause for doubt, such behaviors sometimes follow for those who dissociate from the church. For many, when Mormon belief goes, so does the whole structure of Mormon living. This is not always the case, but it does happen, and it can be even more devastating to a spouse, children, parents, or old friends than the actual departure from the church. Even if one cannot stay connected to full church activity, there is much to recommend in continuing to live the Mormon way.

Those who struggle should not consider any decision made during times of doubt as final. Circumstances change. Life's experiences bring new perspectives. Some people return after many years of doubt or alienation, usually after going through a long, hard process. The strategy for those with intellectual doubts who choose to return typically involves going beyond the level of blog knowledge or an anti-Mormon book or website. They choose to examine the sources and think it through for themselves. Many find that their views soften and change, and they return to a matured position of faith.

Sometimes we tend to think we are either in or out, that we either believe or don't believe. But humans are more complicated than that. We have believing and unbelieving parts in us. We might think we disbelieve, but with some other part of ourselves we believe. It works the other way as well—even devoted believers have questions and problems. The human psyche, including our spiritual life, can rarely be reduced to mere binaries. We experience and live in paradox all the time. As suggested above, it seems that such creative tensions are not necessarily a marker of mortality's flaws but rather the very definition of living on this side of the veil. To find truth, as Joseph Smith suggested, we have to work through and often live within contraries.

Living with contraries is not only the burdensome lot of those who question or who feel they do not fit in. Living with contraries is equally important for those true-blue believers who may feel unsettled by members of their wards and families who seem unorthodox, weird, or liberal. Can we as individuals and a church community deal constructively with the inevitable questions and problems we encounter, or will we see them only as existential threats? Will we reduce those who doubt to the status of lost souls who must correct their views in order for us to maintain association with them, or will we treat them as family members whom we love and care for—and maybe even learn from? Faith crises of various stripes have shaken if not shattered the faith of too many in recent years, and many of those have chosen to leave the church. Regardless of whether the numbers are big or small, the worth of every single soul is "great in the sight of God" (D&C 18:10).

At the same time, many well-informed people who are fully aware of the issues, or who have had some fairly horrendous encounters with certain church leaders, have chosen not to leave. Many among this group are in with both feet, empowered rather than frozen by the paradoxes of mortality and the challenges of discipleship. Though difficult to quantify, I would suggest that we have a stronger corps of informed intellectual Mormons now than ever before, at the same time that we have a growing body of the intellectually disaffected. We have a larger, more active, and more spiritually committed group of Mormon feminists within the church than at any time in our history— the glory years of the *Woman's Exponent* included—yet still we see so many for whom continuing gender inequality is a cross they simply cannot bear.[19] There are more active and temple-worthy gay and lesbian members of the church than ever, just as debates over sexuality and marriage have in recent years vexed us in unprecedented fashion. The people who choose to stay are not simply naive or blind or victims of false consciousness—any more than those who choose to leave are inherently biased, blinded, or wicked. People make choices, sometimes impulsively and sometimes after great deliberation and an agonizing wrestle within their souls. Some choose to minimize their involvement as they work through their issues, without cutting the cord completely. Some of those who leave for a time return. In short, there are models all around us of people who endure and even thrive in the face of paradox, not in spite of it. Disaffection and disaffiliation are not the inevitable routes for those who doubt and struggle.

Mormonism is not the largest planet in the religious solar system, but it exerts a disproportionately powerful gravitational pull. Mormonism has mass and velocity. It combines a remarkably dense system of family and social networks, powerful personal and communal encounters with the divine, cultural cohesion in the midst of diversity, theological profundity, historical depth (if not length), and a way of life that produces real good. At the same time, Mormonism is on the move. Situated in a modern era in which everything changes, often at a dizzying pace, Mormonism changes as well—sometimes with grudging and lumbering steps, but at other times with elegance and agility. However, in contrast with the prevailing centrifugal logic of modernity, which risks spinning individuals off as lone atoms, Mormonism applies a strong centripetal force on its constituent members, seeking to bring people into the center, in closer and more meaningful relationship with one another—for Zion cannot be built upon fracture.[20] Some people find Mormonism's gravity oppressive, while others—no doubt the majority of church members—find it to be the most important, and perhaps only, thing preventing them from hurling off into outer space.

A certain romance and exhilaration arises from floating freely in space. This is the lure of Thoreau in his cabin, of the cowboy in the frontier West, or of the one who dares stand out in a sea of corporate gray suits. Yet while Mormonism teaches in a way that no other religion does that we are independent intelligences, coeternal with God, it simultaneously affirms God's original utterance that it is not good for any of us, man or woman, to be alone (Genesis 2:18). The astronaut exploring space with her jetpack must eventually return to the ship, and the ship must eventually return to the earth. Even the space station is tied in its orbit to the earth's gravitational pull, just as the very possibility of life on earth inextricably relies upon its orbit around the sun. True, there are many orbital paths around the sun, but not all are equally suited to maximize opportunities for life to flourish.

My plea to those who are struggling in the church and feel adrift is simple: Find some kind of tether that works for you. Find something or someone in the church to connect to, even while everything else seems tenuous. Find a way to stay in the orbit of the church as it orbits around the Son. For those who already feel their feet are planted on solid ground, my plea is also simple: Be the type of friend, family member, or fellow church member who provides the safe connection that we all so desperately need.

10

Embracing Mormonism

OVER THE YEARS I HAVE BEEN A MEMBER of many wards. I've never been in a bad one—though I've heard stories. In every place I've lived I have found a community of ordinary people doing their best to follow Christ and live the gospel, which means that along the way some extraordinary things happen. On multiple occasions I have seen in my church home a glimpse of what Zion must surely look and feel like. One glimpse came in South Bend, Indiana, and another in Cairo, Egypt. No one would confuse either locale with paradise: the former is a typical mid-sized Rust Belt city decades past its prime, the other a barely functioning, overcrowded, and polluted megalopolis centuries (millennia?) beyond its heyday. But in both places my wife and I found a deeply meaningful community of care in the local LDS ward or branch.[1]

At church in both South Bend and Cairo, all the markers of human identity that typically divide us—race, class, gender, age, profession, status, politics—mattered less than simply showing up and being willing to serve. Because the membership of the ward or branch was thin and scattered, "We're just glad you're here" was the prevailing ethos. The church became a laboratory for transcending the petty (and sometimes not so petty) differences among us and for bringing a disparate group of people together in common cause, sentiment, and faith.

To be clear, neither place was Zion. We had our fair share of contention, envy, and strife, sometimes based on deep differences of opinion and other times because of basic miscommunication. Disparities in wealth, gender, race, and nationality frequently undermined our unity.

In both South Bend and Cairo we were surrounded by multigenerational poverty, and despite our sincere efforts we failed to make much of a dent. Nevertheless, in both of these graced communities I frequently had a peek at what Zion must look like, an all-too-ephemeral taste of what it might mean to come together "in one, the children of Christ," without regard to "any manner of –ites" (4 Nephi 1:17). Being a member of the church in these places gave me concrete hope that fracture and fissure are not the destiny of human society, certainly not of the body of Christ.

As I explained previously, a crucial aspect of the Latter-day Zion is forced upon us—namely, the fact that we do not choose our congregational home. Mormonism may be the last holdout of the parish system dominant in medieval Europe, in which religious community was defined geographically rather than by personal preference. Choice enters in because of natural socioeconomic divisions, but especially in places outside the Intermountain West, the limited number of church members means that wards and branches are geographically large and typically take in a range of different neighborhoods. This throws together people who would not otherwise associate in virtually any other civic or professional capacity. Although lingering effects of the church's historical race-based policies have understandably and tragically limited Mormonism's appeal to African Americans, Mormon wards are remarkably integrated. Blacks, whites, Hispanics, and Asians all worship together, with no one batting an eye.

While we may still be catching up in terms of racial diversity, there is little doubt that Mormonism encompasses significant socioeconomic diversity. It is not uncommon for a ward to have millionaires and food stamp recipients serving together in a Relief Society or Young Men's presidency. Where else does that happen? The ideal classlessness of Mormon community was exemplified by a comment made by a friend of mine named Kelly, a convert to the church in South Bend. He was a janitor at the University of Notre Dame, where several other members of the ward were either graduate students or professors. On that campus, as at most campuses and other places of work, janitors are practically invisible and occupy a distinctly lower place in the de facto caste system. Professors and janitors just don't normally mix, at least not socially. But Kelly and his wife Kathy were amazing people. They refused to be intimidated by all these people with advanced degrees and fancy words like "hermeneutics" and immediately endeared themselves to the entire ward. They quickly became part of the dinner circuit and joyfully served alongside other ward members in every capacity, sharing lots of laughs in the process. When my mother came to visit, Kelly sought her out, gave her a bear hug, and exclaimed, "Isn't this a great church, where a janitor and a professor at Notre Dame can be friends?" That, in a nutshell, is what it means to have "no manner of –ites." It doesn't always work this way. But the simple fact that we strive for this ideal matters.

Knit together in unity and love

One year, my wife and I invited some friends who are devoted Christians but not members of our church to a ward Christmas party. They knew some of the other members of the ward as well and had attended a handful of church social events. While we were standing in line for dinner, with people all around us engaged in friendly conversation and the kids running wild (as always), they remarked how much they like our church because it seems so much like family and feels so homey. Our friends have other theological beliefs, but they love what they see in a good ward like ours where people really do care for one another and have built meaningful personal relationships over the years. This is based in large part on the service we have rendered together and the interactions we have through teaching and loving one another's children. The very next night, our family joined the youth in caroling to widows, most of whom live in an economically depressed area of the ward where parents otherwise don't want their children to go, especially after dark. Our ward is far from perfect, but at least for that one weekend, we came close to "having [our] hearts knit together in unity and in love one towards another" (Mosiah 18:21).

This image of being knit together, with the children of God in all our diversity inextricably and intricately interwoven, is at the heart of Mormonism's social ideal. It reflects a life-affirming theology predicated on the notion that the entire family of God can and will be eternally bound together—that heaven is less about where we are than who we are with and the quality of our relationships. The exercise of sealing keys, with the power of godliness manifest through sealing ordinances, provides an efficacious means by which Latter-day Saints can help restore and heal the brokenness of the human family.

Descriptions of wholeness, reconciliation, and embrace pervade the scriptures. The images are indelible and poignant. When the prodigal's father saw his son returning, he "ran, and fell on his neck, and kissed him" (Luke 15:20). That should remind us of the reconciliation between once-estranged brothers, when Esau "ran to meet [Jacob], and embraced him, and fell on his neck, and kissed him" (Genesis 33:4). Jesus's application of this ancient text suggests that the same reconciliation is available to each of us. Because of the redemption brought about through Christ's atonement, we can exult along with Lehi, "I am encircled about eternally in the arms of his love" (2 Nephi 1:15). Amulek testified of how the mercy of Christ "encircles [us] in the arms of safety" (Alma 34:16). Mormon described repentance and forgiveness as being "clasped in the arms of Jesus" (Mormon 5:11).

We thus see that one of the most fundamental and recurring images used to describe Christ's offer of mercy to us and our return to a loving and merciful Father is that of embrace. When we extend a physical embrace toward others—especially when that embrace is offered in the spirit of compassion, forgiveness, and reconciliation—then we are doing the work of Christ. Mormons, including Mormon men, are huggers, and appropriately so. When we embrace one another, we are literally embodying our warm and welcoming theology. We not only want our countenances to reflect the image of Christ, but our entire bodies to bear his marks and do his work (see Alma 5:15; 1 Corinthians · 6:15; Galatians 6:17).

Welcoming everyone to the feast

Our physical embraces, however wonderful, must be matched if not exceeded by our figurative, spiritual embraces. We easily accept those who are very much like us and who accept us in turn. Alas, the Savior doesn't let us off so easy: "For if ye love them which love you, what reward have ye? Do not even the publicans the same? And if ye salute your brethren only, what do ye more than others? Do not even the publicans so?" (Matthew 5:46–47). At least this passage gives us license to distance ourselves from unsavory characters like tax collectors, right?

Again, the Savior, whose enemies tried to smear as "a friend of publi-cans and sinners" (Matthew 11:19), set a higher standard:

> And it came to pass, as Jesus sat at meat in the house, behold, many publicans and sinners came and sat down with him and his disciples. And when the Pharisees saw it, they said unto his disciples, Why eateth your Master with publicans and sin-ners? But when Jesus heard that, he said unto them, They that be whole need not a physician, but they that are sick. But go ye and learn what that meaneth, I will have mercy, and not sacrifice: for I am not come to call the righteous, but sinners to repentance. (Matthew 9:10–13)

As if hanging out with society's undesirables was not enough, Jesus offered this final coup de grâce in response to the questions of the chief priests and elders: "Verily I say unto you, That the publicans and the harlots go into the kingdom of God before you" (Matthew 21:31). Jesus never claimed that the publicans and harlots were righteous; to the contrary, he offered publicans as an example of how the truly righteous should *not* behave. However, he taught that their professional and even moral choices were entirely incidental to their true identity as children of God. Jesus dined with them and suggested they would precede the religious authorities—whose hypocrisy seems to have riled him more than anything else—into his kingdom, presumably because in their spiritual lowliness the transparently sinful would accept the gospel of repentance he graciously offered them.

As we put ourselves into the story, we have to ask which role we are playing. Jesus did not reject the chief priests and Pharisees—he dined with them too—but many of them rejected him. Throughout the Gospels it is the humble sinner, the recipient of bodily or spiritual healing, who embraces the Savior, while the proud and self-righteous keep him at arm's length. Publicans and harlots are exalted not in their sins but in spite of them. The good news of Jesus's kingdom is that there is a place for everyone at the feast, if they will but accept the invitation. I once had a stake president whose policy at the family dinner table was, "There's always room for one more." That attitude emulates precisely the open embrace of the Savior.

I have frequently heard statements to the effect that we should smell more tobacco smoke in sacrament meeting because it means that people who are struggling with the Word of Wisdom are choosing to worship with us rather than staying away from church. Typically this sentiment is vaguely attributed to some recent prophet or apostle, but even if the source is apocryphal the attitude is basically correct.[2] In order to fulfill its mission to invite *all* to come unto Christ, our meetings must be a place where all people feel welcome: smokers and nonsmokers, baptized and unbaptized, women and men, the elderly and babes in arms, blacks and whites and Hispanics and Asians and Pacific Islanders and Native Americans and Arabs (and everyone else), welfare recipients and billionaires, single and married and divorced and widowed, childless and child-blessed, soldiers and peace activists, capitalists and socialists, believers and doubters, straight and gay, every-weekers and once-a-yearers, feminists and nonfeminists, intellectuals and the illiterate, groomed and unkempt, those in suits or jeans and those in dresses or pants, conservatives and liberals, publicans and Pharisees.

This inclusiveness is not by way of contemporary political correctness; it is by way of commandment. First, the resurrected Christ taught the Nephites, "Ye shall meet together oft; and ye shall not forbid any man [or woman] from coming unto you when ye shall meet together, but suffer them that they may come unto you and forbid them not" (3 Nephi 18:22). Then speaking directly to the modern church, he instructed, "Ye are commanded never to cast anyone out from your public meetings; . . . ye shall not cast any out of your sacrament meetings who are earnestly seeking the kingdom" (D&C 46:3, 5). In both of these injunctions the Lord also made clear that his church is not simply a social club with nothing more to offer than a place to hang out and an "I'm okay, you're okay" message. The church invites all people to transform themselves into disciples. It calls sinners—publicans and Pharisees alike—to repentance. In order to fulfill its mission to preach Christ to all of humanity, the church needs to have all of humanity within its doors.

Having all those people in the same building is chaotic. It leads to conflict. It's so much easier to associate and worship with people exactly like ourselves. As Neal A. Maxwell wrote:

> Travel on the straight and narrow path occurs in company with other disciples, imperfect [and different] as we all are. Side by side, as we all are, means that there are ways in which we can become offended or even embittered. Given the imperfections of all of us in the Church, offenses will come and disappointments will occur. How we handle these is crucial. . . . Jealousy, resentment, and self-pity can all keep us from becoming alive in Christ.[3]

Like a church hallway in between classes, if we have done our job to bring as many as we can along with us, the narrow path will be crowded and we will bump into one another. Can we do so in good humor and compassion, taking pleasure in the jostling because we are in the company of fellow seekers? Can we even offer a few embraces along the way, not only for our friends but also for the newcomers and strangers in our midst? If you are the one personally struggling to find a foothold here, can you take upon yourself this same crucial and difficult mission?

In our modern age, if we are truly committed to ministering to all, then we must find a way to accommodate and even truly love and serve those who are different than we are. Diversity, including internal diversity, is simply a fact of life in the modern world and the contemporary church. The test is whether we will respond to it, in the words of the hymn, with "tolerance and love."[4] The essence of genuine tolerance, philosopher Martha Nussbaum has recently written, is to realize that rational people can hold beliefs, practice behaviors, and maintain belongings that are alien to our own. As she observes, "any self-knowledge worth the name tells you that others are as real as you are, and that your life is not just about you, it is about accepting the fact that you share a world with others, and about taking action directed at the good of others."[5] Narcissism is the enemy of discipleship, self-adoration the antithesis of charity. As we hope for tolerance and respect for our own beliefs and behaviors and identities, so we should respect and even come to love (if not always like or accept) those of others. We do not have to agree on all matters to be good friends, to love one another, and to feast together at Christ's table.

All things to all people

In that spirit, Latter-day Saints must find a way not simply to coexist with but to truly embrace the diversity that already exists within the family of God. To that end, believing Mormons must come to understand that disbelief is possible. People can have genuine reasons for opting out of the church without being dissolute sinners (at least, not any worse than the rest of us). Disbelievers can be good, solid people who love their spouse and children and live ethical, productive, meaningful lives. At the same time, disbelievers must understand that educated, informed, and sincere people can believe in the reality of Joseph Smith's revelations, the truth of the Book of Mormon, and the divine inspiration behind the church. They are not covering up secret doubts nor are they victims of false consciousness when they bear testimony. There are informed people who genuinely believe in and belong to the church. I am one of them.

Mormonism is wonderful in all its swirl of paradox, contradiction, and challenge. Mormonism's whole is greater than the sum of its parts. It is not reducible to either its best or worst features. It is a graced community that works out its own salvation in this world and the next. We follow the prophet and listen to our own individual conscience and stumble forward, seeing "through a glass, darkly" (1 Corinthians 13:12). We draw deeply from our history and are never bound by it. We are liberated in and from tradition. In my estimation we are the most radically inclusive and exclusive of religions. We love, serve, hope, pray, fast, offend, hurt, forgive, repent, believe, doubt, know, teach, learn, worship, give, receive, thank, suffer, minister, bless, mourn, comfort, obey, create, endure, study, heal, hug, play, eat, laugh, and love some more. "We believe all things, we hope all things, we have endured many things, and hope to be able to endure all things. If there is anything virtuous, lovely, or of good report, or praiseworthy, we seek after these things" (Articles of Faith 1:13).

Mormonism is an optimistic faith that looks to the future. To be sure, the characteristic Mormon joyfulness can sometimes be little more than a veneer covering a multitude of hurts, griefs, and depressions. In our cynical age, all that apparent happiness can be cloying. More seriously, it can alienate those who simply cannot muster a smile on any given day (or week or year). We can, and do, meet one another in our pains and sorrows. A full-time toothy smile is not requisite for discipleship; Jesus was surely not grinning in the garden or on the cross.

But the fundamental proclamation of the gospel is that Jesus rose the third day. If he can triumph over death, surely the resurrected Lord can handle whatever difficult or disconcerting historical and contemporary issues that come our way. His message to those who anticipate his coming and salvation is to "lift up your head and be of good cheer" (3 Nephi 1:13). His message to his disciples who will travail in his absence is to "be of good cheer; I have overcome the world" (John 16:33). The essence of Christian hope is the belief that we always live at "the beginning of better days," in Joseph Smith's words.[6] We patiently await and work for the fulfillment of that promise.

My plea to stay in and with the church is a call to be a Christian. The Church of Jesus Christ of Latter-day Saints is not the only place to follow Christ, but I don't know of anywhere better. Belief will never be fully clinched, and belonging will never be fully comfortable; to expect otherwise is to misapprehend mortality and the church's place within it. The church is one of the manifold means by which Christ shows his love to and through the world. If any part of us feels that love, it is worth trying to hold on despite the "tribulation, or distress, or persecution" that seeks to "separate us from the love of Christ" (Romans 8:35), even (or especially) those hardships that we experience in and perhaps because of the church.

For its power in shaping devoted Christians and builders of Zion, Mormonism is worth embracing. But if Christ is our compass and Zion our goal, then Mormonism also has an obligation to embrace the diverse identities and experiences of all God's children. The genius of Christianity, which has allowed it to become the largest religion and arguably the most powerful force in human history, is that it followed the admonition of Paul: "I have become all things to all people, so that I might by any means save some" (1 Corinthians 9:22 NRSV). Adaptation, acculturation, and acceptance need not equate with or devolve to relativism; certainly Paul was not wishy-washy on the doctrine of Christ. The church does and will make real claims, many of which must be countercultural if it is to fulfill its prophetic function to preach repentance. The church cannot be so pliable as to have no meaningful form or shape, nor so rigid so as to break (or break people) at the merest application of stress or pressure. The success of Mormonism has come in large part because it pragmatically operates within culture while simultaneously offering testimony and evidence of a godly alternative.

The question facing the members of the church is whether we can create a meaningful sense of belonging for those who accept the core precepts and standards of the church but do not conform to the dominant middle-class, white, conservative, American norm. Provided a person gives all the right answers to baptismal and even temple recommend interview questions, how far are we willing to go to embrace significant social, economic, political, cultural, and ideological diversity? Furthermore, to what degree do we want people among us who cannot give the right answers to those interview questions? And what about those who feel the Spirit in our community and want to join with us but cannot embrace some aspect of our teaching, history, or culture? When people express their honest questions and doubts—in a personal and private way, not as a public challenge to the authority of set-apart priesthood leaders—do we want them to feel that they have to leave the church until they figure it all out? Are there any places within the institutional structure of the church where people can talk honestly about their questions and doubts, or must they suffer in silence, move to the margins, or be relegated to finding their only sense of authenticity and community on the Internet? When individuals sincerely want to stay in the church but can't see any place for themselves there and thus decide to leave, the body of Christ is weakened and we all lose.

Faithful ministry

Fortunately, the ability to minister to those among us who "have not faith" is already within our grasp from among the current structures and institutions of the church. We appropriately dedicate incredible time and resources to gospel teaching, from two hours of classes every Sunday to a church-wide system of seminary, institute, and BYU Religious Education classes. If a high school or college student has a question about biology, he asks his biology teacher and expects to get an answer—if she doesn't have the answer, she will do what it takes to find one. Our young people should have the same confidence in those who are teaching them religion. Of course we rely on untrained, lay, volunteer teachers for Sunday and most seminary classes. That is no longer an excuse (if it ever was) for disseminating bad and false information or for shutting down honest inquiry. Ours is an era of unprecedented democratization of knowledge. In the information age, where destabilizing answers are only a few clicks away, we are finally getting to the point that transparent, accurate, and faith-promoting answers are hopefully one or two clicks closer—not to stop the discussion, but to facilitate it. Church curriculum is constantly being revised to put the best information in the hands of our teachers and thus students. Those with difficult questions will generally not be satisfied with easy answers, but we can have faithful conversations in which we validate rather than vilify or vex the asker.

In addition to education, we have various layers, networks, and structures of personal ministry to support each of us in our various needs. We are marvelous at mobilizing when someone faces challenges to their physical health—it is a true wonder to behold the Mormon machine spring into action when a ward member goes on bed rest or is diagnosed with cancer. Those exact same resources can be brought to bear, though more quietly, for those with doubts and or some other "sorrow that the eye can't see."[7] Family, friends, home and visiting teachers, Relief Society and quorum presidencies, bishoprics, and stake leaders can't cure cancer, but they can provide support, relief, comfort, strength, a listening ear, and love. Most people with honest questions and struggles—which, to be clear, are *not* a form of cancer—want and need no more nor less. Like Job's friends, we can minister to one another, even if a silent solidarity is the best we can muster when simple answers won't do. We can, as the revelation states, seek learning and wisdom in the best books—including but by no means limited to the scriptures—so as to succor those among us who have not faith.

This is not rocket science. This is not beyond the scope of our capabilities. This is not just the job of church historians, bishops, Relief Society presidents, and General Authorities. This is the baptismal covenant of every member of the Church of Jesus Christ—"to bear one another's burdens, that they may be light; . . . to mourn with those that mourn; yea, and comfort those that stand in need of comfort"—not to bury our head in the sand or ignore the problem in hopes that it will go away. We "stand as witnesses of God at all times and in all things, and in all places" when we do the works of mercy and ministry that are in fact the work of God (Mosiah 18:8–9). Through our service to others, facilitated and enhanced by our membership in the church, we remain connected to Christ, the True Vine. In him and his church we remain firmly planted.

Postlude

Conversations and Celebrations

AMONG THE VARIOUS PIECES OF ART that my wife and I have hanging on the walls of our home are two evocative paintings that capture the essence of what I have tried to convey in this book. The first is called *A Conversation with the Master*, by Nathan Florence.[1] The background landscape is itself beautiful, but what is really striking are the two figures in the foreground: a woman walking alongside Jesus, engaging

Nathan Florence, *A Conversation with the Master*, 2008, oil on canvas, 30 × 40 in.

181

him in earnest conversation. She is doing most of the talking, while he is listening pensively. She is intense but not agitated, as his active but serene empathy calms her. They are taking their time; for all we know they have wandered all afternoon through the verdant fields. To him at that moment there is not another person in the world—all that matters is this woman with her cares and concerns. He is not reaching out to heal her with his touch; he is not delivering a discourse or telling her what she must think; he is simply accompanying and listening. For her it is enough.

The second painting, by John August Swanson, is called *Wedding Feast*. It hangs in our dining room and was given to us by a dear friend as a wedding gift. I love the bright, vivid colors and swirl of motion portraying the festiveness of the wedding at Cana, which was the site of Jesus's first miracle. As Swanson says of the painting, the whole scene "celebrates life. The newlyweds want all of us to share in their joy. They bring together their community. We are all invited to their feast. Guests celebrate the couple, the promise of new life in the fruitfulness of love, and the mystery of life itself. They eat, drink, and dance with gusto, toasting 'To Life.'"[2] Jesus acts not just as the dutiful son but as the giver of life and the enabler of joyful community. He invites us to revel and celebrate in his presence and in the presence of one another. There is a time to be alone and weep and mourn, but for now let us embrace and laugh and dance together (see Ecclesiastes 3:4–5).

My deep hope for the community of Saints I love is that we will emulate the Master in accompanying one another in deep, meaningful conversation. I hope that we will also come together in joyful cele-bration of life and love and faith. In Zion we believe in and belong to one another just as we believe in and belong to the Lord. As disciples of Christ we are a community of faith, hope, and charity. God's reve-lation to his church invites us to "Search diligently, pray always, and be believing, and all things shall work together for your good, if ye walk uprightly and remember the covenant wherewith ye have covenanted one with another" (D&C 90:24). We will search together, pray together, believe together, walk uprightly together, and always remember that we are bound together in a covenant of love and fellowship. Christ will be our Lord, we will be his people, and our many hearts and hopes will be knit together as one.

John August Swanson, *Wedding Feast*, 1996, hand-printed serigraph, 26 × 18 in.

Acknowledgments

I AM GRATEFUL TO THE MANY FRIENDS, family members, and colleagues who provided feedback on portions or all of this manuscript: Molly Bennion, Tom Griffith, Matt Grow, Melissa Mason, Matt Mason, Nick Mason, and members of the Claremont Mormon Studies Student Association reading group—Bryan Cottle, Shelby Hamm, Chase Kirkham, Matt Pitts, Randy Powell, and Courtney Rabada. I express special thanks to Dallin Lewis and Jeff Turner, who each provided extensive editorial comments on the entire manuscript and thus made it immensely better. Blair Hodges at the Maxwell Institute has been as good an editor as I've ever had. He has steadily, patiently, and astutely shepherded this manuscript through multiple revisions, and the book is far better for his contributions. I'm thankful as well for the encouragement and guidance of Laurel Christensen Day and Lisa Roper at Deseret Book, who helped save me from myself at various points. This book emerged partly as a product of my own experiences and study but just as much from many long conversations—now too often merely by email—with cherished friends going back to my graduate school days at Notre Dame. You know who you are; thank you for making my life so much richer.

This book would not have been written without Tom Griffith's invitation for me to join as a junior member of the Temple and Observatory Group lecture circuit. Thanks for placing faith in me, Tom. I'm grateful for the Saints in Phoenix, Portland, southern California, and Utah who listened to me present some of these ideas and helped me realize what was more or less helpful in them. And of course I cannot neglect to remark once again on the particular debt I owe to Claudia Bushman, Richard Bushman, and Spencer Fluhman—not just for graciously lending me some of their words and ideas, but even more for their lives of thoughtful and generous faith.

No one encourages or supports me more than my family; I could not be more fortunate on that score. Melissa raised her eyebrows when I said I had another book to add to the pile of others I'm "working on," but as always she is both one of my keenest critics and my most ardent champion. Who'd have thought life would take us to all the places it has so far? I can't imagine a better traveling companion. My children challenge and delight me in all the right ways. You won't get much of an inheritance from your professor father, kids, so I hope you enjoy reading this when you grow up! Finally, my mother LeAnn, to whom this book is dedicated, deserves all the credit that all good mothers do, and then some. No mother has a higher opinion of her children—a fact we kids joke about but which has also given us the confidence to do a few good things in this world. Much love and thanks, Mom, for planting me in good ground.

Notes

Introduction

1. Throughout the book I frequently use *Mormonism* and *Mormons* as convenient shorthand descriptors for The Church of Jesus Christ of Latter-day Saints and for fellow Latter-day Saints.

2. To learn more about this particular issue, the church has produced the useful website http://mormonsandgays.org.

3. See http://josephsmithpapers.org/.

4. The recent pattern for full historical disclosure was set with the Church History Department's research into the Mountain Meadows Massacre, which culminated in an outstanding and award-winning book—Ronald W. Walker, Richard E. Turley, and Glen M. Leonard, *Massacre at Mountain Meadows: An American Tragedy* (New York: Oxford University Press, 2011).

5. See https://www.lds.org/topics.

6. "Church Provides Context for Recent Media Coverage on Gospel Topics Pages," Newsroom, November 11, 2014, http://www.mormonnewsroom.org/article/church-provides-context-gospel-topics-pages.

7. According to church spokesperson Eric Hawkins, the Gospel Topics materials "represent the very best of research on church history and doctrine, and they will, over time, be incorporated into church curriculum, publications and, where appropriate, visitors centers." See Peggy Fletcher Stack, "New Mormon Mission: How to Teach Members the Messy Part of LDS History, Theology," *Salt Lake Tribune*, March 9, 2015. The new Religion 225 (Doctrine and Covenants and church history) manual for seminary and institute teachers, *Foundations of the Restoration*, is illustrative of this trend, incorporating many of the insights from the Gospel Topics essays. It is available online at https://www.lds.org/manual/foundations-of-the-restoration-teacher-manual.

8. Many of the materials available at the Neal A. Maxwell Institute for Religious Scholarship's website (http://maxwellinstitute.byu.edu) can serve this responsive need, as can much of the material made available through the volunteer organization FairMormon (http://fairlds.org) and other similar outlets.

9. This verse uses the Greek *apologia* for "answer" when it speaks of defending the reason for our hope—hence the word *apologetics*. Instead of "meekness and fear,"

other Bible translations use the words "gentleness and respect" (NIV, ESV) or "gentleness and reverence" (NASB). Peter thus observes that the manner of giving an answer (testifying of Christ who is the reason for our hope) matters as much as the answer itself.

10. For an insightful LDS interpretation of the book of Job, see Michael Austin, *Re-Reading Job: Understanding the Ancient World's Greatest Poem* (Salt Lake City: Greg Kofford Books, 2014).

11. Terryl Givens and Fiona Givens, *The Crucible of Doubt: Reflections on the Quest for Faith* (Salt Lake City: Deseret Book, 2014).

12. Letter from Joseph Smith to William W. Phelps, November 27, 1832, online at http://josephsmithpapers.org/paperSummary/letter-to-william-w-phelps-27-november-1832?p=4; see also Ether 12:23–25.

13. Karl Marx and Friedrich Engels, *The Communist Manifesto*, trans. Samuel Moore (New York: Penguin Books, 2011), 68.

Chapter 1: Faith and Trust in a Secular Age

1 Laurie Goodstein, "Some Mormons Search the Web and Find Doubt," *New York Times*, July 20, 2013. Because Hans Mattsson's story was published with his knowledge and permission, I have not changed his name or tried to hide his identity here.

2. This story is recounted in M. Sue Bergin, "Keeping the Faith," *BYU Magazine*, Spring 2014, online at http://magazine.byu.edu/?act=view&a=2888.

3. In my opinion, *faith crisis* is an inexact and inelegant term at best. I agree with Rosalynde Welch's critique of the term: "The encounter with uncertainty is a complex experience, and we should resist the impulse to triage and label. I know that there are many Saints . . . who experience genuine rupture and transformation in their faith, and for them the faith crisis paradigm is a lifeline. I suspect there are others like me for whom the paradigm does not precisely fit, but who nevertheless begin to interpret their experience in terms of crisis simply because that is the available language. The language of faith crisis thus 'overdetermines' the experience of uncertainty, to borrow a term from critical theory: the crisis is prompted partly by an authentic personal turmoil, yes, but also by the available rhetorical frame and by the circulation of that frame in personal narrative. Ironically, the crisis formulation, in casting uncertainty as an acute episode to be resolved rather than as a long-term condition to be lived in, may best serve the perspective of those who have already found certainty, in or out of the church, and who naturally want others to cast their lot with them." Rosalynde Welch, "Disenchanted Mormonism: Practicing a Rooted Religion," address at 2013 FairMormon conference, Provo, Utah, available online at http://www.fairmormon.org/perspectives/fair-conferences/2013-fair-conference/2013-disenchanted-mormonism. Acknowledging the problems inherent in the term, then, I use it here as a convenient shorthand, not as an ideal type.

4. The best history of the Kirtland period is Mark Lyman Staker, *Hearken, O Ye People: The Historical Setting of Joseph Smith's Ohio Revelations* (Salt Lake City: Greg Kofford Books, 2009).

5. For one response to this kind of spiritual strain, see Jeffrey R. Holland, "Cast Not Away Therefore Your Confidence," *Ensign*, March 2000, 6–11.

6. Rosemary M. Wixom, "Returning to Faith," *Ensign*, May 2015, 94.

7. For a powerful illustration of how these principles apply in the situation of a family member who has left the church, see Brent H. Nielson, "Waiting for the Prodigal," *Ensign*, May 2015, 101–3.

8. Charles Taylor, *A Secular Age* (Cambridge, MA: The Belknap Press of Harvard University Press, 2007).

9. "I Heard the Bells on Christmas Day," *Hymns*, no. 214.

10. Gilles Kepel, *The Revenge of God: The Resurgence of Islam, Christianity, and Judaism in the Modern World* (State College: Pennsylvania State University Press, 1993).

11. Robert D. Putnam and David E. Campbell, *American Grace: How Religion Divides and Unites Us* (New York: Simon & Schuster, 2010), 122–25.

12. Michael Lipka, "Millennials increasingly are driving growth of 'nones,'" Pew Research Center, May 12, 2015, online at http://www.pewresearch.org/fact-tank /2015/05/12/millennials-increasingly-are-driving-growth-of-nones/; see also Pew Research Religion and Public Life Project, "'Nones' on the Rise," October 9, 2012, online at http://www.pewforum.org/2012/10/09/nones-on-the-rise/. In addition to the "nones," there has also been recent talk about the "dones," or those who are "done with church." See Thom Schultz, "The Rise of the 'Done with Church' Population," online at http://www.churchleaders.com/outreach-missions/outreach-missions-articles /177144-thom-schultz-rise-of-the-done-with-church-population.html. On the other side of the coin are others who are beginning to practice "God-neutral faith," with organizations and rituals patterned after institutional religion but designed for atheists. See T. M. Luhrmann, "Religion without God," *New York Times*, December 24, 2014.

13. Lydia Saad, "U.S. Confidence in Organized Religion at Low Point," Gallup Politics, July 12, 2012, online at http://www.gallup.com/poll/155690/confidence-organized -religion-low-point.aspx.

14. Dieter F. Uchtdorf, "Come, Join with Us," *Ensign*, November 2013, 21–24. For more on this subject see chapter 6.

15. In a 2007 interview for the PBS documentary *The Mormons*, Elder Jeffrey R. Holland said that a number of explanations for the priesthood-temple ban "had been given for a lot of years," and that "however well intended the explanations were, I think almost all of them were inadequate and/or wrong." The transcript is available at http:// www.pbs.org/mormons/interviews/holland.html. The Gospel Topics essay on "Race and the Priesthood" states that "the Church disavows the theories advanced in the past" to justify the restriction, and furthermore that "Church leaders today unequivocally condemn all racism, past and present, in any form." See https://www.lds.org

/topics/race-and-the-priesthood. An earlier official church statement also condemned racism, "including any and all past racism by individuals *both inside and outside the Church.*" See "Church Statement Regarding 'Washington Post' Article on Race and the Church," February 29, 2012, http://www.mormonnewsroom.org/article/racial-remarks -in-washington-post-article (emphasis mine).

Chapter 2: Testimonies

1. Dieter F. Uchtdorf, "Receiving a Testimony of Light and Truth," *Ensign*, November 2014, 22.

2. Stan Larson, "The King Follett Discourse: A Newly Amalgamated Text," *BYU Studies* 18/2 (1978): 12. Joseph Smith did not consistently differentiate between *intelligence* and *spirit* as has become customary in the church today. In this passage, his use of *spirits* seems to correspond to current LDS teachings about the intelligences that existed prior to receiving spirit bodies.

3. Charles Taylor, *A Secular Age* (Cambridge, MA: The Belknap Press of Harvard University Press, 2007), 3. For a helpful overview of Taylor's work, see James K. A. Smith, *How (Not) to Be Secular: Reading Charles Taylor* (Grand Rapids: Eerdmans, 2014).

4. Thanks to Scott Appleby for this insight.

5. Rosalynde Welch, "Disenchanted Mormonism: Practicing a Rooted Religion," address delivered at the 2013 FairMormon conference, Provo, Utah, available online at http://www.fairmormon.org/perspectives/fair-conferences/2013-fair-conference/2013 -disenchanted-mormonism.

6. John the Baptist said as much to the Pharisees and Sadducees: "Think not to say within yourselves, We have Abraham to our father: for I say unto you, that God is able of these stones to raise up children unto Abraham" (Matthew 3:9).

7. In so doing we are emulating the Savior, for whom part of his messianic mission was to "heal the brokenhearted" and "comfort all that mourn" (Luke 4:17-18; Isaiah 61:1-2).

8. From a discourse given by Joseph Smith on April 7, 1844, in Nauvoo, Illinois; reported by Wilford Woodruff, Willard Richards, Thomas Bullock, and William Clayton; cited in *Teachings of the Presidents of the Church: Joseph Smith* (Salt Lake City: The Church of Jesus Christ of Latter-day Saints, 2011), https://www.lds.org /manual/teachings-joseph-smith/chapter-45.

9. Smith, *How (Not) to Be Secular*, 4.

10. See pages 131–32 in this volume, below.

11. The basic scientific argument was most famously and controversially set forth in Dean Hamer, *The God Gene: How Faith Is Hardwired into Our Genes* (New York: Anchor Books, 2005). Many scientists and theologians responded that even if genetics contributes to the neurobiological functions operating when people have religious

experiences, it is impossible to reduce the entirety of human religious experience down to a single gene. For a more recent study, see Tim Spector, "What Twins Reveal about the Science of Faith," *Popular Science*, August 8, 2013, online at http://www.popsci.com /science/article/2013-08/what-twins-reveal-about-god-gene. Based on his extensive interviews and ethnographic research among irreligious people and "apostates," sociologist Philip Zuckerman also posits "the possibility of whether or not some people are strongly predisposed toward irreligion. They just are secular, in their core. . . . That is, some apostates may be people who have an internal predisposition toward secularity, which then blossoms or emerges in the wake of certain decisive experiences in their social lives—personally secularizing catalysts." Philip Zuckerman, *Faith No More: Why People Reject Religion* (New York: Oxford University Press, 2012), 166, 168–69.

12. David A. Bednar, "The Spirit of Revelation," *Ensign*, May 2011, 87.

13. Michael Rea, "Divine Hiddenness, Divine Silence," in *Philosophy of Religion: An Anthology*, ed. Louis Pojman and Michael Rea, 6th ed. (Stamford, CT: Wadsworth/ Cengage, 2011), 266.

14. Mother Teresa, *Come Be My Light: The Private Writings of the Saint of Calcutta*, ed. Brian Kolodiejchuk (New York: Doubleday, 2007), 186–87. For another reflection on and application of Mother Teresa's spiritual struggles, see Rosemary M. Wixom, "Returning to Faith," *Ensign*, May 2015, 93–95.

15. Rea, "Divine Hiddenness, Divine Silence," 270–73.

16. For a powerful expression of this kind of faith, see Welch, "Disenchanted Mormonism."

17. Other examples are mentioned in Terryl Givens and Fiona Givens, *The Crucible of Doubt*, 115–19.

18. For a variation on this theme, see Craig Harline's incisive and humorous mission memoir, *Way Below the Angels: The Pretty Clearly Troubled but Not Even Close to Tragic Confessions of a Real Live Mormon Missionary* (Grand Rapids, MI: Eerdmans, 2014).

19. Regarding the importance of recognizing the spiritual knowledge given to people outside the church, on February 15, 1978, the First Presidency issued a statement called "God's Love for All Mankind," in which they declared: "The great religious leaders of the world such as Mohammed, Confucius, and the Reformers, as well as philosophers including Socrates, Plato, and others, received a portion of God's light. Moral truths were given to them by God to enlighten whole nations and to bring a higher level of understanding to individuals. . . . We believe that God has given and will give to all peoples sufficient knowledge to help them on their way to eternal salvation, either in this life or in the life to come." Cited in James E. Faust, "The Restoration of All Things," April 2006 general conference, https://www.lds.org /general-conference/2006/04/the-restoration-of-all-things.

20. Dieter F. Uchtdorf, "Come, Join with Us," *Ensign*, November 2013, 23.

Chapter 3: Foolishness and Scandal

1. See Edward J. Larson, *A Magnificent Catastrophe: The Tumultuous Election of 1800, America's First Presidential Campaign* (New York: Free Press, 2007), esp. chap. 7.

2. Stephen Prothero, *American Jesus: How the Son of God Became a National Icon* (New York: Farrar, Straus and Giroux, 2003), 24–26. For excerpts of Jefferson's Bible, published later as *The Life and Morals of Jesus of Nazareth*, see Laurie F. Maffly-Kipp, ed., *American Scriptures: An Anthology of Sacred Writings* (New York: Penguin Books, 2010), 1–31.

3. Quotes in J. Spencer Fluhman, *"A Peculiar People": Anti-Mormonism and the Making of Religion in Nineteenth-Century America* (Chapel Hill: University of North Carolina Press, 2012), 21, 48.

4. One of Joseph Smith's contemporaries, Ralph Waldo Emerson, made a similar diagnosis in his famous "Harvard Divinity Address," although he proposed rather different solutions than did Joseph. See "An Address Delivered before the Senior Class in Divinity College, Cambridge 1838," in *Nature and Selected Essays* (New York: Penguin, 1982).

5. For a modern view, see Gary Gutting, "Debating God: Notes on an Unanswered Question," *New York Times*, October 13, 2014.

6. For more information about Joseph Smith's use of seer stones during the translation of the Book of Mormon, see the Gospel Topics essay "Book of Mormon Translation" at https://www.lds.org/topics/book-of-mormon-translation; and Richard E. Turley Jr., Robin S. Jensen, and Mark Ashurst-McGee, "Joseph the Seer," *Ensign*, October 2015, 11–16.

7. See the Gospel Topics essay "Translation and Historicity of the Book of Abraham" at https://www.lds.org/topics/translation-and-historicity-of-the-book-of-abraham.

8. See the Gospel Topics essay "Plural Marriage in Kirtland and Nauvoo" at https://www.lds.org/topics/plural-marriage-in-kirtland-and-nauvoo.

9. See also 1 Corinthians 1:23 and Jacob 4:15. This linguistic connection is also pointed out in the church's former New Testament manual, *The Life and Teachings of Jesus and His Apostles* (1979), chapter 34, section 7, available online at https://www.lds.org/manual /the-life-and-teachings-of-jesus-and-his-apostles/section-8-pauls-witness-as-a-missionary /chapter-34-that-your-faith-should-not-stand-in-the-wisdom-of-men.

10. Christopher Hitchens also hyperbolically calls religion a "menace to civilization" and "a threat to human survival." *God Is Not Great: How Religion Poisons Everything* (New York: Twelve Books, 2007), 15, 25, 31–32.

11. Doctrine, which derives in part from the same linguistic root as *doctor*, is meant to heal, not to wound.

12. See Prothero, *American Jesus*, for examples of all these diverse ways of admiring Jesus.

13. One of my favorites on this score is Dietrich Bonhoeffer, *The Cost of Discipleship* (New York: Touchstone, 1995).

14. Armand L. Mauss, "Mormonism's Third Century: Coping with the Contingencies," unpublished paper delivered at Utah State University, March 25, 2015, pp. 12-13, available online at http://religiousstudies.usu.edu/htm/about/recent-presentations. See also Armand L. Mauss, *Shifting Borders and a Tattered Passport: Intellectual Journeys of a Mormon Academic* (Salt Lake City: University of Utah Press, 2012), 187–88.

Chapter 4: Unicorns and Rhinoceroses

1. Marco Polo, *The Travels of Marco Polo*, trans. Ronald Latham (London: Penguin Books, 1958), 253.

2. Laurel Thatcher Ulrich, *A Midwife's Tale: The Life of Martha Ballard, Based on Her Diary, 1785–1812* (New York: Vintage, 1991).

3. Both quotations are from Sam Wineburg, *Historical Thinking and Other Unnatural Acts: Charting the Future of Teaching the Past* (Philadelphia: Temple University Press, 2001), 10–11.

4. The following sections draw substantially from both Richard Bushman's published scholarship and his subsequent reflections on it. I am grateful to him for sharing his insights with me and granting me permission to publish them here.

5. (Far West, MO) *Elders' Journal* (July 1838): 43, available online at http://josephsmithpapers.org/paperSummary/elders-journal-july-1838?p=12#!/paperSummary/elders-journal-july-1838&p=11.

6. Keith Thomas, *Religion and the Decline of Magic* (New York: Scribner, 1971); and David D. Hall, *Worlds of Wonder, Days of Judgment: Popular Religious Belief in Early New England* (Cambridge, MA: Harvard University Press, 1989).

7. Alan Taylor, "Rediscovering the Context of Joseph Smith's Treasure Seeking," *Dialogue: A Journal of Mormon Thought* 19/4 (1986): 18–28; Alan Taylor, "The Early Republic's Supernatural Economy: Treasure-Seeking in the American Northeast, 1780–1830," *American Quarterly* 28 (Spring 1986): 6–34; and Jon Butler, *Awash in a Sea of Faith: Christianizing the American People* (Cambridge, MA: Harvard University Press, 1990).

8. Richard L. Bushman, "Treasure-Seeking Then and Now," *Sunstone*, September 1987, 5.

9. See Royal Skousen and Robin Scott Jensen, eds., *Revelations and Translations, Volume 3, Part 1: Printer's Manuscript of the Book of Mormon, 1 Nephi 1–Alma 35*, Joseph Smith Papers (Salt Lake City: Church Historian's Press, 2015), xv–xvi, xix–xxii.

10. Bushman, "Treasure-Seeking Then and Now," 6.

11. Richard Lyman Bushman, *Joseph Smith: Rough Stone Rolling* (New York: Knopf, 2005), 45.

12. Bushman, "Treasure-Seeking Then and Now," 6.

13. "Book of Mormon Translation," https://www.lds.org/topics/book-of-mormon-translation; Richard E. Turley Jr., Robin S. Jensen, and Mark Ashurst-McGee, "Joseph the Seer," *Ensign*, October 2015, 11–16.

14. Jared Farmer, *On Zion's Mount: Mormons, Indians, and the American Land-scape* (Cambridge, MA: Harvard University Press, 2008).

15. For example, see chapter 3 in the *Foundations of the Restoration Teacher Manual* (2015), which points teachers and students to the Gospel Topics essay, "Book of Mormon Translation," which in turn mentions Joseph's use of seer stones in treasure seeking.

16. It should be reasserted that for many at the time, the boundary between folk magic and religious faith was porous, a fact reflected in some early church documents. For instance, Doctrine and Covenants 8 originally spoke of Oliver Cowdery's "gift of working with the sprout," which was soon changed to "working with the rod." This referred to a divining rod, which Moses and Aaron used to learn God's will. However, the text of the 1835 edition of the Doctrine and Covenants read instead the "gift of Aaron" in reference to Exodus 7:9–12 and Numbers 17:8. See Jeffrey G. Cannon, "Oliver Cowdery's Gift," December 15, 2012, https://history.lds.org/article /doctrine-and-covenants-oliver-cowdery.

17. See *Teachings of the Presidents of the Church: Joseph Smith* (Salt Lake City: The Church of Jesus Christ of Latter-day Saints, 2011), https://www.lds.org/manual /teachings-joseph-smith/chapter-45.

18. For a wobbly example in the field of psychology, see Brian Handwerk, "Scientists Replicated 100 Psychology Studies, and Fewer Than Half Got the Same Results," *Smithsonian Magazine*, August 27, 2015, http://www.smithsonianmag.com/science-nature /scientists-replicated-100-psychology-studies-and-fewer-half-got-same-results; Brian Nosek et al., "Estimating the Reproducibility of Psychological Science," *Science* 349, no. 6251 (August 28, 2015): 943, aac4716-1–8.

Chapter 5: A Principled Approach to Church History

1. "Ford Says Edison Is Too Commercial," *(New York) Sun*, May 25, 1916.

2. Sting, "History Will Teach Us Nothing" (A&M, 1987).

3. William Faulkner, *Requiem for a Nun* (1950; repr., New York: Vintage Books, 2011), 73.

4. The Claremont Mormon Women's Oral History Project is one of the many extraordinary endeavors along these lines. For more information, see http://www .mormonwomenohp.org.

5. For one helpful guide by Latter-day Saints along these lines, see Dawn Thurston and Morris Thurston, *Breathe Life into Your Life Story: How to Write a Story People Will Want to Read* (Salt Lake City: Signature Books, 2007).

6. *Teachings of Presidents of the Church: Brigham Young* (Salt Lake City: The Church of Jesus Christ of Latter-day Saints, 1997). For citations of the changed quotations, see http://pt.fairmormon.org/Brigham_Young/Polygamy/Hiding_history.

7. "Plural Marriage in Kirtland and Nauvoo," https://www.lds.org/topics/plural -marriage-in-kirtland-and-nauvoo; "Plural Marriage and Families in Early Utah," https://

www.lds.org/topics/plural-marriage-and-families-in-early-utah; "The Manifesto and the End of Plural Marriage," https://www.lds.org/topics/the-manifesto-and-the-end-of-plural-marriage.

8. Richard E. Bennett and Dana M. Pike, "Start with Faith: A Conversation with Elder Steven E. Snow," *Religious Educator* 14/3 (2013): 1–11; see also http://maxwellinstitute.byu.edu/truth-in-church-history-excerpts-from-the-religious-educators-qa-with-elder-steven-snow/.

9. See Bruce C. Hafen, "On Dealing with Uncertainty," *Ensign*, August 1979, 63–67.

10. Essays are on the Gospel Topics portion of the church's website; see https://www.lds.org/topics.

11. John Taylor, "The Organization of the Church," *Millennial Star* 13/22 (November 15, 1851): 339.

12. Letter from Leonard J. Arrington to Wallace R. Bennett, July 12, 1976, Leonard J. Arrington Papers, Special Collections and Archives, Merrill-Cazier Library, Utah State University.

13. Letter from Leonard J. Arrington to David J. Bennion, October 27, 1980, Arrington Papers.

14. See "Book of Mormon Translation," https://www.lds.org/topics/book-of-mormon-translation; Richard E. Turley Jr., Robin S. Jensen, and Mark Ashurst-McGee, "Joseph the Seer," *Ensign*, October 2015, 11–16.

15. *History of the Church*, 4:588.

16. Particular thanks to Spencer Fluhman for his insights incorporated into this section.

17. Quoted in D. Todd Christofferson, "The Prophet Joseph Smith," Brigham Young University—Idaho devotional, September 24, 2013, online at http://www2.byui.edu/Presentations/Transcripts/Devotionals/2013_9_24_Christofferson.htm.

18. L. P. Hartley, *The Go-Between* (New York: New York Review Books Classics, 2002), 17.

19. Even this seemingly universal point can be complicated and qualified, as in David F. Lancy, *The Anthropology of Childhood: Cherubs, Chattel, Changelings*, 2nd ed. (Cambridge: Cambridge University Press, 2015).

20. Quoted in Sam Wineburg, *Historical Thinking and Other Unnatural Acts: Charting the Future of Teaching the Past* (Philadelphia: Temple University Press, 2001), 10.

21. An excellent example is Thomas Kane, a man we have many reasons to admire. He was one of the Latter-day Saints' most resolute public champions and was also a committed antislavery activist. He went to jail because he defied his own father, a federal judge, over the Fugitive Slave Act. He probably participated in the Underground Railroad. In short, he was one of the more progressive Americans of his day. And yet he was—by modern standards—a racist in that he hated the idea of interracial marriage. See Matthew J. Grow, *"Liberty to the Downtrodden": Thomas L. Kane, Romantic Reformer* (New Haven, CT: Yale University Press, 2009).

22. Jan Shipps, *Mormonism: The Story of a New Religious Tradition* (Urbana: University of Illinois Press, 1987), 109–11.

23. Quoted in Andrew S. Finstuen, *Original Sin and Everyday Protestants: The Theology of Reinhold Niebuhr, Billy Graham, and Paul Tillich in an Age of Anxiety* (Chapel Hill: University of North Carolina Press, 2009), 69.

24. Jonathan Edwards, "Sinners in the Hands of an Angry God" (1741), in *A Jonathan Edwards Reader*, ed. John E. Smith, Harry S. Stout, and Kenneth P. Minkema (New Haven, CT: Yale University Press, 1995), 97–98.

25. Jeffrey R. Holland, "Lord, I Believe," *Ensign*, May 2013, 94.

26. Christofferson, "The Prophet Joseph Smith."

27. President Dieter F. Uchtdorf, "Acting on the Truths of the Gospel of Jesus Christ," 2012 Worldwide Leadership Training, https://www.lds.org/broadcasts /article/worldwide-leadership-training/2012/01/acting-on-the-truths-of-the-gospel -of-jesus-christ.

28. Quoted in Lavina Fielding, "Camilla Kimball: Lady of Constant Learning," *Ensign*, October 1975, 62.

29. Holland, "Lord, I Believe."

Chapter 6: In All Patience and Faith

1. Lester E. Bush, Jr., "Mormonism's Negro Doctrine: An Historical Overview," *Dialogue: A Journal of Mormon Thought* 8 (Spring 1973): 11–68.

2. See Newell G. Bringhurst, *Saints, Slaves, and Blacks: The Changing Place of Black People within Mormonism* (Westport, CT: Greenwood Press, 1981); Armand L. Mauss, *All Abraham's Children: Changing Mormon Conceptions of Race and Lineage* (Urbana: University of Illinois Press, 2003); and Newell G. Bringhurst and Darron T. Smith, eds., *Black and Mormon* (Urbana: University of Illinois Press, 2004).

3. See the Gospel Topics essay "Race and the Priesthood" at https://www.lds.org /topics/race-and-the-priesthood. For scholarly interpretations of James's and Abel's lives, see Quincy D. Newell, "The Autobiography and Interview of Jane Elizabeth Manning James," *Journal of Africana Religions* 1/2 (2013): 251–91; Russell Stevenson, *Black Mormon: The Story of Elijah Ables* (self-published, 2013); Russell Stevenson, "'A Negro Preacher': The Worlds of Elijah Ables," *Journal of Mormon History* 39/2 (2013): 165–254. Note that scholars disagree on the spelling of the last name of Abel or Ables. On Darius Gray, see Tad Walch, "Black LDS leader Darius Gray makes, contributes to history," *Deseret News*, June 16, 2014. For more online biographies of faithful black Latter-day Saints, see http://www.blacklds.org/index-to-key-names. The best new analysis of the history of race and Mormonism in the nineteenth century is W. Paul Reeve, *Religion of a Different Color: Race and the Mormon Struggle for Whiteness* (New York: Oxford University Press, 2015).

4. It is possible to interpret some teachings by modern prophets and apostles as supporting something akin to a notion of prophetic infallibility. To this end, many

commonly cite President Wilford Woodruff's statement, published as a footnote to Official Declaration 1 in the Doctrine and Covenants: "The Lord will never permit me or any other man who stands as President of this Church to lead you astray. It is not in the programme. It is not in the mind of God. If I were to attempt that, the Lord would remove me out of my place, and so He will any other man who attempts to lead the children of men astray from the oracles of God and from their duty." I interpret this statement, and others similar to it, as an affirmation of general prophetic reliability, not infallibility, and a testimony that God, and not mortal prophets, is the true head of the church. Indeed, President Woodruff implicitly accepted the possibility of prophetic fallibility, which is why he asserted that God would remove the errant prophet before allowing him to do anything to destroy the church. My contention in this chapter is that God's respect for the exercise of human moral agency means that he tolerates a wide spectrum of lesser mistakes by his chosen leaders that nevertheless do not constitute them leading the church entirely astray, though particular fallible decisions may have serious and lasting negative consequences.

5. Quoted in George Q. Cannon Diary, January 7, 1898; as quoted in Leonard J. Arrington, *Adventures of a Church Historian* (Urbana: University of Illinois Press, 1998), 4.

6. "Lesson 33: Sharing the Gospel with the World," in *Old Testament Gospel Doctrine Teacher's Manual* (2001), available online at https://www.lds.org/manual/old -testament-gospel-doctrine-teachers-manual/lesson-33-sharing-the-gospel-with-the-world.

7. Joseph Smith was consistent in this honest self-assessment of his own personal flaws, though he also defended himself against charges of gross misconduct. He commented, "Although I do wrong, I do not the wrongs I am charged with doing: the wrong that I do is through the frailty of human nature, like other men. No man lives without fault." *History of the Church*, 5:140.

8. Boyd K. Packer, "The Mantle Is Far, Far Greater Than the Intellect," *BYU Studies* 21/3 (1981): 6.

9. David O. McKay, in Conference Report, April 1962, 5–9.

10. Dieter F. Uchtdorf, "Come, Join with Us," *Ensign*, November 2013, 22.

11. See Roger Terry, "Why the True Church Cannot Be Perfect," *Dialogue* 46/1 (2013): 94–107.

12. "Race and the Priesthood."

13. Gerry Avant, "Pres. Kimball Says Revelation Was Clear," *Deseret News*, January 6, 1979.

14. Quoted in Reeve, *Religion of a Different Color*, 259.

15. Martin Luther King Jr., *Why We Can't Wait* (1963; repr., New York: Signet Classic, 2000), 74.

16. Jeffrey R. Holland, "Lord, I Believe," *Ensign*, May 2013, 94.

17. Letter from Joseph Smith to Noah C. Saxton, January 4, 1833, available at *The Joseph Smith Papers*, http://josephsmithpapers.org/paperSummary/letter-to-noah -c-saxton-4-january-1833.

Chapter 7: Abide in the Vine

1. Stephen H. Webb, "Godbodied: The Matter of the Latter-day Saints," *BYU Studies* 50/3 (2011): 85.

2. John Turner, "The Book of Mormon in 15 (or so) Days," http://www.patheos .com/blogs/anxiousbench/2013/11/the-book-of-mormon-in-15-or-so-days/. See also John T. Turner, *The Mormon Jesus: A Biography* (Cambridge, MA: Harvard University Press, forthcoming).

3. Richard J. Mouw, *Talking with Mormons: An Invitation to Evangelicals* (Grand Rapids, MI: Eerdmans, 2012), 49.

4. Emma Lou Thayne, "Where Can I Turn for Peace," *Hymns*, no. 129.

5. Elder Boyd K. Packer taught that the atonement of Jesus Christ "is the very root of Christian doctrine. You may know much about the gospel as it branches out from there, but if you only know the branches and those branches do not touch that root, if they have been cut free from that truth, there will be no life nor substance nor redemption in them." "The Mediator," *Ensign*, May 1977, 56.

6. (Far West, MO) *Elders' Journal* (July 1838): 44.

7. See Ronald W. Walker, Richard E. Turley Jr., and Glen M. Leonard, *Massacre at Mountain Meadows: An American Tragedy* (New York: Oxford University Press, 2008). See also the Gospel Topics essay, "Peace and Violence among 19th-Century Latter-day Saints," https://www.lds.org/topics/peace-and-violence-among -19th-century-latter-day-saints.

8. Arthur Conan Doyle, "A Study in Scarlet," in *The Complete Sherlock Holmes* (New York: Bantam Classics, 1986).

9. Letter from John H. Gibbs to Joseph Morrell, January 10, 1884, in Joseph Morrell Correspondence, 1883–1906, Church History Library, Salt Lake City.

10. Juanita Brooks, who wrote the first (and still one of the best) historical treatment of the Mountain Meadows Massacre, was afterward shunned by many fellow Latter-day Saints. See Juanita Brooks, *The Mountain Meadows Massacre* (1950; repr., Norman: University of Oklahoma Press, 1991); Levi S. Peterson, *Juanita Brooks: The Life Story of a Courageous Historian of the Mountain Meadows Massacre* (Salt Lake City: University of Utah Press, 2011).

11. Quoted in "Expressing Regrets for 1857 Massacre," *Church News*, September 15, 2007; see also Carrie A. Moore, "LDS Church Issues Apology over Mountain Meadows," *Deseret News*, September 12, 2007.

12. "1857 Mountain Meadows Massacre Remembrance and Reconciliation Quilt," http://www.mtn-meadows-assoc.com/quilt.htm.

13. See Luke 18:9-14; Alma 31:16-18.

14. Martin Luther King Jr., "Where Do We Go from Here?" in *I Have a Dream: Writings and Speeches That Changed the World*, ed. James Melvin Washington (San Francisco: HarperSanFrancisco, 1992), 179.

15. For excellent treatments of the power of religion in motivating civil rights activists, see David L. Chappell, *A Stone of Hope: Prophetic Religion and the Death of*

Jim Crow (Chapel Hill: University of North Carolina Press, 2005); and Charles Marsh, *God's Long Summer: Stories of Faith and Civil Rights* (1997; repr., Princeton: Princeton University Press, 2008).

16. See Blair R. Holmes and Alan F. Keele, comps., trans., and eds., *When Truth Was Treason: German Youth against Hitler* (Urbana: University of Illinois Press, 1995); Rudi Wobbe and Jerry Borrowman, *Three against Hitler* (Salt Lake City: Covenant Communications, 2002). An LDS playwright has dramatized Hübener's life—see Thomas F. Rogers, *Huebener and Other Plays* (Provo, UT: Poor Robert's Publications, 1992).

17. Holmes and Keele, *When Truth Was Treason*, 240.

18. *History of the Church*, 5:342.

19. Charles Mathewes, *The Republic of Grace: Augustinian Thoughts for Dark Times* (Grand Rapids, MI: Eerdmans, 2010), 110. Latter-day Saint theology differs on many scores from the Augustinian theology that Mathewes espouses, but his point here nevertheless holds true.

20. Romans 8:31–39; as translated in Adam S. Miller, *Grace Is Not God's Backup Plan: An Urgent Paraphrase of Paul's Letter to the Romans* (Adam S. Miller, 2015), 44–45.

Chapter 8: The Church Is True

1. See especially sections 76 and 130–32 of the Doctrine and Covenants.

2. Richard Bushman is the author of *Joseph Smith: Rough Stone Rolling* (New York: Knopf, 2005).

3. See Matthew 7:21; James 1:27; 2:8-18; 1 John 4:20.

4. For just two examples, see Greg Epstein, *Good without God: What a Billion Nonreligious People Do Believe* (New York: HarperCollins, 2010); and Phil Zuckerman, *Living the Secular Life: New Answers to Old Questions* (New York: Penguin, 2014).

5. See Mary Lythgoe Bradford, *Lowell L. Bennion: Teacher, Counselor, Humanitarian* (Salt Lake City: Signature Books, 1995); see also Eugene England, "The Legacy of Lowell L. Bennion," *Sunstone*, September 1996, 27–44.

6. First published in 1939, I will be using a later edition: Lowell L. Bennion, *The Religion of the Latter-day Saints* (Provo, UT: LDS Department of Education, 1964).

7. Bennion, *Religion of the Latter-day Saints*, 142.

8. Bennion, *Religion of the Latter-day Saints*, 143–45.

9. Bennion, *Religion of the Latter-day Saints*, 146–48.

10. Bennion, *Religion of the Latter-day Saints*, 148–50.

11. Bennion, *Religion of the Latter-day Saints*, 150–53.

12. Bennion, *Religion of the Latter-day Saints*, 155.

13. Dieter F. Uchtdorf, "Are You Sleeping through the Restoration?," *Ensign*, May 2014, 59.

14. For biographical information, see http://www.eugeneengland.org/eugene -england.

15. Eugene England, "Why the Church Is as True as the Gospel," *Sunstone* volume 10, issue 10, 1986, 30–36; republished with additional material in *Sunstone*, June 1999, 61–69. The updated version of the essay is also available online at http://www.eugeneengland.org/why-the-church-is-as-true-as-the-gospel. All quotations here are from the online version.

16. Doing one's duty in the service of God and our fellow humans has been a major theme in President Thomas S. Monson's ministry. Relevant conference talks from across the decades include: "The Call of Duty" (April 1986); "Duty Calls" (April 1996); "Do Your Duty—That Is Best" (October 2005); and "Willing and Worthy to Serve" (April 2012).

17. See Matthew 10:39; Luke 9:25; John 12:25.

18. See Harold B. Lee, "The Message," *New Era*, January 1971, 6; Jeffrey R. Holland, "An Ensign to the Nations," April 2011 general conference.

Chapter 9: When Church Is Hard

1. It would have been even better for me to follow Jesus's admonition: "Therefore, if ye shall come unto me, or shall desire to come unto me, and rememberest that thy brother hath aught against thee—Go thy way unto thy brother, and first be reconciled to thy brother, and then come unto me with full purpose of heart, and I will receive you" (3 Nephi 12:23–24).

2. See Sheri L. Dew, *Go Forward with Faith: The Biography of Gordon B. Hinckley* (Salt Lake City: Deseret Book, 1996), 64.

3. See M. Russell Ballard, "Stay in the Boat and Hold On!," *Ensign*, November 2014, 89–92.

4. Special thanks to Claudia Bushman and Spencer Fluhman for much of the language and good advice contained in these sections.

5. "Uniformity and Adaptation," chapter 17 in *Handbook 2: Administering the Church* (2010), available online at https://www.lds.org/handbook/handbook-2-administering-the-church.

6. For an analysis of what the surge of sister missionaries might mean for the church, see Courtney L. Rabada, "A Swelling Tide: Nineteen-Year-Old Sister Missionaries in the Twenty-First Century," *Dialogue* 47/4 (2014): 19–46.

7. As far as I know, this is primarily an American Mormon practice. In many countries, couples are legally required to be married civilly before being sealed in the temple, which substantially ameliorates the problem.

8. A helpful resource discussing how members of the church can proactively work within the church's own parameters, especially on gender issues, is Neylan McBaine, *Women at Church: Magnifying LDS Women's Local Impact* (Salt Lake City: Greg Kofford Books, 2014).

9. Julie M. Smith, "Book Review: Crucible of Doubt," *Times and Seasons*, August 30, 2014, http://timesandseasons.org/index.php/2014/08/book-review-the -crucible-of-doubt/.

10. These were common titles for Eliza R. Snow and other nineteenth-century female leaders in the church. See Jill Mulvay Derr, "Eliza R. Snow and the Woman Question," *BYU Studies* 16/2 (1976): 250-64.

11. Maxine Hanks, ed., *Women and Authority: Re-emerging Mormon Feminism* (Salt Lake City: Signature Books, 1992).

12. FairMormon is a volunteer organization that responds to criticisms of the practices and beliefs of The Church of Jesus Christ of Latter-day Saints. See http:// www.fairmormon.org/.

13. Personal notes from Maxine Hanks lecture, "Working with the Church: Another Narrative," and her participation on a panel, "Charity Never Faileth: Seeking Sisterhood amid Different Perspectives on Mormon Feminism," FairMormon Conference, Provo, Utah, August 1, 2013. See also Blair Hodges, "A Few Notes from the 2013 FAIR Conference," http://maxwellinstitute.byu.edu/a-few-notes-from-the-2013 -fair-conference/. Hanks was given a standing ovation at the conference.

14. See Terryl L. Givens, *People of Paradox: A History of Mormon Culture* (New York: Oxford University Press, 2007), chap. 1.

15. Letter from Joseph Smith to L. Daniel Rupp, June 5, 1844, in *History of the Church*, 6:428.

16. Quoted in Eugene England, "Joseph Smith and the Tragic Quest," in *Dialogues with Myself: Personal Essays on Mormon Experience* (Salt Lake City: Signature Books, 1984), 10.

17. Elder Bruce C. Hafen observed, "If we are not willing to grapple with the frustration that comes from facing bravely the uncertainties we encounter, we may never develop the kind of spiritual maturity that is necessary for our ultimate preparations." See "On Dealing with Uncertainty," *Ensign*, August 1979, 63–67. See also Richard G. Scott, "The Sustaining Power of Faith in Times of Uncertainty and Testing," *Ensign*, May 2003, 75–78.

18. I emphasize that there may be exceptional instances, such as in cases of abuse, where temporary separation from the church may be appropriate, even while reconciliation in Christ remains the ideal. Professional counseling may be needed to deal productively with emotional or spiritual traumas and their corresponding feelings of anger, betrayal, and woundedness. A second caveat: My analogy of outer space is not meant to suggest that there is literally nothing happy, productive, or godly outside the Church of Jesus Christ of Latter-day Saints. It is a fact that many people who leave the church end up living joyful, fulfilled, Christ-centered lives, sometimes in association with other churches. Mormonism does not have a monopoly on community or healthy relationships, though at its best it does foster Zion-like communities that are as close to heavenly society as anything I've experienced.

19. The *Woman's Exponent* was a periodical published by Latter-day Saint women for Latter-day Saint women from 1872 until 1914. Digital scans are available on BYU's Harold B. Lee Library website. See http://contentdm.lib.byu.edu/cdm/ref/collection /WomansExp/id/963.

20. For a brilliant interpretation of the restoration along these lines, see Philip L. Barlow, "To Mend a Fractured Reality: Joseph Smith's Project," *Journal of Mormon History* 38/3 (2012): 28–50.

Chapter 10: Embracing Mormonism

1. The following paragraphs are adapted from Patrick Q. Mason, "Glimpses of Zion," in *A Book of Mormons: Latter-Day Saints on a Modern-Day Zion*, ed. Emily W. Jensen and Tracy McKay-Lamb (Ashland, OR: White Cloud Press, 2015).

2. Such a quote is often attributed to Spencer W. Kimball, as in Peggy Fletcher Stack, "Active, Inactive: Do Mormon Labels Work or Wound?" *Salt Lake Tribune*, October 4, 2011.

3. Neal A. Maxwell, "Becoming a Disciple," *Ensign*, June 1996, 19.

4. Mabel Jones Gabbott, "In Humility, Our Savior," *Hymns*, no. 172.

5. Martha C. Nussbaum, *The New Religious Intolerance: Overcoming the Politics of Fear in an Anxious Age* (Cambridge, MA: Harvard University Press, 2012), xiii.

6. Joseph Smith, in Relief Society Minute Book, Nauvoo, Illinois, April 28, 1842, LDS Church History Library, 40; available online at http://josephsmithpapers.org /paperSummary/nauvoo-relief-society-minute-book.

7. Susan Evans McCloud, "Lord, I Would Follow Thee," *Hymns*, no. 220.

Postlude: Conversations and Celebrations

1. Nathan Florence, *A Conversation with the Master,* © 2008. Used by permission. Digital image available at http://history.lds.org/media/ac-2009-02-234-wca9953.

2. *Wedding Feast,* © 1996 by John August Swanson. Used by permission. Visit http://www.johnaugustswanson.com/default.cfm/PID=1.2.9.14.

Suggested Reading

THROUGHOUT THIS BOOK I have referred to and cited books and articles by scholars whose work has shed light on the issues that have provoked questions for many Latter-day Saints. Academic scholarship on Mormonism has exploded in the past half century, making it impossible (or at least highly unwieldy) to list all the published titles on related subjects. For readers interested in learning more about some of the topics discussed in *Planted*, I have included here a list of the Gospel Topics essays on lds.org and a sampling of the available scholarship, as well as select general conference talks and other devotional materials.

For an online database with searchable bibliographic information about academic scholarship related to Mormon history, see Studies in Mormon History at http://sites.lib.byu.edu/mormonhistory/. Peer-reviewed scholarship and book reviews on Mormon history, theology, and culture are regularly published in periodicals including *BYU Studies Quarterly, Dialogue: A Journal of Mormon Thought, Journal of Mormon History,* and *Mormon Studies Review.*

Gospel Topics essays on lds.org (as of 2015)

"Are Mormons Christian?" https://www.lds.org/topics/christians.
"Becoming Like God." https://www.lds.org/topics/becoming-like-god.
"Book of Mormon Translation." https://www.lds.org/topics/book-of
-mormon-translation.
"Book of Mormon and DNA Studies." https://www.lds.org/topics/book-of
-mormon-and-dna-studies.
"First Vision Accounts." https://www.lds.org/topics/first-vision-accounts.

"The Manifesto and the End of Plural Marriage." https://www.lds.org /topics/the-manifesto-and-the-end-of-plural-marriage.

"Plural Marriage and Families in Early Utah." https://www.lds.org /topics/plural-marriage-and-families-in-early-utah.

"Plural Marriage in Kirtland and Nauvoo." https://www.lds.org/topics /plural-marriage-in-kirtland-and-nauvoo.

"Peace and Violence among 19th-Century Latter-day Saints." https://www. lds.org/topics/peace-and-violence-among-19th-century-latter -day-saints.

"Race and the Priesthood." https://www.lds.org/topics/race-and-the -priesthood.

"Translation and Historicity of the Book of Abraham." https://www.lds.org /topics/translation-and-historicity-of-the-book-of-abraham.

Faith and doubt

Givens, Terryl, and Fiona Givens. *The Crucible of Doubt: Reflections on the Quest for Faith.* Salt Lake City: Deseret Book, 2014.

Hafen, Bruce C. "On Dealing with Uncertainty." *Ensign,* August 1979, 63–67.

Hinckley, Gordon B. "A Time of New Beginnings." *Ensign,* May 2000, 87–88.

Holland, Jeffrey R. "Lord, I Believe." *Ensign,* May 2013, 93–95.

Millet, Robert L., ed. *No Weapon Shall Prosper: New Light on Sensitive Issues.* Provo, UT: Religious Studies Center, Brigham Young University, 2011.

Nielson, Brent H. "Waiting for the Prodigal." *Ensign,* May 2015, 101–3.

Uchtdorf, Dieter F. "Come, Join with Us." *Ensign,* November 2013, 21–24.

———. "Receiving a Testimony of Light and Truth." *Ensign,* November 2014, 20–23.

Wixom, Rosemary M. "Returning to Faith." *Ensign,* May 2015, 93–95.

Joseph Smith and early LDS history

Brown, Samuel Morris. *In Heaven as It Is on Earth: Joseph Smith and the Early Mormon Conquest of Death.* New York: Oxford University Press, 2012.

Bushman, Richard Lyman. *Joseph Smith: Rough Stone Rolling.* New York: Knopf, 2005.

———. "Treasure-Seeking Then and Now." *Sunstone*, September 1987, 5–6.

Harper, Steven C. *Joseph Smith's First Vision: A Guide to the Historical Accounts.* Salt Lake City: Deseret Book, 2012.

The Joseph Smith Papers. Salt Lake City: Church Historian's Press, 2008–. Also available online at http://josephsmithpapers.org/.

Newell, Linda King, and Valeen Tippetts Avery. *Mormon Enigma: Emma Hale Smith.* 2nd ed. Urbana: University of Illinois Press, 1994.

Turley, Richard E., Jr., Robin S. Jensen, and Mark Ashurst-McGee, "Joseph the Seer." *Ensign*, October 2015, 11–16.

Mormon history and historians

Arrington, Leonard J. *Adventures of a Church Historian.* Urbana: University of Illinois Press, 1998.

Baugh, Alexander L., and Reid L. Neilson. *Conversations with Mormon Historians.* Provo, UT: Religious Studies Center, Brigham Young University, and Salt Lake City: Deseret Book, 2015.

Bushman, Richard Lyman. *Believing History: Latter-day Saint Essays.* Edited by Reid L. Neilson and Jed Woodworth. New York: Columbia University Press, 2012.

The Mountain Meadows Massacre and Mormon violence and peacebuilding

Baugh, Alexander L. *A Call to Arms: The 1838 Mormon Defense of Northern Missouri.* Dissertations in Latter-day Saint History. Provo, UT: Joseph Fielding Smith Institute for Latter-day Saint History; BYU Studies, 2000.

Brooks, Juanita. *The Mountain Meadows Massacre*. Stanford: Stanford University Press, 1950.

LeSueur, Stephen C. *The 1838 Mormon War in Missouri*. Columbia: University of Missouri Press, 1987.

Mason, Patrick Q., J. David Pulsipher, and Richard L. Bushman, eds. *War and Peace in Our Time: Mormon Perspectives*. Salt Lake City: Greg Kofford Books, 2012.

Walker, Ronald W., Richard E. Turley Jr., and Glen M. Leonard. *Massacre at Mountain Meadows: An American Tragedy*. New York: Oxford University Press, 2008.

Nineteenth-century LDS history

Arrington, Leonard J. *Great Basin Kingdom: An Economic History of the Latter-day Saints, 1830–1900*. New ed. Urbana: University of Illinois Press, 2004. First published 1958 by Harvard University Press.

Farmer, Jared. *On Zion's Mount: Mormons, Indians, and the American Landscape*. Cambridge, MA: Harvard University Press, 2010.

Fluhman, J. Spencer. *"A Peculiar People": Anti-Mormonism and the Making of Religion in Nineteenth-Century America*. Chapel Hill: University of North Carolina Press, 2012.

Leonard, Glen M. *Nauvoo: A Place of Peace, A People of Promise*. Salt Lake City and Provo, UT: Deseret Book and Brigham Young University Press, 2002.

Mason, Patrick Q. *The Mormon Menace: Violence and Anti-Mormonism in the Postbellum South*. New York: Oxford University Press, 2011.

Shipps, Jan. *Mormonism: The Story of a New Religious Tradition*. Urbana: University of Illinois Press, 1985.

Staker, Mark Lyman. *Hearken, O Ye People: The Historical Setting of Joseph Smith's Ohio Revelations*. Salt Lake City: Greg Kofford Books, 2011.

Turner, John G. *Brigham Young: Pioneer Prophet*. Cambridge, MA: Harvard University Press, 2012.

Polygamy and its aftermath

Compton, Todd. *In Sacred Loneliness: The Plural Wives of Joseph Smith.* Salt Lake City: Signature Books, 1997.

Daynes, Kathryn M. *More Wives Than One: Transformation of the Mormon Marriage System, 1840–1910.* Urbana: University of Illinois Press, 2008.

Flake, Kathleen. *The Politics of American Religious Identity: The Seating of Senator Reed Smoot, Mormon Senator.* Chapel Hill: University of North Carolina Press, 2004.

Gordon, Sarah Barringer. *The Mormon Question: Polygamy and Constitutional Conflict in Nineteenth-Century America.* Chapel Hill: University of North Carolina Press, 2002.

Hales, Brian C. *Joseph Smith's Polygamy.* 3 vols. Salt Lake City: Greg Kofford Books, 2013.

Race and the priesthood-temple ban

Bush, Lester E., Jr. "Mormonism's Negro Doctrine: An Historical Overview." *Dialogue: A Journal of Mormon Thought* 8/1 (1973): 11–68.

Kimball, Edward L. "Spencer W. Kimball and the Revelation on Priesthood." *BYU Studies* 47/2 (2008): 5–78.

Mauss, Armand L. *All Abraham's Children: Changing Mormon Conceptions of Race and Lineage.* Urbana: University of Illinois Press, 2003.

Reeve, W. Paul. *Religion of a Different Color: Race and the Mormon Struggle for Whiteness.* New York: Oxford University Press, 2015.

Stevenson, Russell W. *For the Cause of Righteousness: A Global History of Blacks and Mormonism, 1830-2013.* Salt Lake City: Greg Kofford Books, 2014.

Young, Margaret Blair. "'The Lord's Blessing Was with Us': Jane Elizabeth Manning James, 1822–1908." In *Women of Faith in the Latter Days*, vol. 2, *1821–1845*, edited by Richard E. Turley Jr. and Brittany A. Chapman, 120–35. Salt Lake City: Deseret Book, 2012.

Scriptural studies

Barlow, Philip L. *Mormons and the Bible: The Place of Latter-day Saints in American Religion.* Updated ed. New York: Oxford University Press, 2013. First published 1991.

Faulconer, James E. *The Book of Mormon Made Harder.* Provo, UT: Neal A. Maxwell Institute for Religious Scholarship, 2014.

Givens, Terryl L. *By the Hand of Mormon: The American Scripture That Launched a New World Religion.* New York: Oxford University Press, 2003.

Hauglid, Brian M. "Thoughts on the Book of Abraham." In *No Weapon Shall Prosper: New Light on Sensitive Issues,* edited by Robert L. Millet, 245–58. Provo, UT: Religious Studies Center, Brigham Young University, 2011.

Hardy, Grant. *Understanding the Book of Mormon: A Reader's Guide.* New York: Oxford University Press, 2010.

Perego, Ugo A. "The Book of Mormon and the Origin of Native Americans from a Maternally Inherited DNA Standpoint." In *No Weapon Shall Prosper: New Light on Sensitive Issues,* edited by Robert L. Millet, 171–216. Provo, UT: Religious Studies Center, Brigham Young University, 2011.

Peterson, Daniel C., ed. *The Book of Mormon and DNA Research.* Provo, UT: Neal A. Maxwell Institute, 2008.

Sorenson, John L. *Mormon's Codex: An Ancient American Book.* Salt Lake City: Deseret Book and Neal A. Maxwell Institute for Religious Scholarship, 2013.

Theology

Bennion, Lowell L. *The Religion of the Latter-day Saints.* Provo, UT: LDS Department of Education, 1964. First published 1939.

Brown, Samuel M. *First Principles and Ordinances: The Fourth Article of Faith in Light of the Temple.* Provo, UT: Neal A. Maxwell Institute for Religious Scholarship, 2014.

England, Eugene. "Why the Church Is as True as the Gospel." *Sunstone,* June 1999, 61–69.

Givens, Terryl L. *Wrestling the Angel: The Foundations of Mormon Thought: God, Cosmos, Humanity*. New York: Oxford University Press, 2014.

Givens, Terryl, and Fiona Givens. *The God Who Weeps: How Mormonism Makes Sense of Life*. Salt Lake City: Ensign Peak, 2012.

McMurrin, Sterling M. *The Theological Foundations of the Mormon Religion*. Salt Lake City: University of Utah Press, 1965.

Miller, Adam S. *Letters to a Young Mormon*. Provo, UT: Neal A. Maxwell Institute for Religious Scholarship, 2013.

———. *Rube Goldberg Machines: Essays in Mormon Theology*. Salt Lake City: Greg Kofford Books, 2012.

Paulsen, David L., and Martin Pulido. "'A Mother There': A Survey of Historical Teachings about Mother in Heaven." *BYU Studies* 50/1 (2011): 70–97.

Twentieth-century LDS history

Alexander, Thomas G. *Mormonism in Transition: A History of the Latter-day Saints*. 3rd ed. Salt Lake City: Greg Kofford Books, 2012.

Bowman, Matthew. *The Mormon People: The Making of an American Faith*. New York: Random House, 2012.

Bushman, Claudia L. *Contemporary Mormonism: Latter-day Saints in Modern America*. Lanham, MD: Rowman & Littlefield, 2008.

Kimball, Edward L. *Lengthen Your Stride: The Presidency of Spencer W. Kimball*. Salt Lake City: Deseret Book, 2005.

Mauss, Armand L. *The Angel and the Beehive: The Mormon Struggle with Assimilation*. Urbana: University of Illinois Press, 1994.

Prince, Gregory A., and Wm. Robert Wright. *David O. McKay and the Rise of Modern Mormonism*. Salt Lake City: University of Utah Press, 2005.

Women and feminism

Beecher, Maureen Ursenbach, and Lavina Fielding Anderson, eds. *Sisters in Spirit: Mormon Women in Historical and Cultural Perspective*. Urbana: University of Illinois Press, 1987.

Bushman, Claudia L. *Mormon Sisters: Women in Early Utah*. Logan: Utah State University Press, 1997.

Bushman, Claudia L., and Caroline Kline, eds. *Mormon Women Have Their Say: Essays from the Claremont Oral History Collection*. Salt Lake City: Greg Kofford Books, 2013.

Derr, Jill Mulvay, Janath Russell Cannon, and Maureen Ursenbach Beecher. *Women of Covenant: The Story of Relief Society*. Salt Lake City: Deseret Book, 2002.

Dew, Sheri. *Women and the Priesthood: What One Mormon Woman Believes*. Salt Lake City: Deseret Book, 2013.

Dew, Sheri, and Virginia H. Pearce, eds. *The Beginning of Better Days: Divine Instruction to Women from the Prophet Joseph Smith*. Salt Lake City: Deseret Book, 2012.

Hanks, Maxine, ed. *Women and Authority: Re-Emerging Mormon Feminism*. Salt Lake City: Signature Books, 1992.

McBaine, Neylan. *Women at Church: Magnifying LDS Women's Local Impact*. Salt Lake City: Greg Kofford Books, 2014.

Turley, Richard E., Jr., and Brittany A. Chapman, eds. *Women of Faith in the Latter Days*. 7 vols. Salt Lake City: Deseret Book, 2011–.

Scripture Index

Index

Patrick Q. Mason is the Howard W. Hunter Chair in Mormon Studies at Claremont Graduate University. He is author of *The Mormon Menace: Violence and Anti-Mormonism in the Postbellum South* (Oxford University Press, 2011), which examines anti-Mormon prejudice against nineteenth-century LDS missionaries. He is a nationally recognized authority on Mormonism who has contributed to articles in the *New York Times*, *Los Angeles Times*, *Washington Post*, and *Chicago Tribune* and has also appeared on National Public Radio and PBS.

A
Living Faith
Book

LIVING FAITH books are for readers who cherish the life of the mind and the things of the Spirit. Each title is a unique example of faith in search of understanding, the voice of a scholar who has cultivated a believing heart while engaged in the disciplines of the Academy.

Other LIVING FAITH books include:

Adam S. Miller, *Letters to a Young Mormon*

Samuel M. Brown, *First Principles and Ordinances: The Fourth Article of Faith in Light of the Temple*

Steven L. Peck, *Evolving Faith: Wanderings of a Mormon Biologist*